JEANNE BEKER
FINDING MYSELF IN FASHION

VIKING
CANADA

VIKING CANADA

Published by the Penguin Group

Penguin Group (Canada), 90 Eglinton Avenue East, Suite 700,
Toronto, Ontario, Canada M4P 2Y3 (a division of Pearson Canada Inc.)

Penguin Group (USA) Inc., 375 Hudson Street, New York, New York 10014, U.S.A.
Penguin Books Ltd, 80 Strand, London WC2R 0RL, England
Penguin Ireland, 25 St Stephen's Green, Dublin 2, Ireland
(a division of Penguin Books Ltd)
Penguin Group (Australia), 250 Camberwell Road, Camberwell, Victoria 3124, Australia
(a division of Pearson Australia Group Pty Ltd)
Penguin Books India Pvt Ltd, 11 Community Centre, Panchsheel Park,
New Delhi – 110 017, India
Penguin Group (NZ), 67 Apollo Drive, Rosedale, Auckland 0632, New Zealand
(a division of Pearson New Zealand Ltd)
Penguin Books (South Africa) (Pty) Ltd, 24 Sturdee Avenue, Rosebank,
Johannesburg 2196, South Africa

Penguin Books Ltd, Registered Offices: 80 Strand, London WC2R 0RL, England

First published 2011

1 2 3 4 5 6 7 8 9 10 (RRD)

Copyright © Jeanne Beker, 2011

*Penguin is committed to publishing works of quality and integrity. In that spirit, we are proud to offer this
book to our readers; however, the story, the experiences, and the words are the author's alone.*

Manufactured in the U.S.A.

Library and Archives Canada Cataloguing in Publication Data available
upon request to the publisher.

Visit the Penguin Group (Canada) website at **www.penguin.ca**

Special and corporate bulk purchase rates available; please see
www.penguin.ca/corporatesales or call 1-800-810-3104, ext. 2477 or 2474

For Bekky and Joey

"But when it does work, when it all comes together
and we have one foot poised to take another step on life's perilous
tightrope … it's the most magnificent feeling on earth."

CONTENTS

FINDING MYSELF

The older I get, the more the old adages of childhood ring true. Like Dorothy in *The Wizard of Oz*, who discovers that her ruby slippers have the power to take her home, I have learned, through my high-flying adventures in fashion over the past two and a half decades, to appreciate my roots and to see the beauty of my own backyard.

UP IN THE AIR

THERE'S A SMALL BLOCK PRINT hanging in my office at work. It's based on a line drawing I created on my fiftieth birthday, at an artist's studio in San Miguel de Allende, Mexico. The subject is a girl holding an umbrella and gingerly walking a tightrope strung between two trees. I call the image *Balancing Act*. The girl is me, and the precarious feat pictured is the essence of my personal story.

I pinch myself several times daily, forever amazed that I live, have lived, and still plan on living a most extraordinary life. The fact that much of my career has taken place against the backdrop of one of the most glamorous and creative arenas on the planet is just an added bonus. As much as I adored fashion when I was growing up, I never imagined that I'd wind up being a player in this rarefied world, hobnobbing with famous designers and models, attending international runway shows, reporting on trends and analyzing the sartorial zeitgeist on a multitude of media platforms. I never actually aspired to be a fashion journalist. I was initially hell-bent on having a life in the theatre. But somewhere along the way, I decided that starving in a garret was not an option for me. So slowly and serendipitously, I began carving out a new niche for myself—one that would still allow me to savour grand theatrics and human expression, but on a more practical and potentially lucrative level.

Strange as it may sound, I was a Paris-trained mime artist when I started reporting on the arts for CBC Radio in St. John's, Newfoundland, in the mid-1970s—an opportunity that materialized thanks to both my own drive and the foresight of a young producer, John Dalton, who saw my potential and gave me my first reporting gig. And because I was ambitious, and adamant about propelling myself to greater heights, I made my way back to Toronto at the end of that decade and launched into the next leg of my journey, TV reporting. I suppose it was my ability to think outside the box, coupled with my unbridled energy, fearlessness, tenacity, and love of people, that got me here. But there was also another important factor in my success: I was determined, no matter what, to lead a balanced life. As much joy and satisfaction as I glean—have always gleaned—from my work, I know that it's those I cherish, my friends and family, who keep me going. Just as starving in a garret was never an option, loneliness wasn't either. Of course, many believe that we're all ultimately alone. And I do spend an inordinate amount of time physically on my own, both when I'm travelling and when I'm writing. But I feel that my loved ones, from my late father and my doting mother to my precious daughters to my best friends, are always with me in spirit— cheering me on, comforting and inspiring me. It's this deep sense of family, belonging, and unconditional love that grounds me and enables me to get out of bed every day.

Still, despite all this emotional support, I do sometimes engage in pep talks with myself just to keep going. These internal conversations occur in all kinds of places. Some of the more memorable ones have taken place on moving sidewalks in airports around the world. You see, I board planes the way some people board buses. It's become a wonderfully familiar routine, and I pride myself on the fact that I really do have this travelling thing down pat. There was never any choice, really, since I wanted to operate on an international platform. Hauling my butt around the globe is part and parcel of what I do for a living.

People often ask me how many days a year I spend on the road, and how many kilometres I travel. I have never counted. Each week, each month, each year is different. Opportunities to travel to exotic destinations constantly present themselves, and I happily take advantage of as many as I can. The only certainty is that I will travel to my favourite city, Paris, at least four times a year, for both the ready-to-wear and the couture collections. And I try never to miss the New York collections. Besides these regular jaunts, my schedule is replete with other assorted trips—some for as little as a day or two, some for up to ten days. Suffice it to say that I pack my bags and board a plane at least a couple of times a month. In spite of all the practice, I do usually forget something banal—like toothpaste, my favourite cosmetic, a certain purse, a particular bra. It's a bother, but it's never anything irreplaceable. Why I always manage to do this is a mystery. Maybe I'm secretly intent on leaving a piece of myself behind.

Granted my kids are a lot older now: Bekky is twenty-four, and Joey is twenty-one. But I'll never forget how those sweet little girls used to run alongside the airport limo as I sat crying quietly in the back seat, pulling away once again for yet another work-related adventure. It still breaks my heart a little bit when I think back to those days. I don't know how I mustered the strength to leave at all. But I'm thrilled to say that they've grown into amazing, independent young women. So of course, while it may never totally dissipate, my guilt about leaving them behind is less intense now. Also, I know how badly I yearned— still yearn—for the kind of inspiration that a city like Paris can bring. Truthfully, though, there's a big part of me that longs for the simple life, and I often find myself wishing I could just work in the comfort of my own little home office each evening, spinning stories at my own familiar desk and sipping ginger tea late into the night, before disappearing under my cozy duvet with my big dog, Beau, softly snoring at the foot of my bed.

However, I can't afford to get too sentimental. Fashion is an eternal quest for what's new, and that has become part of my DNA. That's why switching into travel mode has become automatic for me. I always manage to gather the required energy, run the appropriate errands, get all my packing done, and make my flights on time. Often, I'm surprised by just how smoothly I sail through it all, relishing that moment when I finally board the plane, settle into my seat with a stash of great magazines or a good book, and hunker down for yet another transatlantic crossing. I figure I'm good at going away because of my ability to detach. It's as if I stop thinking. Stop feeling. Pump myself up with drive and determination and duty. Got to go! Got to get out there and do this job I've worked all my life for! Why? Well, because it's what I do—what I've struggled and fought for, slaved and sacrificed for. Can't give up now! Not ever. It's who I am, or at least who I *think* I am. And as crazy as this lifestyle may be, I'm addicted to it. It's my drug.

In this modern age, we want it all, and why not? The fact that we often nearly kill ourselves trying is society's big joke on us all. It's as though we've been told to knock ourselves out, and sometimes that's exactly what we do. But when it does work, when it all comes together and we have one foot poised to take another step on life's perilous tightrope, secure in the knowledge that our kids are tucked away all safe and snug, it's the most magnificent feeling on earth. I wouldn't trade those moments for anything.

I've learned a lot about what it takes to get through this high-wire act. Fashion's trenches have provided me with far more than mere eye candy. This past decade has been especially enlightening. Through all its ups and downs, I've learned many lessons: how to heal, how to stand on my own two feet, how to raise my two girls, how to fall in love again, and most important, how to continue dreaming and doing and devouring every last bit of this delectable life.

HOME AND AWAY

I KNOW that I'm blessed. A vast array of incredible opportunities has come my way—from travelling and meeting interesting people to fulfilling countless personal fantasies—and I have never, not for one second, taken any of it for granted. But I also know this about myself: I have never been one to sit back and let life happen. From a young age, I knew that if I wanted to lead not just a good life, or even a great life, but an *extraordinary* life, I'd have to make things happen for myself. That's why, when I was sixteen and a totally inexperienced young actress, I put myself on the line and went to an open casting call that a friend had told me about at the CBC.

I don't know where I got the chutzpah to think that I could compete with the scores of professional actresses who were auditioning for the same role. My performing experience was limited to the drama classes I took when I was twelve years old and a couple of summer camp plays. But somehow, my ambition paid off, and I found myself juggling high school classes and a recurring role in a nationally televised sitcom. Three years later, not content to await discovery in my native land, I rode a Greyhound bus to New York City to enrol at the Herbert Berghof Studio, a prestigious West Village acting school. I found a low-rent apartment on Riverside Drive and revelled in every aspect of my Big Apple existence, studying my craft and befriending a host of colourful characters who were also working to make their dreams come true.

A couple of years later, I was back in Toronto, frustrated with my studies in York University's theatre department. Determined to go all out for my art, I gathered up all the tips I had made as a cocktail waitress in the summer of 1973 and headed to the City of Light to study with Étienne Decroux, the legendary mime master who had mentored Marcel Marceau. I wanted to perfect a technique, to master the art of illusion on stage, and I was determined to learn from the best. The following year, I came to the realization that while I was devoted to being an artist, what I really craved was security. So I moved back home, enrolled in theatre at York once again, and started plotting what to do next.

An opportunity to move to St. John's, Newfoundland, presented itself when my boyfriend was offered a fellowship to study at Memorial University. Embarking on a major East Coast adventure with the man I loved struck me as the most proactive thing I could do. So we got married, on September 2, 1975, and moved to sleepy St. John's the next day. We didn't know a soul in town, and my new hubby immediately entered his postgraduate studies at MUN's folklore department, leaving me to fend for myself. I set out to find a job, planning to give mime classes on the side. As the only mime artist in Newfoundland, I miraculously and ironically landed a gig in radio. I had the gall to pitch myself as an arts reporter, and since there was a vital arts scene in St. John's, but no one reporting on it for radio, I was given the chance to be a full-time writer/performer for CBC's *Radio Noon* show. In addition to my reporting duties, I also produced a variety of arts specials for the network. And that was the beginning of my media career.

Three years later, in 1978, my husband was ready to launch into his thesis on urban folklore, going beyond the tales of local fiddlers, fishermen, and sailors to explore the lives of cabbies, strippers, and cocktail waitresses. Now that I had cut my teeth on local radio, I also felt ready for a move back to the big city. So we returned to Toronto, where my husband began working on his thesis, while I, armed with my arsenal of demo tapes, approached every program director at every radio station in the city. A couple of weeks later, 1050 CHUM, the number-one Top 40 AM station, bit. Largely because its program director, J.R. Wood, liked my "young-sounding" voice, I was recruited to be CHUM's "good news girl," working out of the station's gritty little Yonge Street newsroom, booking, producing, writing, recording, and voicing seventeen different ninety-second lifestyle featurettes a week. My eclectic contributions were called "CHUM Reports," and my regular sign-off—a cocky "I'm Jeanne Beker"—became a calling card for me, getting my name out there in a bold and snappy way.

That same year, CHUM Radio purchased Citytv, a hip downtown cable television station. Almost immediately, the CHUM execs decided to cross-promote their radio personalities on TV. I was chosen to co-host *The New Music*, a weekly magazine series on City, with a handsome young deejay named J.D. Roberts (better known today as John Roberts, formerly of CNN and now with Fox). The show was groundbreaking and took viewers behind the scenes of the music world, interviewing rock stars in their hotels and dressing rooms, on the road, in studios, and backstage. One Toronto pop critic dubbed J.D. and me "video virgins," and indeed we hadn't done any television reporting before (though I had TV performing experience from my acting days). But most of the musicians we were putting on the show were just as green: this was 1979, pre-MTV, and the art of talking on TV was foreign to most pop stars. We were all flying by the seats of our pants. But the musicians soon began to develop their TV personalities, and so did we, and before long, we flitted between radio and television effortlessly.

Shortly after my stint on *The New Music* began, my first marriage ended. My husband was offered the chance to return to Memorial University to teach, even before his Ph.D. work had been completed. It was an offer he couldn't refuse. But for me, the prospect of going back to Newfoundland when my Toronto television career had just started to take off was unthinkable. We had grown apart, and I knew I had to follow this new path of my own. So I stayed behind, eager to embrace all the possibilities that were coming my way.

Around the same time, I began having a relationship with the all-night deejay at CHUM—a charming and personable guy who had the most exquisite blue eyes I had ever seen. His on-air name was Bob Magee, but his real name was Denny O'Neil. We fell madly in love, and six years later, on February 7, 1986, we eloped and got married. A year after that, our first beautiful daughter, Rebecca Leigh—Bekky— was born. And in 1989, we were blessed once again with the birth of Sarah Jo—or Joey.

I was drunk with happiness. My life had blossomed into everything I could ever have hoped for—a gorgeous, loving husband; adorable kids; and a fantastic, creative job. I had learned that if you want exceptional things to happen in your life, you have to fuel the fires and work at conjuring that magic for yourself. But you also have to learn to bite the bullet sometimes, and hang tough. Often, those things you've toiled at so relentlessly are the same things that can tear you apart. Suddenly, there I was with two little kids who needed to be tucked in every night and a job that required me to travel the world. Denny was incredibly supportive, and a great father to our little girls. And five days a week, we had a loving housekeeper/nanny who helped fill in the blanks. But for me, not always being able to be there for them was an endless source of anxiety. I was conflicted to the point that feeling torn became second nature to me.

The guilt started right after Bekky was born in 1987. I was thirty-five years old, having waited patiently for my career to take off before I ventured into motherhood. I felt tremendously fulfilled. Still, I couldn't stop to savour the joys of parenthood for long. My career seemed just as demanding as my newborn baby. In retrospect, I can hardly believe that my little Bekky was only four months old when I first left her to go on a two-week trip to London and Paris. I'm not sure how I found the strength. But there wasn't any option—this was what I'd signed up for.

It was Moses Znaimer, the innovative mastermind behind Citytv, who deserves credit for toughening me up. *Fashion Television* had been on the air for less than two years, and the show—and the team—was just hitting its stride. I was about eight and a half months pregnant— and determined to work for as long as I possibly could—when Moses, in his wily way, started putting the show's lovely young production co-coordinator on camera, encouraging her to hone her reporting skills. Whether or not this ambitious young woman was ready for "prime time" wasn't the issue. Call it old-fashioned insecurity, but I had the sneaking suspicion that this gal was after my job, and Moses appeared more than happy to dangle the notion that I could be easily replaced. He also taunted me at least once with the questionable greeting "Hi chubby!" when he passed me in the hallway. Add to all that my hormonal rage, burgeoning belly, hefty weight gain (I gained something like forty-five pounds during my first pregnancy!), and you had the perfect recipe for professional paranoia.

One of the lovely young production co-coordinator's duties was to pull my wardrobe for the show—not an easy job at a time when people still tried to disguise pregnant bellies with tent-like maternity wear. To make matters worse, it was the year Lycra gave new meaning to body-conscious fashion, and skinny silhouettes were all the rage. I remember this enthusiastic young woman bringing me a silver leather jacket that made me look like a human Sputnik. "Oh, gawd!" I wailed. "This is so wrong!" Granted, I must have come off as some difficult diva, but the co-coordinator snapped and said something unsympathetic, like, "Well, what do you expect?" It was depressing, but it fuelled my determination to hang on to what I had achieved. So when Moses made a point of reminding me that my job might be in jeopardy if I didn't hop right back as soon as I possibly could, I took the bait.

"When do you plan on coming back after you have the baby?" Moses asked me about a week before my due date.

"Well, I hadn't really thought about it," I replied.

"Because you know there's a long lineup of twenty-two-year-olds outside my office door, all vying for your job," he said.

"Oh, don't worry about me," I replied instantly. "I'll only take a couple of weeks off."

And so, much to the chagrin of my potential competition, I convinced my producers that there'd be no need to replace me. They'd only have to go into two or three repeats, I assured them, because I would be back in a flash.

True to my word, I was out covering my first story only two and a half weeks after delivering my baby. Actually, I was back even before that. Two days after I got home from the hospital, my producer sent a crew to my house to record some voice-overs. To this day, I'm not quite sure how I did it.

Unquestionably, it had a lot to do with the weekends we spent together as a family, all cozied up at our quaint Muskoka cottage, and with the comforting bedtime routines we followed whenever I was in town. In later years, when I was away, I had a cellphone with me at all times. I smile when I think of the times I was just about to interview some VIP halfway round the world when my phone rang and I had to field a question about homework or weekend plans or a favourite piece of clothing that had disappeared. I was there for my kids as much I could be. They were on my mind every moment I was away from them. These were the days before text messaging and email, so I kept the home fax line busy, sending loving missives, and Denny would help the girls send their notes and drawings to hotel fax machines wherever I was staying. Every spare minute was spent shopping for the kids, seeking out the perfect little gifts. I always delighted in seeing their faces when I finally got home and unpacked my bags to reveal the treasures I had brought back.

I may have looked back a few times over the years and wondered how things would have played out if I hadn't been so career-driven, but I can't say I would have done things any other way, even if I were given the choice. Has it torn me to pieces sometimes, this excruciating split between home and work? Without a doubt! But it's a torment that I've thrived on in a way—the kind of crazy head/heart dilemma that makes me feel alive sometimes. Nothing worth anything comes easy in this life. We'd all be bored if it did.

SURVIVAL MODE

WHEN WE CELEBRATED the twenty-fifth anniversary season of *Fashion Television* in the fall of 2010, interviewers kept asking me how I had managed to beat the odds in an industry that eats its young. Not only had I hung in there for over a quarter century, but I had thrived, and fresh fuel was continually being added to my career fires. "How do you do it?" reporters asked. "How do you explain your longevity?" There are a thousand reasons. But one answer, the most succinct and all-encompassing, says it best: because I'm a survivor. It's just who I am, and how I was raised—as the daughter of two courageous people who were themselves true survivors.

For as long as I can remember, my mother was adamant about sharing her personal story. Actually, both my parents felt compelled to talk about how they had survived the Holocaust: the terror, the anguish, the hunger, the pain, the loneliness, and then the miracles. Their poignant stories became part of my DNA, and took me to a place that was light years away from where most of the kids I played with dwelled. I knew from a very young age that I was on this planet thanks to my parents' wits and some kind of divine intervention. And even though I remember hiding under my bed when I was about five years old, just so I wouldn't have to listen to any more "war stories," I'm thankful my parents expressed themselves so openly, sharing the experiences that helped define them.

My parents were both from Kozowa, a small town in eastern Poland (now Ukraine), which was invaded by the Germans in 1941. My father, Joseph, was born in 1913—the son of Beryl, a cobbler, who died when my dad was just fourteen years old. Since he was the eldest in the family, my dad had to leave school and find work to support his mother, Gitl (Genia in Polish), after whom I'm named, and his two brothers and sister. In 1937, my father joined the Polish army and became an officer. A couple of years later, when the Polish army was overwhelmed by the Germans and then the Soviets, he defected and returned to Kozowa, to be reunited with my mother, whom he had been dating secretly (to avoid the disapproval of her religious father).

My father, seven years older than my mother, was a handsome, strapping man who had an incredible zest for life, a great love of people, a huge heart, a strong sense of entrepreneurship, and an uncanny ability to reinvent himself. His strong work ethic inspires me still. He used to tell us about the diverse opportunities he created for himself in his native Poland, from raising honeybees and selling horses to organizing big-band dance parties. After he and my mother immigrated to Canada in 1948—both penniless and unable to speak a word of English—he began laying the foundations for his own company, since he was adamant about being his own boss. By the early 1950s, Quality Slippers, a tiny slipper-manufacturing company, was born. For the rest of his life, my dad worked seven days a week, usually twelve hours a day, just so he could put a roof over our heads. He was selfless, brave, tenacious, and wildly generous. Undoubtedly, it was his heroic spirit that helped see both him and my mother through the war.

My mother, Bronia Rohatiner, was born in 1920. Her father, Moses Baruch, was a very religious, revered, and learned man who was a successful village merchant—a purveyor of leather goods. His first wife died giving birth to his ninth child. Nine months later, my grandfather married a woman twenty years his junior—Esther Malka Gold, a nineteen-year-old who would bear him another two children: my mother and my beautiful aunt Sarah. My mother always delighted in telling stories about her magical Polish shtetl, Kozowa—a lively place filled with colourful characters—and her joyful girlhood. But in 1941, with the arrival of the Germans, her perfect world came crashing down.

After the Nazis gunned down two of my mother's half-brothers in a mass killing in a nearby forest, ten members of her extended family moved into her parents' large house. With the help of neighbours, they dug a small cave in the cellar. "There were two pipes for air circulation," my mother explained to me countless times. "Often, all of us had to spend hours down there. Sometimes, we stayed there for a whole day, when the Nazis came and were looking for people to kill. We heard them walking around upstairs, and only when we were sure they had left would we come out of the cave."

Before long, my mother's mother died of typhoid fever. Two months later, in April 1942, there was word that the Nazis were coming to liquidate the Kozowa ghetto. The family—my mother; her father; her only remaining half-brother and his two daughters; the wife of one of her late half-brothers and their three children; and my mother's sister, Sarah—went that night to their hiding place. In the morning, they heard the Nazis walking around upstairs. "They were shouting, and yelling, and searching for our family," my mother would tell me. The Nazis couldn't find the entrance to the cave, but they must have spotted the two air pipes. They stuffed them with something, blocking the flow of air. "I was the first to faint," my mother recalled. "That was because I'd just recently recovered from typhus myself." When the Germans finally left, some people from the ghetto came to open the cave, and they pulled out the family, one by one. Everyone had suffocated, except for my mother. She would often tell the story of how her family's corpses were being loaded onto wagons to be taken away when someone noticed her eyelids fluttering. They poured cold water on her, and she was revived. The next thing she knew, she was in her bed, surrounded by strange people and the town's one remaining doctor. "He told me what happened. I was shocked and angry, and asked him, 'Why did you revive me? Now I'm all alone!'" That day, the Nazis killed one thousand Kozowa Jews.

My father arrived on the scene and took my mother to his family's home. But shortly afterwards, they heard of the Nazis' plans to make the town *Judenrein* (clean of Jews). My parents fled, and for the next fourteen months, relying on their wits and the kindness of gentile strangers, they scrambled to hide from the Nazi terror. My mother would tell me how she and my father had to ration scraps of food; how she "made friends" with cute, tiny field mice; how she dreamed of being able to read a book or eat a piece of bread with butter. I remember being puzzled as a kid whenever my mother would yawn and let out a big, loud sigh. She explained to me once that she yawned so loudly because she could never make a noise when she was in hiding for all those months. From then on, her loud yawns became music to my ears.

My parents were open about their hellish memories, and adamant about raising us to appreciate that nothing should be taken for granted. Their stories built a kind of fire in my belly that fuelled that passion and desire to lead a truly exceptional life—one that would allow me to realize all the dreams they never could, and then some.

My mother often spoke about her longing to return to Poland, and maybe even visit Kozowa, now in Ukraine. But it was hard for her to get up the nerve to confront her past. After my father died, my mother said she would consider going back only if my sister and I accompanied her. The opportunity never arose. And frankly, I was afraid that a trip to Poland might be too emotionally exhausting for my mother. But fate has a funny way of delivering things that are meant to be.

In 1995, thanks to the LINK Group, a fashion promotion agency that had bought the rights to *Fashion Television* for satellite broadcast in Poland, I was given the opportunity to travel to Warsaw. Apparently, our show had been pirated across the Eastern European airwaves for years, and I was a well-known entity there—a mini-celeb, if you will. Now that *FT* was going to be delivered to Poland legitimately, the broadcast execs wanted to celebrate by bringing me over. It was too good an opportunity to pass up, especially because I knew the perfect roommate and translator—I asked my mother to accompany me. My supervising producer, Marcia Martin, and the Toronto exec who had made the deal were also on board for this first-class trip.

Days before we were to leave, my mother expressed concern as we filled out our visa applications. "It's asking what my father's name was," she said apprehensively. "I don't want to write 'Moses.'"

"Why not? That was his name, wasn't it?"

"Because then they'll know we're Jewish," she explained.

"Mum, you don't have to be afraid anymore," I told her. "You're a Canadian citizen now. And the war is over."

The next day my mother phoned to tell me how excited she was about our impending trip. "But please try to understand," she said. "I was so scared for so long."

Our welcome at the Warsaw airport was ultra glam: four gorgeous models dressed in prim grey suits, each carrying a huge bouquet of roses, marched towards us upon our arrival. It was 8:30 in the morning, and there was a posse of Polish TV crews and newspaper photographers there to capture the excitement. My mother turned to me in disbelief. We felt like rock stars.

Our host in Warsaw was Jack Orlowski, an affable fellow who headed up the LINK Group. He had known my mother was coming, and he offered to drive her directly to the Natan Rappaport Memorial, which commemorates the Warsaw Ghetto Uprising of April 19, 1943. The massive monument depicts Mordecai Anielewicz and other members of the community who barricaded the gates of the walled ghetto against the Nazis. (By the time the uprising ended, on May 16, 1943, at least seven thousand people had been killed, and tens of thousands more had been captured and transported to concentration camps.) In the trunk of Jack's Mercedes was a glorious wreath he had thoughtfully brought for my mother to place at the monument.

We arrived at the Umschlagplatz, the centre of the infamous ghetto, and stepped out of the car onto the cobblestone square. Jack carried the flowers. My mother's eyes were misty. She turned to me, incredulous that she had made it this far. "If you live long enough," she observed, "you live to see everything." She gingerly climbed the stairs and rested the wreath at the base of the monument. I was overwhelmed by disparate emotions—joy, sorrow, peace, loss, and a sense of profound reverence. In a strange way, I felt as though I had come home. I closed my eyes and sensed those thousands of tormented souls, screaming out to be remembered. When I opened my eyes, my mother hugged me and, wiping away her tears, thanked me for bringing her on this amazing trip. As frivolous as I've sometimes found the fashion arena to be, I silently thanked it for making all this possible.

We spent most of the rest of the day riding around the old city in a horse-drawn carriage. My mother was cooing like a kid in her native Polish. "How I dreamed of visiting Warsaw when I was a girl. This was the big city!" she said as she took in the sights. "But who could ever afford to come here in those days?"

The next morning we visited a seventeenth-century palace that had been transformed into a kind of private club used by the business community. This is where I was to introduce *FT* to about twenty journalists. At the beginning of my speech, I mentioned that this was a kind of homecoming for my mother. When it was time for questions, an elderly gentleman asked if she would say a few words. To my surprise, my mother had prepared a little speech, just in case someone asked her to speak. She pulled a paper out of her purse, and then, in her perfect Polish, provided the audience with a riveting description of how she had survived the war and how emotional it was for her to return after all these years. You could have heard a pin drop. My heart swelled with pride as I realized yet again what a remarkable, fearless woman I had for a mother.

When the press conference ended, several journalists approached her. The elderly gentleman who had asked her to speak flashed me his card. He was a former White House correspondent. "You were the sunshine of this press conference," he told her. My mum was kvelling, especially because of her ability to speak Polish so well after so long, and she was amazed that having left this country as a second-class citizen fifty years earlier, she'd come back as the toast of the town.

Back at the Bristol, our lavish five-star hotel, my mother took a call from a reporter with a Warsaw newspaper who had been unable to grab her at the press conference. After a twenty-minute interview, she hung up. "I wonder if I told him too much," she mused. Later that night, a full-scale fashion show was staged in our honour at a local theatre. The director of Polsat TV approached my mother to tell her that she had been featured on the national newscast earlier that evening. They had aired part of her speech from the press conference. We all teased her about her new-found fame as Poland's media darling.

"I don't care," she said defensively, biting into a perogy at the post-show dinner. "Make fun of me all you want." A few beats later, evidently pretty satisfied with herself, she smugly added, "You know what? My perogies are better!" I had never seen my mother so self-assured, so fiercely proud. And this time, it wasn't because of her children or her grandchildren. She was radiantly happy with herself. I had never loved her more.

It was well past midnight when we crawled into our beds, complaining about our aching feet, exhausted but giddy, laughing and kvetching about how tough it was to be a celebrity. As I fell asleep, I thought about the last time we had shared a hotel room. In 1983, we had accompanied my dying father to a renowned hospital in Boston in a last-ditch effort to save his life. His heart condition was rapidly worsening, and we were desperate. That night, at this ritzy Warsaw hotel, I distinctly felt my dad's presence, as if he were watching us share this wondrous homecoming.

The next day, we drove to Kraków in a Polish TV minivan. As rows of farmhouses and strips of countryside darted past our windows, my mother spun some of the war stories I had heard a thousand times before. There were tales about how gallant Polish families had hidden my parents in their barns and brought them bread and milk. I wondered if the farmhouses we were passing were like the ones in which my parents sought refuge. My mother was too preoccupied reliving the past for me to ask.

In Kraków, our guide took us to the old Jewish quarter, where Steven Spielberg shot scenes for the film *Schindler's List*. My mother teared up as we walked through the stone gates of the sixteenth-century Ramu Synagogue, the oldest in Kraków. There we met an old Yiddish-speaking man in a yarmulke. He told us there used to be tens of thousands of Jews living in Kraków. Today, fewer than a thousand remain. The courtyard of the synagogue was filled with tombstones. It was quiet, cold, and lonely. I wept silently for all Jews, and for family I'd never known. Those buried at the synagogue were fortunate to have marked graves; those who perished at the camps never did. I remembered my mother's story about a town near hers where all the tombstones in the Jewish cemetery had been torn down and made into sidewalks.

Back in Warsaw that night, I was violently ill, likely the result of food poisoning. Just as she had when I was a little girl, my mum stayed up with me, a familiar worried look on her face. In the morning, a doctor arrived to give me some anti-nausea pills for the flight home. He reminded my mother that fifty-five years ago that day, on September 1, 1939, war broke out in Poland. My mother looked at the gold signet ring she had worn all those years and remembered that on that day, fifty-five years ago, her brother had given her that ring. This was the fifty-fifth anniversary of the day her life changed forever. This was also the day she would leave Poland with a new sense of herself, and at peace with her past.

NEW BEGINNINGS

We've all heard that it's darkest before the dawn. It was a proverb I clung to with all the faith I could muster when my marriage ended. The rug had been pulled out from under me, and my entire belief system was shaken. Dark days, indeed. But as the new millennium dawned, I started picking up the pieces of my shattered life. Despite the inspiring example my parents had set for me, I had to discover for myself what it takes to forge ahead. And I did. By seeking out a new country retreat and briefly returning to my original passion, I began to remember who I really was.

THE BUBBLE BURSTS

I ACTUALLY THOUGHT I had it all—supportive husband, fantastic kids, brilliant career, beautiful city house, cozy country home—when, in January 1998, Denny dropped a bomb: He suddenly and unexpectedly told me he was leaving our marriage. He gave me little more than a couple of weeks to digest the news.

I should have seen it coming. Exactly one year earlier, in January 1997, after nearly two decades with CHUM, Denny found out that his *Magee in the Morning* radio show had been axed—his position was terminated. His frustration mounted as he tried to find another job. For the first time in our eighteen-year relationship, my ever-positive husband admitted that he was discontented. I was desperately worried, and pleaded with him to tell me what was wrong and how I could help.

One cold Friday afternoon, after I had just come home from my first trip back to St. John's, Newfoundland, in over twenty years—a cathartic experience that reminded me how much I'd grown and how far I had come—Denny finally told me he was "ready to talk." The girls had a couple of friends over, and their laughter as they ran through our big old house jarred with my anxiety over what I was about to hear.

Denny took me into the bedroom, closed the door, and sat me down on the bed. My heart was beating like crazy.

"I guess you realize that I've been very unhappy for some time now," he said solemnly.

"Yeah, honey, I know. I want to help you so much. It's the work thing, isn't it?" I asked.

"No. It's more than that. It's the relationship."

"The relationship?" I retorted. I had no idea what he meant.

"Yeah. I don't want to be in the relationship anymore. I've decided I don't want to be married anymore. I want to leave."

My heart plummeted. "But surely you just need to get away for a while—go on a trip, take some time. We can work it out …"

As I looked into his eyes, I was suddenly swept up in a monstrous blur of confusion, smashed by a tsunami of the most acute pain I'd ever known.

"Oh, my God," I muttered. "What are you telling me?" Every last bit of me was writhing in disbelief, screaming out that this must be a bad dream and demanding that I please, please wake up because this couldn't possibly be happening!

But Denny was implacable. "I simply don't desire the relationship. I don't desire you. I'm not in love with you anymore," he said softly and with frightening finality.

I ran into the bathroom and leaned over the toilet. My stomach was heaving, but nothing came up. Heart racing, I looked in the mirror and was repelled by what I saw: me, dressed in black like a new widow, with pasty white skin and frightened eyes. I looked drawn, horrified, pathetic. No wonder he didn't love me anymore! Still, I came back for more.

"There's someone else, isn't there?" I asked, madly grasping for some explanation.

He shook his head. "No. Absolutely not. I wish there was someone else. Then it would make it easier for you to hate me. There's no one else."

"Don't I turn you on anymore?" I asked pathetically.

"You know you don't."

I had no idea that was the case. My world exploded. I heard the children playing outside our door. My God! What about the kids? We're not the only ones breaking apart here. We have these kids ...

"What about the children?" I asked.

"Oh, kids are resilient. They'll be fine," he answered. Obviously, he had rationalized it all. He sounded so flippant to me. And then he started weeping. If this was what he really wanted, I asked, why was he crying?

"Because it's all so sad," he said. "There's so much history there."

I couldn't believe he was so adamant. He was determined to get out, and quickly. He said he was leaving in two weeks. I begged him to stay for three, just so I could catch my breath.

In retrospect, as shocked as I was, it's clear that I immediately went into survival mode. I was determined to hang on to the bitter end to whatever vestiges were left of the relationship. In between imploring him to get some counselling—which he vehemently refused to do—I cooked him gourmet meals every night, organized a family outing to the zoo, and asked him to take me to see a movie in the middle of the afternoon. Ironically, it was *Titanic*. And as I sat in that dark theatre with him, holding hands and watching that big ship go down despite all the love, passion, and romance on board, I realized that life as I knew it would never be the same.

The dark depression that overtook me in the following weeks was almost intolerable. But I knew I had to hang tight to my sense of self, and to my precious girls. They were the only things I could be sure of now. I was also profoundly grateful for my work, though I went into automatic pilot for a while, going through the paces like some kind of zombie. Actually, there were aspects of my work that I suddenly couldn't stand—the schmoozing, the politics, the hype and hustle of it all. And I remember being sickened by the sight of all those glossy fashion magazines on the newsstands, emblems of the superficial world that I believed had cost me my marriage. At least part of me suspected that this monstrous career of mine was to blame for the fact that Denny didn't love me anymore. Perhaps he felt it had consumed me. Or maybe he just didn't desire me because, at forty-five years of age, I had lost my lustre, my sexual appeal. The fact that he was out of work and might have been going through a midlife crisis did not enter my mind at the time. Also, I didn't learn until five months later that he had been involved in a relationship for three years with someone decades younger than him. At the time of his departure, I was convinced that he had decided to leave because of some fault of mine.

Despite the devastation I felt, I was never angry with Denny, and I made up my mind not to resent him, no matter what. While I couldn't possibly understand at the time what it was that had led him to this decision, I was determined to try to have a good, solid relationship with him as we co-parented our precious girls. Although it was officially decided that we would have shared custody, we agreed that the girls would live in the house with me, and that Denny, who moved into his own apartment, would be with them every Wednesday and every other weekend. I'll never forget the first weekend he took them. I was beside myself, frantic about seeing them go off without me. My dear friends Christopher Hyndman, who was my makeup artist at the time, and his partner, Steven Sabados (this was a good couple of years before they launched their *Designer Guys* TV series), along with another sweet friend, Dan Duford, compassionately took me on a fun but totally tacky weekend trip to Niagara Falls just to distract me! I could not imagine ever getting used to this new reality of not having my girls with me whenever I wanted. It was a torment for me—especially when Denny took them up to the cottage. The thought of not being able to go to Muskoka with my family, as we had done so joyously for almost a decade, made me feel like I was being kicked out of my own life.

A few weeks after Denny moved out, I took the girls to California for March Break. My mother had been holidaying in Palm Springs for the winter, and I knew I had to break the sad news to her person-ally. It was one of the hardest tasks I had ever undertaken. My mother worshipped Denny and often asked me if he was really as wonderful as he appeared. "He seems too good to be true!" she used to marvel. I always assured her that her handsome son-in-law was, in fact, the real deal. Now I had to tell her that this whole chapter in my life had indeed been "too good to be true." I was crestfallen. Fighting my creeping depression, I gathered up every ounce of courage and optimism I could possibly muster and told her that everything was under control. I'd be okay. I just had to come up with a strategy to get myself back on track. But deep down inside, I doubted I would ever be happy again.

MY OWN
PRIVATE PARADISE

OUR FAMILY'S COTTAGE—that charming, humble gem of a place, built in the 1930s on the southern shore of Penn Lake—was paradise to me for nearly a decade. Denny and I had bought the property in the fall of 1990, when our girls were three and one. We wanted a family retreat where they could grow up and be close to nature—something neither Denny nor I had had as children, and something we'd always longed for. Our tiny, perfect cottage felt better to us than we ever could have imagined, and we travelled there religiously just about every weekend, forty-eight weekends a year, no matter what the weather. It was unquestionably the happiest, most comforting home I'd ever known. At the end of every week we would pack up the two cats, the two kids, and even our pet turtle, Sheldon, and make the two-and-a-half-hour trek to Muskoka, all cozy in the car, often singing along the way. Sometimes, if I had been on a business trip, Denny and the kids would pick me up at the airport, and we'd all head directly to our little piece of heaven—and the blessed chance to be together as a family for a couple of precious days. For me, it was part of striking the perfect balance, and I loved this aspect of our lives most passionately.

After Denny and I broke up in 1998, we attempted to share the cottage for about a year and a half, using it on alternating weekends. I started piling kids and cats and turtle into my car, and we headed up to the cottage on our own. But it drove me crazy. I took the greatest pains to make sure that everything was "just so" every time I left, from the way the bed was made to the way the boat was put away. I knew nothing would escape Denny's scrutiny. So while I had mastered weekend highway driving, lighting roaring fires, calling the plumber, and even discarding dead mice, I realized that I wasn't getting any closer to real independence, and the pain of constantly being reminded of what we'd lost there was just too much for me to bear. I finally asked Denny to buy me out, and I made up my mind to find another country home where the girls and I could create a new brand of family togetherness and cozy, happy times.

I knew I wanted nothing that would even remotely remind me of Muskoka. I was entertaining a new dream. Since our dear cottage was made of wood and was situated on the water, I fantasized about a stone house on an expanse of land. I envisioned myself on a farm with a French country motif, a poetic place full of bucolic charm that would speak a very different romantic language to me.

In the fall of 1999, I began scouting properties to the north and west of Toronto. I had decided a trek like the one to Muskoka was a little too long to make by myself every weekend. I wanted someplace that would be a bit more accessible—no more than an hour and a half away. But the places that were available within my price range were nowhere near charming, and all seemed to require a fair bit of work. I wanted a place I could settle into right away, without the fuss of a major renovation. It was a tall order—a stone house with character that didn't need any major work, on a decent piece of land, no more than ninety minutes from Toronto.

I was getting discouraged, but I wasn't quite ready to give up. I had faith that if I really was supposed to find this new home, I somehow would. And then, serendipity set in.

There was an art auction preview one October evening at a stately Toronto home. It was there that I met Bruce Bailey, a stylish, charismatic, slightly eccentric, and very prominent Toronto art collector. We instantly clicked. I began telling him my story: I was in the throes of getting over a sad divorce, I said, missing Muskoka terribly, but trying to put down some new country roots. I told Bruce I'd looked at several properties, but nothing had grabbed me.

"Have you tried Northumberland?"

"Where is that?" I asked, never having heard of it.

"Just east of Toronto. The prices are fabulous! You'll get much more value for your money," he said.

Bruce went on to tell me that he owned a glorious two-hundred-acre farm in Northumberland County, where he raised thoroughbreds. Then he asked me what I was doing on Sunday. I told him it was Joey's tenth birthday. "Well, it's my son's birthday on Sunday too, and I'm having a big birthday party for him at my farm. You must come and bring the girls!"

It started to feel like kismet, and the thought of taking Bekky and Joey to a wonderful farm, complete with horses, on an early fall day was tempting. I had a gut feeling we would all love it. So I accepted Bruce's friendly invitation, and that Sunday, Bekky, Joey, and our nine-month-old Golden Retriever, Beau, piled into the car and headed for Northumberland.

It was a spectacular sunny day—exactly the sort of early October day on which Denny and I had discovered our little bit of Muskoka, nine years earlier. The fall colours were in all their glory, and life was finally feeling close to perfect once again. Bruce's property was sensational, and we spent the day socializing with his guests, riding through the fields in a small horse-drawn carriage, playing with kittens in the barn, and chasing after our rambunctious puppy, who was delirious with excitement. It was one of the best days I'd had in a long, long time. I decided then and there that come spring, I would try to find a country home for us in this exquisitely beautiful neck of the woods.

In May 2000, a friend recommended a real estate agent who specialized in the area. The agent told me about a "quirky" property in Alnwick Township, about fifteen minutes away from Bruce's farm. The property included a charming little stone house, built in 1842, which had been very well cared for and, except for some redecorating, wouldn't need much work at all. The property, which had been on the market for a while, even had a pond on it, perfect for Beau. The only downside, according to the agent, was its size: a whopping 123 acres! The house was smack dab in the middle of all this land, so while there was privacy, the agent felt that the property in general was a little enigmatic, and that's why it hadn't sold. I made plans to see the place that weekend.

The magic set in the moment I turned onto a winding dirt road and started the gradual uphill climb past patches of forest and golden meadows. When I finally got to the front gate, I was charmed when I noticed that atop the two stone pillars were two stone roosters, each with a distinct air of antiquity and a cocky sense of pride and permanence. I could swear they were calling my name. My heart melted as I turned into the long tree-lined driveway. The light was radiant and everything was in bloom: towering lilac bushes; flowerbeds brimming with tall, unruly hollyhocks; overgrown patches of giant-leafed rhubarb; endless expanses of emerald lawns; and vast corn- and wheatfields and wildflower pastures that stretched beyond the rustic log fences. To add to the charm, an assortment of eclectic birdhouses perched atop several tall wooden posts. Even before I set eyes on the old farmhouse, I knew I had come home. This setting was light years away from the rugged beauty of Muskoka and that sparkling lake I so adored. But somehow, the sad memories of all those painful months—when I knew I was losing our beloved cottage—began to dissipate. I had discovered a new country haven, and it was exactly as I had envisioned it. My guardian angel—perhaps my late dad—was taking care of me once again.

The farmhouse was the most idyllic little stone house imaginable, like something out of a storybook, complete with shuttered windows, a big brass doorknocker, and an angel weather vane. A weathered shed nearby sported a shingle roof covered in moss. Inside, the house oozed charm and personality, with three fireplaces, chintz wallpaper, wide plank floors, quaint crystal chandeliers, an old-fashioned bathtub, and three bedrooms on the second floor. Perfect for me and the girls! The upstairs floors were black-and-white checkerboard, and the bedroom doors were whimsically painted bright red. I knew that Bekky and Joey would be enchanted: I couldn't wait to bring them to see it all! I flashed on the cocky stone guardians at the front gate and decided then and there to call my new-found haven Chanteclair, after the proud rooster in the old children's story.

"What does a single mother with two girls need a 123-acre farm for?" demanded my well-meaning mother. I tried to make her understand that I was trying to recapture some of my lost happiness. My mum, who was very much against my letting go of the cottage in the first place, wasn't convinced. But she gave me her blessing anyway, reluctantly admitting that my dad would have been very proud of this impressive, if daunting, acquisition.

A few weeks before I took possession of Chanteclair that summer, I brought Bekky and Joey out to see it. We were all so excited on the way that when we passed a sign that read "Kittens: Five Dollars," we couldn't resist stopping, just to have a look. Of course, we then couldn't leave without taking one of the irresistible creatures with us. We named him Marcel, put him in a cardboard box, and continued on our way. The girls fell instantly in love with the charming old stone house. They claimed their rooms, Bekky dubbing hers "Alice in Wonderland" and Joey settling for something more bucolic, "The Cow Room." In the car on the way back, we continued dreaming and scheming, with Marcel merrily mewing away in his cardboard box and Beau sleeping in the back, exhausted. This new feeling of independence was exhilarating. I didn't have to consult with anyone about financing, or what colours to paint the walls, or what furniture to buy, or what kinds of deals to make with which farmers and tradesmen to help me keep the place going. It was one of the happiest days of my life.

But as the possession date drew nearer, I started to experience a bit of buyer's remorse, a kind of insecurity about whether I would really be able to handle this grand property on my own, and even a little fear about the isolation and loneliness that it might bring, knowing that I would have the girls there with me only on alternating weekends. Maybe my mother was right and I was a little crazy after all. I tried my best to ignore these nagging doubts and throw myself into sprucing up the place. But in my heart, I secretly prayed for some sign that I had indeed made the right decision.

I wanted Chanteclair to have a French country vibe, so I went on a mad shopping spree, buying a variety of things that spoke of Provence, from hand-painted blue-and-yellow dishes and an antique harvest table to a yellow-and-cream-striped couch and a huge Edwardian birdcage, which I planned to place on the big pine windowsill with its door flung wide open—a symbol of my new freedom. One of the most endearing little things I purchased was a hand-painted plaque with the words "Believe in Yourself" to hang just inside the front door, so I'd see it every time I entered the house.

Just around the time I was set to move in, my friends Steven and Christopher began production on their first season of *The Designer Guys*. Chris called me and asked if they could have a hand in decorating my farmhouse for the second episode of the show. I balked, not sure if I really wanted a designer-perfect place. I told them I had already started buying things. But Chris and Steven said they would incorporate my purchases, assured me they would only do the living room, and guaranteed that since they knew me so intimately, their riff on the French country theme I'd chosen would be everything I had dreamed of and more.

They asked that I check out a few things they were considering purchasing for the house and urged me to visit a large Toronto furniture store called Elte Carpets. It was located in the northwest end, a part of the city I didn't frequent, so I begged off and told them I completely trusted their taste. Not long after, however, I found myself in that neck of the woods and decided to drop by Elte just to see what all the fuss was about.

The upscale store was housed in an enormous warehouse type of space. I walked through the front doors, not knowing exactly what I was looking for. But almost instantly, I spotted a big Ralph Lauren sign at the back of the store and decided that area might feature some pleasing items. As I entered the Ralph Lauren section, I saw a round table laden with old trophies—about twenty of them. As a lover of flea-market finds and interesting old memorabilia in general, I gravitated towards this table. One trophy in particular caught my eye. Sleek and elegant, it was shaped like a kind of loving cup. I picked it up to read the inscription, supposing it had been awarded for something exotic, like curling or maybe even lacrosse. I was stunned when I read the big letters on the front of the cup: "Public Speaking Trophy." That was pretty seductive. If I ever won a trophy, I thought to myself, I'd want it to be for public speaking. What I read next blew my mind: "Presented by Alnwick Council." Chanteclair was in Alnwick Township! I turned the trophy around and saw a long list of names inscribed on the back. The very first one my eyes hit was "Edward Coyle, 1954." Chanteclair had been built by the Coyle family! The hair on my arms stood up as I continued to read the names of winners dating back to 1931. Many of the names were familiar to me, since they could also be found on various landmarks, roads, and villages in the township. The Doris M. Robins who had received the honour in 1945 was likely of Robins General Store fame. The 1933 winner was Audrey A. Mouncey, as in Mouncey Road, just down the highway from my farm. Judith McCracken, possibly from the farm family the next property over, took the award in 1961. The neighbouring village of Fenella was cited beside the names of some of the winners. What were the chances, I wondered, of finding this trophy so far from where it had originated, in this obscure place—a shop I hadn't even wanted to visit? I had to have this trophy and take it back home where it belonged. I knew this was just the sign I'd been praying for.

It took a while to talk the store manager into selling it to me. It was being used as a prop in the Ralph Lauren department and wasn't even for sale. But my little story was just too compelling, I guess. The manager eventually sold me the trophy for two hundred dollars, and I left Elte Carpets with the precious artifact in tow, now totally convinced that the gods wanted me to have this special property in divine Alnwick County.

I decided to bring the trophy to Chanteclair on the day Steven and Chris were shooting. On the way to the farm, I stopped by Bev Robins's store in Roseneath. Standing behind the counter, Bev was flabbergasted to see me with the trophy his sister had brought home some fifty years ago! He began reminiscing about almost every name inscribed on it, relaying bits and pieces of old gossip about these locals along the way.

I was thrilled that I had such a monumental piece of Alnwick memorabilia in my possession—and I took it back to my farmhouse.

When I got there, I was amazed by the splendid job Chris and Steven had done, and overcome by all their creative touches. The room had been painted a soft, buttery yellow. The house's original old windowpanes, found abandoned in the shed, had been lovingly transformed into magnificent wall pieces, one featuring small mirrors, another antique botanical prints. They had brought the outdoors inside by placing urns filled with tall, striking branches they had gathered from around the property on either side of the couch. There were two moss-filled white urns on the windowsills and a lovely hooked rug in the centre of the room. Faux white shutters adorned the huge, deep-set windows. An array of beautiful pillows made out of yellow-and-burgundy toile and blue plaid complemented my yellow-and-white-striped couch. My new pine coffee table had been painted white and then distressed to make it look like an antique. The lovely old birdcage with its open door had been placed on the large windowsill in front of my desk, so I could face this emblem of freedom and gaze out the window at this inspiring new setting while I wrote. A gorgeous French floral print hung over the fireplace, with lovely topiaries atop the mantle. And there in the centre, the guys had placed a small framed photograph—one of my favourites—of my father happily clapping his big hands, eyes closed in joy, that fabulous grin of his just beaming at me.

The Designer Guys camera crew was there to capture my reaction to Chris and Steven's brilliant handiwork. The living room looked like a dream, and I suddenly felt very much at home. I unwrapped the trophy and showed it to Chris and Steven, recounting the incredible story of its discovery. I then placed it on the mantle, right next to the photograph of my father, and that's where it still sits a decade later, a constant reminder of the magic that is Chanteclair. That amazing memento also serves as a kind of pat on the back from my late, great dad, who, I'm convinced, concocted this sign for me, just to let me know that he approved of my buying this unique and charming country home.

TAKING CHANCES

COMPLACENCY IS OFTEN a danger of aging. We can become so comfortable in our far-from-perfect lives that we just accept them as they are, rather than going out on a limb and trying to make things better. But how can you improve the quality of your life if you don't take a risk? How can you find what you really crave if you don't step outside your safety zone?

Call it a midlife crisis, but about six weeks before my forty-ninth birthday, I was overcome by the feeling that I was at the end of a road. I was seized by the notion, more enthralling than disturbing, that I had to do something wild and crazy, push my personal envelope, challenge myself to visit dark places, expose my inner secrets, and get closer to my own truths. I decided to celebrate my midlife awakening by purchasing a brightly painted, life-size fibreglass moose. It was one of several dozen that had been painted by local artists, sold to sponsors, and placed throughout the city in 2000, in an effort to raise money for Toronto's failed bid for the 2008 Olympics. The project was commissioned by Mayor Mel Lastman, and after the novelty of the moose wore off, the mayor's wife hosted a charity ball to sell off about fifty of the antlered creatures to enthusiastic bidders, with the proceeds benefiting a number of good causes. The five thousand dollars I spent on my moose went to a women's shelter. It was definitely a feel-good thing, and the outrageous, friendly looking creature still stands by the side of the pond at my farm, emblematic of that restless, exciting time in my life.

But something else happened to me the week I bought the moose: I was offered a three-week stint in *The Vagina Monologues*. This controversial, much-celebrated work, based on a book by the American writer Eve Ensler, is a compilation of interviews with women talking in graphic detail about their often-ignored genitals. Ensler originally delivered a selection of these sometimes amusing, often poignant monologues in 1996, in a one-woman show that played cities from Jerusalem to Stockholm. The presentation never failed to garner rave reviews, and before long, some of America's best-loved actresses, from Whoopi Goldberg to Susan Sarandon to Glenn Close, had been invited to deliver selected monologues for benefit performances. Eventually, *The Vagina Monologues* evolved into a three-woman show, with two regular actresses joined on stage by high-profile celebrities—people such as Brooke Shields, Alanis Morissette, Calista Flockhart, Claire Danes, Andrea Martin, Julianna Margulies, Amy Irving, and Marlo Thomas. *The Vagina Monologues* soon became the stuff feminists and great actresses longed to wrap their heads and hearts around. Now, a Canadian company was bringing the show to Toronto, and I was approached to participate.

Up to this point, I had felt no compulsion to see *The Vagina Monologues*. As a matter of fact, when a friend told me she was going, I cringed, suspecting the whole deal was mere exploitation. I was determined to keep my vagina to myself, thank you very much, and the last thing I wanted to hear was how other women were dealing with theirs. Maybe I was a prude, but the whole concept seemed weird and unsavoury to me. I shuddered at the thought of a room full of women fixating on their privates. I may have burned my bra with the best of them in the 1960s, but what lurked behind my zippered fly was nobody's business.

So there I was, going through this midlife moment, having bought this extravagant beast of an *objet d'art*, when the theatre producer

Stephen Shinn left a message on my voicemail inviting me to take part in one of the hottest and most talked about shows of the moment. I called back and told him how flattered I was but said it wasn't my cup of tea. He begged me to reserve judgment until I'd read the script. "Okay," I said. "Send it over."

I immediately called a number of male and female friends to get their take on the offer. The response was unanimous: I had to accept! The experience might stir up some forgotten talent in me—maybe I would find a new old calling. My New York acting-school training would serve me well. This was my big chance to revisit places deep within my creative psyche. My anticipation mounted.

The script was delivered the next day in a plain brown envelope. I looked at it as if it were some forbidden fruit, a mysterious package that could change the direction of my life—or at least my sexual aware-ness—forever. I grabbed it and ran upstairs to my bedroom, closing the door behind me for the privacy I craved. Stephen Shinn had said I could choose three or four monologues. I disappeared even further into my inner sanctum. Finally, in my ensuite bathroom, confident I was out of earshot of both nanny and kids, I began reading the script out loud. By the time I got to the end of the third monologue, there were tears in my eyes. I was mesmerized by the honesty and intimacy of the words I was reading, and I slowly got hooked on the profound sense of sharing I knew the performance would provide.

The material was superb—heartfelt, emotional, brave, funny, tragic. I immediately understood why so many women related to it, and why so many famous actresses had jumped at the chance to be part of this unique production. After I got over the initial discomfort of having to articulate some of these sacred and profane thoughts and feelings, I realized these passages were overflowing with a pain and joy that was oddly liberating. I was reminded of my humanity, innocence, passion, and victimization. Suddenly, I couldn't wait to get up there and present these daring and powerful monologues. I called Stephen and enthusias-tically accepted the honour. I had no idea how I would explain it all to my eighty-year-old mother, who was vacationing in Palm Springs but would be back just before opening night. She was bound to hear about my return to the stage and would be eager to see what all the fuss was about. No way I could allow that!

For my appearance, I was teamed up with two wonderful Toronto actresses, Krista Sutton and Karen Robinson, and we were directed by Kate Lynch, who was a complete joy to work with. Actually, the show was one of the best experiences of my creative life. I'll forever be grateful for the thrill—after so many years of secretly longing to get back on the stage—of getting the chance to express myself in that intimate little theatre, before a receptive audience.

The monologues I chose included one by an elderly woman talking about having some kind of unexpected discharge, tantamount to a basement flood, "down there"—as in, "There was a flood down there!" I decided to assume a broad character for this dramatically endearing piece, choosing to play her as an old lady from the Bronx, complete with heavy New York accent. This monologue went over extremely well, and people were enchanted by my delivery—especially those who had no idea I had ever been an actress. I was proud as punch that I still had my chops. And there was another factor I secretly relished: I was in the early throes of menopause at the time. Undergoing intense hot flashes up there onstage, as we three performers spun tales of woman-hood and the female experience, was strangely invigorating. Both the play and the performance resonated with me profoundly, and it was all because I had taken that risk, ventured out on some scary turf, and transcended my initial small-mindedness.

While I did invite Bekky, who was fourteen at the time, to see the show, I thought that Joey, at eleven, was a little too young. And I never did let my mum come. I told her it might freak her out too much. She reluctantly acquiesced. In retrospect, I regret that decision. After all, it was the role of a lifetime for me. Perhaps I could have been a little more courageous when it came to showing my mother the stuff I was made of. But that stint onstage served its purpose: It helped remind me that I was a true performer whose absolute delight is telling stories. Happily, it wouldn't be the last time.

IN FASHION

I've always been charmed by William Blake's notion
that a world can be seen in a grain of sand. For the past
quarter century, that grain of sand, for me, has been
fashion. Granted, it can be an arena filled with artifice
and illusion. But perhaps because its star players are
just people at the heart of it all, the fashion world also
provides an astoundingly rich backdrop for insight into
the human spirit.

APOCALYPSE THEN

FOR A LONG TIME, I was enamoured with the fashion world because it seemed so rarefied. Those of us who work in its trenches are, for the most part, die-hard romantics, hell-bent on keeping our glorious bubble intact. This is a world where we all aspire to express ourselves through beautiful and stylish imagery—whether we're creating it, reporting on it, selling it, or wearing it. So when we all got a loud and unexpected wakeup call smack dab in the middle of New York Fashion Week on September 11, 2001, we fashion warriors were affected in profound and peculiar ways. My own 9/11 experience had me questioning the validity of the business, and left me wondering about fashion's future.

New York Fashion Week had just got underway. I spent Sunday afternoon at the swish Fifth Avenue penthouse of Denise Rich, the estranged wife of Marc Rich, an international commodities trader who had been indicted in the United States on charges of tax evasion and making illegal oil deals with Iran. (Rich received a presidential pardon from Bill Clinton on his last day in office.) Rich himself was based in Switzerland, but his and Denise's artistic daughter, Ilona, had come up with a cool new clothing line, and she was showing it to the press at an intimate presentation in her mother's apartment. Amid Denise Rich's hugely impressive art collection, a privileged assortment of top editors and stylish socialites sat sipping champagne, eating petit fours, and looking out at the glorious view of Central Park. I remember thinking this was everything I had ever imagined the good life in New York to be about. I was living the dream.

The next evening, my dear friend Carol Leggett accompanied me to the Marc Jacobs show, which was held in a big warehouse and tent down on Pier 54 on the Hudson River, about five kilometres north of the World Trade Center. Marc's shows always attracted a huge celebrity crowd, and this night was no exception, with luminaries like Sarah Jessica Parker, Chris Noth, Debbie Harry, Sophie Dahl, Sofia Coppola, Zoe Cassavetes, and Rosanna Arquette there to cheer Marc on and celebrate his upbeat 1960s-inspired collection, as well as the launch of his first eponymous fragrance.

It was a warm, clear, gorgeous night. Just a few blocks away, the Statue of Liberty was in full view. Carol and I marvelled at the opulence and perfection of the evening, which was also a fundraiser to benefit a dozen New York charities. Marc had proved to be a great success at the creative helm of Louis Vuitton, and his *savoir faire* as one of the world's most influential designers was in evidence in an entire wall lined with exquisite white gardenias—the scent of his new perfume. Post-show, hundreds of people feasted at long tables laden with sumptuous food. Wall Street and the Twin Towers loomed in the distance. In an ironic twist, a small fire-fighting tugboat shot mammoth sprays of water into the air, pumping up the inspiration for the scent: gardenias in water. The decadent spectacle was nothing short of exhilarating. "This reminds me of what led to the fall of the Roman Empire!" I joked to Carol. We never guessed it was the calm before the storm.

The next morning, I was up early for the Oscar de la Renta show, which was taking place in the tents at Bryant Park at Thirty-ninth Street and Sixth Avenue, just a few blocks from where I was staying. It was close to 9:00 a.m. when I turned on the TV to NBC's *Today Show*. A Toronto colleague, Serena French, who was reporting on fashion for the *National Post*, called and we started chatting about the designer shows we'd seen to date. Serena had her TV on as well, coincidentally also tuned to *The Today Show*. During the course of our conversation, we both became aware that Katie Couric was saying something about a small plane having flown into one of the World Trade Center's towers. The report seemed to indicate that it was a private plane, and Serena and I remarked how freaky that was. Suddenly, we both witnessed an incredible image: What looked like another small plane was flying directly into the second tower! We stopped talking. And for about another fifteen minutes, we both kept silent—my jaw had literally dropped—as we watched the riveting, colossal tragedy unfold.

Serena finally broke the silence. "My God," she said, "I've got to go and call my paper," and we hung up. I continued watching the TV screen in horror, dumbfounded as the enormity of the disaster began to sink in. Another plane had gone down in a field in Pennsylvania. A fourth one had hit the Pentagon. The phone rang. It was the news director at Citytv.

"Your cellphone's not working. Are you aware of what's happening?" he asked.

"Yeah, I've just been watching it on TV," I said.

"Well, can you get Arthur"—he was referring to my cameraman, Arthur Pressick—"and go down there to try to talk to some people?"

"Are you serious?" I asked. After all, my beat was fashion, not news. "I don't think that's such a good idea right now. But let me call Arthur and get right back to you."

Arthur had just woken up, but he already knew what had happened.

"They want us to go down there," I told him.

"Are they crazy?" he retorted. "I'm not risking my life."

I totally concurred. Besides, the authorities had issued strong warnings for people to stay indoors and not go anywhere near the towers. The Oscar de la Renta show was obviously cancelled. I wondered if they would cancel Fashion Week altogether. The phone lines hadn't gone dead yet, so I called my mother to let her know I was okay. Then I contacted my sister in L.A., waking her up and telling her to turn on the TV. Finally, I called my boyfriend at the time, Jack, who was in a board meeting and was oblivious to what was happening. Carol called me from her downtown apartment, hysterical. "Can you believe this!?"

she asked. And before I could answer, she started screaming, "Oh, my God! That entire building just collapsed! I have to go ..." And she was gone. Everything had become a blur. I rang Arthur's room again. "Do you think maybe we should just go down as far as Bryant Park, to try to get some reactions from people?" Arthur reluctantly agreed, and so we warily made our way out of the hotel and across Forty-fourth Street.

Hilary Alexander, the fashion editor of *The Daily Telegraph*, was the first person we ran into. She seemed a little frantic and was definitely wide-eyed. "Did you hear that there were supposed to be eight hijacked planes but only four have been accounted for?" she asked. The implication was that the others could strike anywhere, at any time. I couldn't begin to imagine what that meant, but we were determined to carry on. Sixth Avenue and the streets around it were utterly free of traffic, save for the odd police car or ambulance screeching downtown. Arthur and I bravely walked south as scores of people streamed towards us heading north. They were moving faster than usual, eager to get as far away from Ground Zero as possible—eager to get home. The subway system had been shut down, and the odd bus that passed us was crammed with passengers. Small groups were huddled around boom box radios, hungry for the latest information. Every conversation I could tune in to revolved around the horror of the terrorist attack. Some people were sobbing, and others stared straight ahead, like zombies. Sirens could be heard everywhere, but there were no vehicles, just a sea of pedestrians, packs of frightened people trying to make sense of the insanity. I heard jets overhead. Could any of these be the "unaccounted for" planes that Hilary had mentioned? Maybe they were planning to strike the fashion tents at Bryant Park? As crazy as that sounds now, it seemed like a plausible notion at the time. After all, if these were terrorists, why wouldn't they want to make their voices heard at a place where they knew the international press had gathered? My imagination was running rampant, and with one eye on the sky above, I felt my heart starting to beat faster and faster.

Finally, we arrived at the Bryant Park tents, their sides decorated with the gritty graffiti of the New York artist and designer Stephen Sprouse, who would die just a few short years later. A row of security guards stood at the entrance. The day's shows had been cancelled, and no, I couldn't get a comment from anyone from the Council of Fashion Designers of America—everyone was tied up in an emergency meeting. I told Arthur that I wanted to interview people about what they were feeling. I saw the friendly face of the runway photographer Randy Brooke. I had known Randy for years—he was a laid-back, cheerful guy. But now, the fear in his eyes was palpable. He started telling me about a buddy who had been near the World Trade Center at the moment of the first crash. "Are you rolling?" I asked Arthur. Randy proceeded to give us a graphic description of what his friend had seen. We were entranced.

All of a sudden, like a tidal wave of terror, everybody started running and pushing and yelling. I looked up at the sky, certain that a fiery jet was coming right for us in Bryant Park. Cops were running in all directions, and the throngs of people on the street in front of the big tent scattered, everyone dashing every which way. I saw Arthur out of the corner of my eye. Amazingly enough, he was straddling the curb, still rolling in an attempt to capture the insanity. I huddled up against a wall with some young guy I recognized as another fashion reporter. I was shaking. Chaos reigned. It might have been a few seconds. It felt like a hundred years.

Gradually, things calmed down. "It's all right, everybody," a cop called out. "It's okay. Somebody said they were blowing up the Chrysler Building. Evidently, it was a false alarm. Just try to get inside now." The young guy hugged me and told me that he was scared too, but it was going to be all right. All I could think about were my girls and how I had to call them immediately. I raced to a phone booth and tried to call home, but the line was dead. I had never felt so scared and alone. I flashed on my parents and the war stories they had told me growing up—the desolation, the panic, the fear, the random way they would run into certain people and totally lose track of others. This is what war must feel like, I thought. Maybe the Third World War was breaking out. My safe, cozy, charmed life was over.

I searched the sea of faces for a familiar one, and there was Barbara Atkin, the fashion director of Holt Renfrew.

"Jeanne, where's your hotel?" she asked.

"Just a few blocks away," I told her. "Let's go!"

A couple of others who were on their own joined us. No one wanted to be alone. When we got back to the hotel, the lobby was filled with people and television sets. Everybody was glued to the screens, trying to figure out how the world had changed, and how they would get home. There was a conscious, deep awareness that home was the only place that really mattered now, and the sudden desperation to see loved ones had everyone on tenterhooks. But getting home would be a challenge.

All the airports had been closed, along with all the tunnels and bridges and borders. People were saying that there was still limited train service, and some scrambled to make reservations. Another good friend, the retail dynamo Bonnie Brooks, who was in from Hong Kong, got hold of me at the hotel and asked how I was getting back to Toronto. She wanted to come back with me so she could see her mother. Barb's boss, Andrew Jennings, the president of Holt Renfrew, had come in that morning, on a flight that landed shortly before the disaster. As he drove into the city and realized what was going on, he decided to turn around and have his driver take him all the way back to Toronto. Barb spoke to Andrew, and he assured us he would arrange for another car to pick us up as soon as the roads were open again.

I went up to my room and checked my voicemail. I was overwhelmed by the number of calls that had come in—friends, relatives, even casual acquaintances who knew I'd be in New York for Fashion Week, all checking to see whether I was okay. It was moving to feel that loved. The *Toronto Sun* called and asked whether I could write a first-person account of what I had experienced. The Internet was down, so after I wrote my story, I called the *Sun*'s newsroom and dictated the article to them word by word. I then did another live phone report for *CityPulse* news. My voice was breaking as I recounted the morning terror. I kept saying that all this had jarred me into remembering what was really important in life. And all I yearned to do was get home so I could hug my kids.

The next morning, a driver named Errol in a black sedan collected Barb, Bonnie, and me for the long drive back home. Traffic was horrendous, and many roads were still closed. Errol warned us that he would take us only as far as the Peace Bridge—it would just take too long to get through. We could walk across the bridge, he said, and arrange for another car to take us home from the other side.

As we hit the highway, I looked back at what we were leaving behind. The huge smokestacks receded in the distance, and I thought about all the hype and glamour and dazzle that were synonymous with New York. And I wondered whether things would, or could, ever be the same.

A couple of hours after we got on the New York State Thruway, we made a pit stop for gas and decided to stock up on munchies for the ride. We were poking through the convenience store when Bonnie told me she thought she saw Tommy Hilfiger one aisle over. "You're nuts!" I said, figuring that the events of the day had made her giddy. But as I turned the corner, I heard a voice calling my name. I looked up, and there was Tommy with his wife and daughter! It felt like another one of those war stories my parents had told me, where you randomly bump into all kinds of unexpected people because things have been so shaken up. Tommy was going to Upstate New York to visit his ailing brother. I kept thinking that the episode was like a bizarre dream: "And then we had to flee New York because the whole city was going up in smoke. So we piled in a limo to drive back home and made a pit stop, and there, between the pretzels and potato chips, was Tommy Hilfiger ..." Sometimes life really is stranger than fiction.

I honestly believed at that point that fashion might be over forever. I mean, who could ever be moved by a beautiful dress again? Who could seriously fret over what to wear in light of what had happened? How could I continue in this business, scrambling around the world to trend-spot and pick designers' brains? Overnight, fashion had seemed to turn into something horribly shallow and unspeakably insipid. I couldn't imagine anyone ever really caring about it again.

When we finally got to the Peace Bridge, there had been a bomb threat, so Errol drove us to an alternate border crossing at Niagara Falls, where a new driver picked us up. When I arrived home, my girls were waiting at the door. "We were so scared," said Joey. "I wish you didn't have to travel ever, ever again." I hugged them, held them, and told them it would all be okay.

But I had a slight problem: Just a few days later, I was slated to fly across Canada to launch my new Jeanne Beker clothing line for Eaton's. And if that wasn't enough, the collection was inspired by my hectic, jet-set lifestyle and had been designed with the travelling woman in mind. How ironic! Most of us never wanted to get on a plane again. But travelling was such a vital part of my life. How would I cover the international scene if I was balking at the thought of boarding an airplane? Was it time to reassess what I did for a living? Or would the fear eventually subside?

By the weekend, emotional exhaustion had set in. The morning papers carried headlines about a possible impending war, with page after page of doom-and-gloom stories. Suddenly, in the front section of the paper, I spotted a huge ad: "Meet Jeanne Beker … Monday … as she launches her new clothing line." My heart sank. There I was, looking smug and cool and glamorous, a coat slung over my shoulder, confidently standing inside an airport terminal—the modern woman on the go—as assorted pieces from my collection went round the luggage carousel. The concept had seemed so clever at the time. Now, the notion of a clothing line geared to travelling seemed laughable. I should have been thrilled—a new project had come to fruition, a dream had come true. But I was overwhelmed by sadness and wept at the helplessness, and hopelessness, of fashion. Nevertheless, friends and colleagues turned out at the downtown Toronto Eaton's store on Monday morning to attend the launch and cheer me on. We weren't in a celebratory mood, but it felt good to be together again, especially after the aborted Fashion Week. It was apparent that we needed this arena as an escape—a friendly diversion in a world that was growing increasingly dark.

You could have heard a pin drop at the airport when I boarded the plane for Vancouver a couple of days later. It was less than a week after 9/11, and hardly anyone was flying. Having eagerly boarded planes my whole life, I was now frightened, but I fought to put the paranoia to rest. After about an hour in the air, acceptance set in. I came to the conclusion that life does go on. Despite the devastation, the fear, the uncertainty, it's our duty to forge ahead. This is what makes us human. When I addressed the crowd gathered at the Vancouver Eaton's store—a big, friendly sea of faces eager to escape for a few minutes and watch beautiful women glide down a runway—I remembered what's at the very heart of fashion: the need to dream, to imagine, to see ourselves in a perfect world, where the right clothes can actually transform us, lead us in new directions, and help us live carefree lives. Great style will never save the world, but sometimes, it can make things a little more tolerable.

By spring, the beast that is fashion had indeed marched on. Fashion is just too big a business to stop for long. The collections that came down the runways for spring '02 had been conceived prior to "the day the world changed," and fashion that season tenaciously held to themes of innocence and romance. The heavy doses of femininity and escapism, and the new Boho Chic trend, offered a welcome bit of relief and a much-needed sense of optimism in a dark world.

By fall '02, one short year after fashion had been the last thing on anybody's mind, designers were more determined than ever to embrace all that was positive in the business. "This is about fashion," Calvin Klein told me. "And fashion is always supposed to make a woman or a man feel good, regardless of the economy, politics, whatever is going on in the world. Fashion should never make you feel depressed. Otherwise, what's the point?" We were backstage at the Milk Studios, just after he had presented his sensual spring '03 collection. "It's time to feel happy again," agreed Anna Sui as she sent out an ultra-upbeat, sport-themed collection, which included a sparkling football jersey reminiscent of the one Geoffrey Beene gave us back in 1968—a piece that heralded a "loosening up" of glamour. Anna Sui's vision was all about slowing down and smelling the flowers. It was just the kind of feel-good statement we had been longing for.

The celebrity quotient at the shows that season was stronger than ever too, with a bevy of stars coming out to support their friends. Oprah Winfrey and Holly Hunter were at Vera Wang; Hilary Swank and Sandra Bullock sat in the front row at Marc Jacobs; Julianne Moore and Ellen Barkin turned up at Rick Owens; Gwyneth Paltrow was at Calvin Klein; Britney Spears caused a stir at Pat Field; Sarah Jessica Parker came out for Narciso Rodriguez; Bette Midler added to the fun at Cynthia Rowley; Elizabeth Hurley cheered on Ralph Lauren. These celebs were all chatting up the importance of style, and telling us it was time to go shopping again.

The events of 9/11 had robbed us of our innocence and changed the world in some basic way. But by that next September, optimism had unquestionably returned to New York. I remember taking in a street fair on Sixth Avenue one Saturday morning during that Fashion Week. I had an hour between shows, and I wanted to soak up some sunshine. Vendors were out selling balloons and toys and kebabs and crepes and lemonade and CDs and jewellery and T-shirts and spices and handbags—and just about everything else imaginable. The road was teeming with families and couples and bargain hunters and cops and kids and dogs. Everyone was smiling and helpful and kind and friendly. It was pure joy seeing that remarkable city so wholeheartedly back in motion. I was awed by the human resiliency and took pride in our limitless potential.

On my way back to the tents, a woman came up to me and asked if I was a designer. "No, I'm just reporting on the shows," I told her. "Well, you should come see me," she said. "I'm a psychic, and I see lots of good things coming your way. Big changes. Many good things." She scribbled down her name and address. And as I watched her disappear down the street, I somehow believed in her forecast, awed by the new-found optimism in the New York air.

ON THE EDGE

THE FIRST INTERNATIONAL DESIGNER I interviewed, even before the launch of *Fashion Television*, was the Italian-born genius Pierre Cardin. It was *circa* 1984, and Cardin had just acquired the legendary French restaurant Maxim's. In an effort to promote the country's culture, Air France had generously offered our entertainment news department a free trip to Paris to interview the celebrated designer, who revolutionized the fashion industry in 1960 when he famously, and controversially, introduced the idea of licensing his name. Cardin also treated our crew to a couture show at his Espace Cardin. I was awed by this charming but egotistical creator, who dreamed of one day opening a restaurant on the moon.

As recently as 2010, I had the pleasure of interviewing Cardin at length in his Paris office across from the Élysée Palace. At eighty-eight, he was as spry, astute, and productive as ever. Days earlier, he had sent a new spring collection down a Paris runway. And he delighted in showing me the sketches for a futuristic building he had designed, which was being erected outside of Venice. I was stunned by Cardin's ability to recall names, dates, and experiences. Could it be that the secret to his sharp mind and ageless spirit was his active sex life? I commented on the fact that he was so impressively sound of mind and body. And then I asked him what shape his heart was in, romantically speaking. "Oh, I'm never alone in my bed!" he said, laughing mischievously. Evidently, his passion for work had kept Cardin young. But I was happy to hear him insinuate that a good helping of sex wasn't hurting. It was no surprise to me that the billionaire couturier enjoyed an association with history's most notorious playboy, the Marquis de Sade.

Now, it isn't every day that a girl gets invited to the château of the Marquis de Sade. But when Cardin bought the historic castle of the infamous libertine, he was eager to show it off, and to establish the village of Lacoste as a cultural destination. So in July 2001, when Paris couture week wrapped, the visionary entrepreneur and philanthropist, who was then seventy-eight, invited me and 880 other guests to an unparalleled Provence experience: Cardin's arts foundation was hosting a *grande soirée* at the marquis' abandoned château, complete with a full-scale production of a new musical Cardin had commissioned, based on the legend of Tristan and Yseult, which also happened to be the name of Cardin's new fragrance. Evidently, Cardin's marketing savvy was still going strong.

The coveted invitation requested that we dress "*léger, en noir et blanche*"—lightly, in black and white. As a tribute to the infamous marquis, I was tempted to get outrageously decked out in skimpy black leather. But at the last minute, I opted for prudence, donning a lacy cocktail number and a pair of strappy Sergio Rossi stilettos, which definitely had the right S&M attitude—I knew they would be torturing me by the end of the night! And so, feeling a little like a true fashion victim, I drove past the fields of sunflowers and lavender to Lacoste, about forty kilometres east of Avignon.

I knew little of the history of de Sade's château—only that it was to him what Walden was to Thoreau: a place of inspiration. I imagined a lush and decadent fortress. But when we finally reached the summit where the château stood, I was disappointed to find little more than ruins—a few half-demolished rooms, parts of walls and ramparts. The forty-two-room château had been destroyed in 1792. Midway through the past century, the remains of the château and its surrounding terrain

My parents, Joseph and Bronia, after the war in Lodz, Poland. They'd been to hell and back, and were eager to rebuild their shattered lives.

TOP: For my sweet sixteen in 1968 at Yorkdale's Encore Restaurant, my mother and I had a dressmaker copy an glitzy outfit that was featured on the cover of *Harper's Bazaar*.

BOTTOM LEFT: Just back from studying acting at the HB Studio in New York in 1972, I posed for my dramatic new 8x10 glossies.
(MIKE GLUSS)

BOTTOM RIGHT: Mime became a new creative mode of expression for me when I returned from studying the art form in Paris in 1974.
(ANDRÉE GAGNÉ)

TOP: Radio station promotions, such as this one for a CHUM bike-a-thon in the summer of 1979, were especially fun once I started dating the handsome all-night deejay, Bob Magee (a.k.a. Denny O'Neil).

BOTTOM: This Toronto subway poster heralded my new position as 1050 CHUM's "Good News Girl" in 1978. Note the incorrect spelling of my first name. The marketing department thought the original spelling of *Jeanne* wouldn't read properly. (Lucky they didn't insist on adding a *c* in *Beker* … though they tried!) (COURTESY OF CTV)

TOP: J.D. Roberts (a.k.a. John Roberts) and I were dubbed "video virgins" by the media when we began co-hosting Citytv's groundbreaking magazine show *The New Music* in 1979. (COURTESY OF CTV)

RIGHT: The early '80s were an exhilarating blur of concerts and rock star interviews for me as co-host of *The New Music* and news anchor on MuchMusic, which we launched in 1983. (COURTESY OF CTV)

TOP: Posing for our first formal family portrait. The birth of our daughter, Rebecca Leigh (Bekky), in 1987 brought Denny and me incredible joy. I was beginning to feel as though I had it all.
(TIBOR HORVATH)

MIDDLE: Time spent at our sacred little Muskoka cottage with Bekky and Joey through the early '90s was one of my life's greatest blessings.

BOTTOM: Joey and Bekky on-set with the Olsen twins in Toronto during the filming of *It Takes Two* in 1995.

TOP: Chanteclair, the magical little 1842 stone farmhouse I acquired in 2000, became emblematic of my independence and provides the perfect sanctuary from the wilds of the high fashion world.

LEFT: The moose that I bought at a charity auction in 2001, painted by artist Linda Blix, stands guard near the pond at my farm.

RIGHT: My old friends Steven Sabados and Chris Hyndeman helped comfort me after my marriage breakup and decorated the living room at Chanteclair for their first show, *The Designer Guys*.

TOP: I've always felt a kind of solace whenever I've visited Ireland, and was delighted to take my girls on holiday to the west of Ireland in 2001, which included a trip to the Aran Islands.

LEFT: The first exotic vacation I took with my girls after my marriage breakup was to Curacao in 1999, an experience that helped us see ourselves as an adventurous trio.

RIGHT: Our beloved golden retriever, Beau, came into our lives in 1999. It was as though he completed our brave team and solidified us as a new family unit.

TOP: Taking my mother, Bronia, back to her native Poland in 1995 and riding in an open carriage through the streets of Warsaw was a dream come true for us.

RIGHT: My romantic trip to Bali with Jack at the end of 1998 healed my broken heart and was a wonderful way to end what had been the worst year of my life.

LEFT: Jack was always up for travelling, and he accompanied me to Hong Kong in 1999, where I went to judge the Smirnoff International Fashion Awards.

were purchased by a local schoolteacher and his wife, who built a large theatre in the stone quarry on the property. It was here that the rock opera Cardin had commissioned was going to be staged.

Cardin was wandering the moonlit grounds of the château as his guests arrived. They were all dressed in black and white, with outfits that ran the gamut from jeans to evening gowns, while the designer himself looked a bit like an absent-minded professor, defying his own dress code in casual khaki and beige, glasses perched on the end of his nose, his thinning grey hair badly in need of a cut. The Champagne flowed as the spectacle began, with a Chinese acrobatic troupe dressed in space-age outfits acting as a kind of chorus. The play was bizarre and banal, and after being subjected to it for nearly two hours, guests began leaving their seats to go off in search of more Champagne.

Finally, the show ended, and then another theatrical offering was afoot. I was standing next to Cardin as we watched a horse and wagon pull up in the yard, with a white-wigged passenger, meant to be the marquis himself, aboard. The "marquis" was handcuffed and dragged off the cart. He was then escorted to a jail cell and sat down at a desk to write. Suddenly, over the loudspeaker, we heard the marquis' words, quotes from his philosophical writings. Out of nowhere, a vinyl-clad dominatrix appeared, leading a maiden on a leash. I wasn't sure I wanted to watch much more, but the proceedings were too preposterous to miss. Cardin looked intrigued. The dominatrix led the maiden behind a backlit screen. We watched their silhouettes as the maiden fell to her knees and slowly began licking the thighs of the dominatrix. Cardin was fixated, but I couldn't tell whether he thought this was all very hot or all very silly.

Within a couple of minutes, the lewd act ended. I engaged Cardin in a conversation about the synergy between fashion and art. He told me that he had wanted to be an actor and dancer when he was young, but instead he began designing costumes for Jean Cocteau, the great poet, playwright, and filmmaker. I asked Cardin if he identified with the Marquis de Sade at all, at least in terms of his efforts to entertain and enlighten people. "Not exactly," he said. "That's not my mentality. But he was such a free writer, such a free man. And that was two centuries

ago. The one thing we can at least do today is say, 'Thank you, sir …
Merci, Monsieur Marquis.'"

I reluctantly left the party at 2:00 a.m. True to form, my Sergio
Rossis were killing me! But I heard that the hedonistic dancing at the
château that night went on until dawn. I'm not sure just how raunchy
the party got, but the Marquis de Sade would have undoubtedly been
proud—and probably would have thanked Pierre Cardin not only for
hosting such a theatrically wild celebration, but for trying to keep a
dark sense of daring alive.

ACHING FOR ART

OF ALL THE FASCINATING PEOPLE I'm privileged to rub shoulders with on a regular basis, it's the designers I admire the most. Their passion and creativity, coupled with their technical mastery and disciplined work habits, are a constant source of inspiration for me. Their sheer tenacity to come back each season and reinvent the wheel, as well as the courage they have to oppose convention and make their voices heard, fills me with reverence. While none of them may ever save the planet, they all make the world a more beautiful place.

For some designers—like many sensitive souls who sacrifice so much for their art—life is especially complicated and difficult. They experience a level of suffering that becomes part of their personal fabric. Of all the great designers I have met over the years, I always had the suspicion that the inimitable Yves Saint Laurent, a gentle giant of a man, had a particularly painful life. As celebrated as he was, he always seemed to exude a profound and unrelenting sadness as he struggled to come to terms with his place in an arena whose ideals and values were so rapidly changing.

Saint Laurent was born in Algeria, and his career ambitions formed when he was still in high school. He won third place in a sketching competition organized by the International Wool Secretariat and was invited to Paris for the awards ceremony. While he and his mother were there, they met the editor of the French edition of *Vogue*, Michel de Brunhoff, who encouraged Saint Laurent to pursue his fashion dreams. The aspiring young designer enrolled at the famous Chambre Syndicale as soon as he finished high school. Before long (and shortly after winning a design competition against a young German student, Karl Lagerfeld), Saint Laurent was hired as Christian Dior's assistant. He was only seventeen. Four years later, Dior told Saint Laurent's mother that he had chosen her talented son to succeed him. He was only fifty-two at the time, so Saint Laurent's mother was puzzled by his remark. But a few months later, Dior died suddenly of a massive heart attack. At the age of twenty-one, Saint Laurent took the reins at the illustrious fashion house.

He shot to international stardom with his spring 1958 collection. But the fashion world can be distressingly fickle, and his subsequent collections were panned by the press. In 1960, Saint Laurent was conscripted by the French army. After less than three weeks in the barracks, where he was hazed by fellow soldiers, he was institutionalized at a military hospital. There, he was pumped full of sedatives and subjected to electroshock therapy. He was also informed that he had been fired from Dior. In later years, Saint Laurent blamed many of his mental problems and his addiction to drugs on this wretched time in his life.

Right after his release from hospital, Saint Laurent sued Dior for breach of contract and eventually started his own label with his lover, Pierre Bergé. He democratized fashion by becoming the first French haute couturier to come out with a full line of ready-to-wear, and he opened his first Rive Gauche store in 1966, just to sell this prêt-à-porter collection. (Catherine Deneuve was his first customer.) While not always applauded by the critics, Saint Laurent's vision was embraced by legions of stylish women, and he empowered them by offering clothes that were wearable, artful, and always in tune with the cultural zeitgeist. He and Bergé went on to rule a fashion empire that inspired a generation.

On January 7, 2002, the sixty-five-year-old designer read a statement to a group of journalists announcing his retirement. And while he spoke in that speech of his personal battles with solitude, depression, and drugs, these weren't the reasons that Saint Laurent was stepping down. It was, according to the great designer, simply time.

Three years earlier, his company had been taken over by the French billionaire François Pinault, who also controlled the House of Gucci. It was a lucrative deal that still allowed Saint Laurent to retain control of his precious haute couture business, but it put the YSL ready-to-wear collections and accessories under the management of Gucci. The word was that Saint Laurent was outraged by the way Pinault's company was using the YSL name, and that he became resentful of the creative direction Gucci's head designer, the suave and talented Tom Ford, was taking with the YSL brand. Saint Laurent was simply disillusioned by how crassly commercial the fashion world had become.

"I'm afraid Yves Saint Laurent is the last one to think about elegant women," Pierre Bergé, the designer's long-time business partner and former lover, had told me six months earlier, at what was to be YSL's last full couture collection. "Now things are different ... Life's changed. Maybe, in a way, it's more modern and easier ... I don't want to argue with that. Everybody has a right to design clothes the way they feel. But for Saint Laurent, who loves and respects women and their bodies, it's very difficult to understand the feel of today." Bergé went on to explain that creativity, not marketing, always came first for Saint Laurent. And because of that, he was at odds with the way the fashion world now functioned. At the end of that show, Saint Laurent hinted at his impending departure. He told me, "The work is very, very hard for me now. I'm beginning to be old, and I must think about retirement." I was saddened to think that this brilliant man would soon leave the arena that he had helped define.

Two weeks after announcing his retirement, as a kind of last hurrah and to close the spring '02 couture collections, Saint Laurent threw open his phenomenally rich archives and staged a forty-year retrospective. It was drizzling in Paris on the night of January 22, 2002, as two thousand ardent fashion fans made their way to the Pompidou Centre to honour the man whose name had been synonymous with style for more than four decades. The three-hundred-piece gala presentation, which was watched by the public on giant screens outside the Pompidou Centre, was aimed at showing us all why Saint Laurent so rightly deserved the title of king.

It was the hottest ticket in recent Paris memory, and I was both thrilled and honoured to be among the recipients. Unfortunately, the invitation was solely for me—I wasn't allowed to bring my cameraman, since podium space for TV crews was limited. *Fashion Television* would have to make do with a house tape of the show. Any quotes I got from the invited guests would have to be used for my newspaper reportage alone. And so, notebook in hand and wearing a little black dress, I took a taxi to Beaubourg, knowing that the coming fashion show would be one of the most poignant and moving I would ever see.

Outside the Pompidou Centre, scalpers were charging up to 350 euros for the chance to see the master's last runway presentation and gawk at the bevy of international designers who had assembled to pay tribute, including Jean-Paul Gaultier, Yohji Yamamoto, Kenzo, Oscar de la Renta, Vivienne Westwood, Fernando Sanchez, Sonia Rykiel, Paul Smith, Alber Elbaz, and the retired Hubert de Givenchy. Saint Laurent's devoted clients—from Bianca Jagger and Paloma Picasso to Nan Kempner, Diane Wolfe, and the biggest collector of them all, Mouna Ayoub—also came out in droves.

As I took my seat, watching the glitterati assemble and waiting for the show to start, I thought back to the first time I met Saint Laurent, in the mid-1980s, shortly after the launch of *Fashion Television*. In those days, his presentations were held in the posh mirrored ballroom of the Paris Intercontinental Hotel, with its ornate ceilings, luxe chandeliers, and small, elegant gilt chairs. The intimate atmosphere was a far cry from the media circus that high-profile fashion presentations have evolved into today. There may have been a couple of local TV news crews backstage, along with Elsa Klensch's CNN crew, but that was about it. The media's appetite for fashion had barely been whetted then. In retrospect, it was a peaceful time, the likes of which we'll never see again. Nonetheless, it was wildly exciting for me to be in the midst of such grandeur, and to witness the kind of refined artistry that today has become more rare.

Saint Laurent's vision for spring that season was particularly upbeat, with a dramatic and joyful rose motif. As we filed backstage to voice our praise, I was delighted to run into the designer's mother, Lucienne, a thin, bird-like woman dressed to the nines in YSL couture. Madame Saint Laurent's staunch support of her son's work was well known, and we briefly chatted about the pride she took in his success. Backstage in the crush of well-wishers, my cameraman and I found the tired but smiling designer. Saint Laurent was known for his fragile nerves, but on that morning, he was the portrait of calm. Eyes twinkling, he generously allowed me to engage him for a few moments.

"You seem very happy today, Mr. Saint Laurent," I said. "What makes you so happy?"

He closed his eyes briefly, basking in contentment, drinking in the moment. After a few beats, he looked into my eyes and, grinning, shrugged his huge shoulders and answered, in a great, deep voice, "I don't know," as if he too was surprised by his own fleeting happiness.

"*Est-que c'est dur d'être un artiste?*" I asked him.

"*Oui,*" he said, and laughed, evidently charmed by the question. "*Très, très dur.*"

"He is completely consumed by his work. He doesn't conceive of the creative process without a sense of gravity, of urgency," explained David Teboul, a filmmaker I interviewed just before the premiere of *5 avenue Marceau*, his 2002 documentary about YSL. "There is an air of good feeling," Teboul told me, speaking of the master's work, "but the good feeling only comes when it's over." Teboul, who had the privilege of shadowing Saint Laurent for the three months leading up to the designer's final fall/winter couture collection, shared some touching insights with me. He said that while Saint Laurent approached his work like a suffering artist, he was very strong mentally. "Suffering doesn't accompany those who are mentally fragile," Teboul told me.

The night of the grand YSL retrospective, I was jarred by the contrast between the modern design of the industrial Pompidou Centre and the romantic, old-world splendour of the Intercontinental's ballroom, where Saint Laurent traditionally held his shows. It struck me as emblematic of the way the fashion industry had changed. But the moment the first models came down the runway, sporting 1962-era navy pea jackets and wide, white pants, walking to the beat of the Stones' "I Can't Get No Satisfaction," we were all transported to the time when we first fell in love with fashion. For the next hour, Saint Laurent reminded us of the cupid's role he had played in our style-conscious lives. From a dramatically simple black jumpsuit to the safari jacket worn by Claudia Schiffer, relaxed pantsuits, sheer blouses, Mondrian dresses, pop-art frocks (sent out to the tune of the Beatles' "It's Getting Better"), and the wild green fox jacket strutted by Naomi Campbell, the fashion dreams of my youth came rushing back. Then the exoticism crept in with a vivid rainbow of 1970s "Ballets Russes" fantasies—lavishly embroidered peasant blouses teamed with fur-trimmed vests and sumptuous ball skirts, all followed by a tribute to modern Chinoiserie. It was the stuff of which fairy tales are made.

The luxe vision continued with a larger-than-life canary-yellow evening cape worn over a sleek black velvet gown; a silver matador suit and *senorita* clad in black lace; gold lamé East Indian saris draped to perfection; a beautiful bride in black; jungle prints; Naomi again, this time wrapped in cream feathers and strutting to the tune of Marilyn Monroe's "Bye Bye Baby"; and the incomparable Jerry Hall, a vision in a white satin halter gown, her feather-trimmed chiffon duster blowing in the runway breeze as speakers blared "La Vie En Rose." It was a kaleidoscope of sensual elegance, and the essence of what Saint Laurent always stood for. The grand finale was a stream of tuxedoed models— there had been so many variations over the years. YSL's signature "Le Smoking" tux is still a hot evening wear trend to this day.

At the end of the show, Catherine Deneuve, the designer's first ready-to-wear customer—and his friend and muse since 1966, when he created her wardrobe for Luis Buñuel's film *Belle de Jour*—took the stage from her front-row seat and sang "Ma Plus Belle Histoire d'Amour, C'est Vous" as Saint Laurent stoically marched down the runway for the last time. The audience members rose to their feet, applauding wildly, relentlessly. And with tears welling up in our eyes, we bid adieu to an era.

Post-show, the guests were enthralled, buzzing about the brilliance of the parade they had just witnessed and how it had affected them all so personally. "In a funny way, watching that show, I felt like I was getting old!" quipped the striking Mouna Ayoub, who was gloriously decked out in YSL's 1989 gold crystal jacket. For her, the grand runway had been rife with nostalgia. And she wasn't alone. Paloma Picasso, too, told me the evening had "brought back so many memories of my whole life as a woman."

The last time I saw Yves Saint Laurent was in January 2007, at Mathis, the intimate restaurant/bar in Paris. He was having a quiet dinner with his long-time muse and confidante, the former model Betty Catroux, with his faithful little French bulldog at his feet. It was surreal to see this larger-than-life icon out of his usual professional context, and as he struggled out of the restaurant on an unsteady gait, I realized he wasn't well. I was overcome by a strange combination of emotions—a kind of awe and amazement, coupled with sadness. This gargantuan genius, this artistic innovator and romantic visionary who had so manipulated and nurtured our style aesthetic, helping to define an entire age in fashion, had returned to civilian life—a mere mortal casually dining at the next table with a friend and his dog in tow. I imagined how long he must have suffered for his art. And I couldn't imagine him not suffering now that he was away from it. The following year, in June 2008, Yves Saint Laurent died of brain cancer. When I heard the news, I flashed on what the iconic British designer Vivienne Westwood had told me on the way out of the Pompidou Centre, just after Saint Laurent's spectacular farewell. "He was the world's greatest lover," she'd said. "He made it easy for women. He's probably the greatest designer that ever lived."

HEART ON SLEEVE

THE FASHION WORLD revolves around image. This notion both attracts and repels me. As much as I revel in fashion's surreal landscape and high theatrics, I often ache for unbridled truth and honest passion. And that's precisely why I adore the effervescent, forever youthful New York designer Betsey Johnson—one of my personal heroines—who, well into her sixties now, continues to grab life by the horns and not let go.

"And at the very end, I'm gonna try doing my cartwheel right into the swimming pool! What d'ya think?" It was just before 10:00 a.m. on a sunny August morning in 2002, and Betsey's blue eyes twinkled as she shared her secret surprise with me. A Raggedy Ann doll come to life, with her copper hair extensions bopping in the breeze, Betsey had opened her charming cottage in the Hamptons to four hundred of her closest friends and family, and for the first time, the media. The occasion was her sixtieth birthday, a day that also marked the twenty-fourth anniversary of her company. Three big busloads of models, dressers, hairstylists, and makeup artists had already made the two-and-a-half-hour trek from Betsey's Manhattan headquarters. Another busload of editors and photographers was scheduled to arrive at noon. By 3:00 p.m., the rest of Betsey's guests would have made their way to the sea-blue cedar-shingled house on Grape Arbor, which had been Betsey's country home for three years. I brought along one of Betsey's biggest fans, my twelve-year-old, Joey, to join in the festivities.

There was a giant pink tent pitched on the property, and the gardens were a sprawling rainbow of blooms. Hip young women in turquoise tank tops, with the words "My Blue Heaven" scrawled in sparkles across their chests, were carrying cases of Pommery POP Champagne to various stations around the grounds. Perfect little flowerbeds sprinkled throughout the emerald lawns sported nursery rhyme signposts: "Little Bo Peep," "Mary, Mary Quite Contrary," "Little Miss Muffet." The dreamy setting awaited the role-playing models, who, dressed in vintage Betsey-wear, would conjure memories of lost innocence. The Beatles' "Strawberry Fields" blasted from the kitchen as Betsey rounded up the girls for rehearsal.

Inside, the two-storey house was a riot of chintz and tchotchkes, each antique-filled room camera-ready for the impending vignettes. From bon-bon-eating beauties and Snow White languishing beside a basket of rosy apples to a princess sleeping atop a tall stack of mattresses piled upon a pea, the theatrical stage was set for an experiential fashion show aimed at charming the little girl in all of us. On the deck off Betsey's bedroom, a couple of steamy sirens were getting ready to frolic in a hot tub filled with rubber duckies. Upstairs, naughty lovelies clad in skimpy lingerie were sneaking too many cigarettes, and in the downstairs den, a couple of babe-acious twins were watching *The Parent Trap*. All the girls were wearing tiaras, vintage Betsey frou-frou, and gobs of makeup.

"She's obsessed," confided Lulu, Betsey's twenty-something daughter. "She worked on every detail for days. She stressed me out so much yesterday, I cried all day!" Evidently, life with a mum like Betsey wasn't easy. But could it possibly be more fun? It was Lulu, for years Betsey's muse and right-hand woman, who had urged her mother to get a place in the Hamptons, where the social scene ruled. Still, the senior Ms. Johnson's passion, first and foremost, had always been her work. And for the past few years, she'd had a cause to fight for as well. In 1999, Betsey was diagnosed with breast cancer. With her sense of humour intact, she had shown her spring '00 collection on Playboy Bunnies. The concept garnered an unprecedented amount of publicity, and happily, Betsey made a full recovery.

Today the birthday girl bounced out of the house wearing a royal-blue tulle skirt with a matching corset and dazzling tiara. "This is me!" she gushed. "This is my dream … my collection … my home. I really want to share it with all the people who've supported me for all these years."

"But what really keeps you going, Betsey? How do you explain all the success and personal fulfilment you've achieved so far?" I asked.

"The secret is, you've got to be terrified," she told me. "Every time I do anything, I'm always scared. I think that's really important."

"Guess that's what keeps you on your toes," I said.

"Absolutely! I'm always insecure. Like even today … I'm thinking this is such a crazy idea. What are all those people gonna think of me? What if they think I'm just a dumb little girl, with this dumb little cottage? I'm never sure anybody will like what I have to offer. But it doesn't matter. Gotta do what I've gotta do!"

Betsey spent the next couple of hours rushing around from room to room, directing and coaching her models, pumping them up to play out her fantasies. The attention to detail was astonishing. Betsey knew exactly what she wanted, and the young girls were inspired.

"She's incredible," a Ukrainian model told me. "Such an amazing woman!"

"I want to be just like her when I get older," said a Belgian beauty.

I relayed the compliment to Betsey.

"Yeah, I guess it's important to have leaders. For me, it was always Tina Turner!" she said, laughing.

Down by the front gate, Betsey smashed a mini Champagne bottle and cut a ribbon. The guests streamed in as a rendition of "My Blue Heaven" wafted through the air. The models in the gardens were working it—Mary, Mary Quite Contrary watered her flowers; Miss Muffet fed a fake spider; and Bo Peep gazed through binoculars for stray sheep. People drifted in and out of the house, enchanted by what they saw, high on Betsey's dream. The designer Nicole Miller sat on a bench with her little boy. "She's really stuck to her vision," she commented. Nikki Hilton rushed by in a transparent pink Versace top. "My sister and I have been wearing Betsey's stuff since we were little," she told me. The *Sex and the City* stylist Pat Field talked about how she and Betsey had started in the fashion biz at the same time. And then we all gathered around the pool for the runway presentation, with the Stones' "Miss You" filling the air. The models marched out in gold mega-platform sandals, each sporting a classic Betsey look: a capri jumpsuit in olive-green chiffon; an aqua ruffled micro-mini adorned with rosettes; a chintz crinoline skirt with an emerald lamé bra. One by one, the models disappeared into a cabana, emerging again moments later, pageant-style, with mirrored aviator glasses and tiaras intact. A woman next to me with a chihuahua in her bag squealed with delight. Madonna's former stylist, Lori Goldstein, looked on with glee.

There was wild applause. And then the inimitable Betsey trotted out and did her trademark cartwheel into the pool—an unabashedly beautiful fashion moment. A minute later, the bedraggled designer was presented with a whopping hot-pink birthday cake. She posed for the press, sopping wet, smiling like crazy, refreshingly unselfconscious and truly sensational at sixty.

Seven years later, the indefatigable Betsey and I had a lengthy tête-à-tête in her colourful Manhattan showroom. At sixty-seven, she was looking better than ever, and made no bones about the fact that she had done her share of nipping, tucking, and injecting. "You have to get into the idea of whether you like plastic surgery and needles," she told me matter-of-factly. "I don't think I look good with skin that falls down. You want to look as good as you possibly can. So I'm into it. Anything to look better to myself." Betsey, then between relation-ships, was also delightfully candid about her love life. "I'd love to be in love," she told me. "But you can't make the guy thing happen. I think we finally have to get happy without that thing happening." However, the grandmother of two was quick to add, "But I do love a hot little love affair!"

People like Betsey, with the courage to wear their hearts on their sleeves, never fail to inspire me. It's something I always seek to do—though naturally there are times when I have to mask my feelings, to protect others or myself. Most often, though, I'm pretty candid. My mother has frequently complained that I'm honest to a fault.

"Do you have to tell everything?" she'll ask me after reading a piece I've penned in the paper or hearing me interviewed.

"Why not?" I ask, proud of the fact that I have nothing to hide.

Then she'll mumble something about how people don't need to know everything. I understand her point. But I don't agree. We humans are on this planet for such a limited time. All we have is one another. Sharing our stories, our hopes, our fears, our feelings is the best gift we can give to one another. And though my mother might beg to differ, she can actually take part of the credit for teaching me this lesson. It's the people with an unabashed sense of themselves who have taught me the most.

GLOSSED OVER

WHEN ONE DOOR CLOSES, another opens. In March 2003, twenty-five years after I started to work at CHUM, the company that still employed me, my supervising producer, Marcia Martin, took me out to a nice dinner at Celestin, a chic Toronto restaurant. Halfway through the second course, Marcia—or Marcie (she had become a good friend over the years)—sighed deeply and launched into a rather grave and potentially devastating subject: my future with *Fashion Television*. Marcie regretted to inform me that while I was still doing a great job, my potential with the show was limited. I was getting older, she noted, and perhaps after eighteen years, *Fashion Television* was in need of some younger blood—someone not necessarily to replace me, but to co-host with me. Marcie also told me that even though I was the one who'd stood in front of the CRTC in Ottawa to pitch for the Fashion Television channel licence a couple of years earlier, there wasn't really any money for new programming now—or not yet anyway. "It hurts me to have to tell you this, but I have to prepare you," she said. "Next year, your salary's going to be cut. There's just not enough for you to do anymore. I can't see you doing anything besides this show for us." And that, quite simply, was that.

Marcie suggested that I start thinking about what other work I might want to get into. I could start a production company myself, perhaps. She was trying to be helpful and realistic, but to me at that moment, she seemed to be saying, "Prepare to die!" My heart raced as a kind of panic set in. I couldn't believe my ears. After all those years of working my butt off, building a brand, slaving and sacrificing, pushing and climbing, the end was nigh. I hadn't a clue what I would do next. The thought of sharing hosting duties with some unseasoned rookie was completely unnerving and, frankly, threatening. I couldn't believe that everything I had helped build, everything I had fought for, was being pulled out from under me.

On September 1, 2003, I was told that my salary was going to be slashed by about 40 percent. There was no doubt that I would have to find something else to make up for the income I was losing. Friends said that this was effectively constructive dismissal, and that I should seriously consider getting a lawyer and suing. But I couldn't bear to jeopardize my future, or to lash out at a company I so loved. Besides, CHUM owned close to two and a half decades of archival material—my life's work—and I might want to access that one day. I didn't want to have an acrimonious relationship with this company. So I prayed very hard that I would find some way of reinventing myself.

Around this time, my trainer, Shelby Pilot, told me about a glamorous new guy in town—a young, international, jet-setting entrepreneur named Michael King, who was making the rounds of all the hot spots and hobnobbing with the cool crowd. Shelby explained that King was the creative helm of *Inside Entertainment*, a spirited glossy magazine that was distributed through the *National Post*, the paper for which I had been writing a weekly style column for the past few years. She thought that Michael King might be an interesting person for me to know and suggested I try to meet him. But I figured that if my meeting this exotic Mr. King was in the cards, kismet would make it happen sooner or later. After all, Toronto is a pretty small town when you get down to it.

About a week later, I was a guest at a wine event, and at one point towards the end of the crowded evening, a handsome young man with a winning smile came over and introduced himself as Michael King. He had a charming New Zealand accent and was the personification of style. I was instantly taken by his charisma and energy.

"I've been looking forward to meeting you," I told him.

"Same here," he said. "I'm going to call you in the next little while. There's something I want to talk to you about."

True to his word, Michael called a couple of days later and told me that his magazine, *Inside Entertainment*, was planning a special style issue for May, to coincide with the Cannes Film Festival. "How would you like to guest edit the issue for us?" he asked.

I told Michael I had never done anything like that before, and asked him what the assignment would entail.

"Basically, we need your fashion expertise," he explained. "Besides writing a couple of pieces for the magazine, maybe you could also suggest some stories, and we could certainly use some of your contacts."

It sounded simple enough, so I told him I was up for the challenge. After all, adding the role of guest editor to my resume certainly couldn't hurt. A few days later, I went to the magazine's office and met with Michael's business partner, the marketing whiz Geoffrey Dawe, as well as the editorial and art teams. Within a few minutes, the ideas were flying.

Right from the get-go, there was a tremendous synergy at play with this group. I suggested a number of features, from a piece on stylists (the unsung heroes of Hollywood) to a profile of the Lebanese couturier Elie Saab, whose red-carpet business was booming since he'd dressed Halle Berry for her 2002 Oscar win. It was exhilarating to see these features go into production, as well as to help decide which writers to hire and which art to use. My excitement escalated as the pieces starting falling into place and this special issue took shape. This was a true education, and even though it was only a one-shot deal, I was thrilled at how much I was learning about how a magazine is put together. I loved every aspect of the process. Most important, I was proud of the results, and most people seemed pretty impressed with what we came up with. Little did I realize that I was being put to the test!

A few days after the magazine came out, Michael called me to the offices of the Kontent Group, the publisher of *Inside Entertainment*.

"Geoffrey and I want to put together a striking new high-style magazine," he said, "to be distributed through *The Globe and Mail*. It would be a quarterly, but with a high-end, oversized format. We're calling it *Fashion Quarterly*, or *FQ*. Sound interesting?" he asked.

"Absolutely!" I said. "Did you want me to contribute to it?"

"Well, actually, we want you involved in any way you'd like to be involved," Michael said. "You could write features for us, or you could edit. You could even be editor-in-chief. You can choose your title."

I could barely digest the amazing offer. It was something I wanted, and needed, even more than I admitted to myself. So gathering every ounce of confidence I could muster, I decided, quite simply, to go for it.

"Okay," I said, taking a deep breath, "I'll be editor-in-chief, then." And the celebratory fireworks began blasting away in my brain.

Because I was such a novice in the publishing business, I knew I'd have my work cut out for me. And I wasn't about to abandon my beloved *Fashion Television*. But I also knew that my passion, coupled with all those years of experience working in fashion's trenches, would see me through. A door in the TV world may have been closing, but a door in the publishing world was opening up. I couldn't wait to step through it.

Michael turned out to be a real visionary. With the help of a talented art director, Ric Little—who had coincidentally designed the hang tags for my clothing line a couple of years earlier—and his associate, Gerry Mamone, a mock-up was made. It was far bigger than any other glossy fashion magazine on the stands, and the visuals were arresting—extremely stylized, ultra classy, refined, and decadent. It recalled the look of *Harper's Bazaar* and *Vogue* back in the early 1950s, when photographers like Richard Avedon and Irving Penn brought unparalleled artistry to the pages of fashion magazines. Our seasoned publisher, Shelagh Tarleton, and Geoffrey Dawe took the *FQ* mock-up around town, and they were happy to report that there was indeed a market for this kind of over-the-top style publication. We immediately had commitments from top luxury sponsors—everyone from the high-end retailer Holt Renfrew and labels like Chanel and Ports to designer fragrances, cosmetic companies, and even Cadillac cars. The support was phenomenal. We were filling a niche in the market: Luxury was taking off, and we were determined to pump up the glamour quotient as no one had ever done before.

Besides the art team, which had already been assembled, and the sales staff, which Geoffrey and Shelagh had hired, we needed a managing or executive editor to work under me and a senior editor, as well as an editorial intern. I suggested to Michael that we hire Kate MacDonald, a sophisticated and stylish woman who was a seasoned magazine pro, having written and edited fashion and beauty features for a number of publications. Kate was forty-two, married to a successful Toronto doctor, and the mother of three young boys, with a lovely Rosedale home and an incredible passion for fashion. In my mind, she epitomized the style-savvy reader we were after. Kate had been working at a commercial publishing house, but I knew she was dying to get back on board a fashion magazine. She was kind and lovely, talented and dedicated, and had been a strong supporter of mine in the past. I felt she'd be a perfect collaborator for *FQ*. Michael met her and instantly liked her. "She was even wearing a little pink Chanel suit," he told me after meeting her for the first time. "She's perfect for our brand!"

Kate introduced us to a candidate for senior editor, the feisty and quick-witted Shawna Cohen. Shawna also was a perfect addition to the team, which was filled out with two of my discoveries, interns extraordinaire Hayley Atkin, a real go-getter and the daughter of Holt Renfrew's fashion director, Barbara Atkin, and Kayla Radke, the daughter of Toronto model Kerry Jewitt. The chemistry between us all was instantaneous. We were excited, committed, proud, and passionate. We couldn't wait for the adventure to begin.

There was a resurgence of 1930s deco on in the fall of 2003. I suggested the trend as the theme for our inaugural issue, and the creative cogs started turning. We planned an elaborate fashion shoot at a newly refurbished downtown Toronto event venue called the Carlu, which had been designed in 1930 by the famed French architect Jacques Carlu. I conscripted an author friend, Marian Fowler, whose specialty was historical books about fashion, to write a feature on the deco era. We wanted *FQ* not only to entertain but also to edify—to shed some light on the eras and icons that so often inspired designers in their work. We intended to be mindful of the past, while keeping our gaze firmly focused on the future. But above all, unlike most conventional fashion magazines, we were determined not to tell our readers how to dress. We wanted to show them how to dream.

Regular departments that we introduced in the inaugural issue of *FQ* included "Icon," for which we profiled Jean-Paul Gaultier; "Up Close and Personal," which featured my recent conversation with Isaac Mizrahi about his much-ballyhooed comeback with a collection for Target; and "Signature Style," in which we dissected the personal style of a celebrated person from the past whose choices were still relevant today. For that first issue, our subject was Frank Sinatra, who had a penchant for a colour that was just then making a comeback on the runways—orange. Every issue would also run a report, in the form of a diary entry, which I composed about the international collections, both ready-to-wear and couture. We introduced another diary feature as well, slugged as either "Diary of a Diva" or "Diary of a Dandy," depending on who penned it. Our first "Diary of a Dandy" was written by Bruce Bailey—my art collector pal and the man who had turned me on to the wonders of Northumberland County. His piece was based on his recent sojourn to the Venice Biennale. And it was considered a coup that I managed to convince the illustrious journalist and fashion-ista Barbara Amiel, wife of Conrad Black, to write a regular column in a department we playfully dubbed "Babs." Barbara would share her insider perspectives on high style, beginning with what it was like to go on a shopping spree with *Vogue's* inimitable André Leon Talley. We reserved the last page of *FQ* for "F-Stop," a look back at a vintage photo that encapsulated the theme of each issue. For the deco issue, we found a stellar photograph of Joan Crawford, standing in front of a set of revolving doors, in the dramatic black-and-white gown she wore in *Grand Hotel*. But perhaps my favourite department in *FQ* was "Doll House," our nostalgic take on the paper dolls of the past—the precious playthings that were my introduction to fashion as a girl. This was a novel way of featuring hot runway trends each season. I would choose the outfits that best captured the current zeitgeist, and our illustrator would recreate them as paper-doll garments, suitable for both collecting and dreaming.

With so many rich and intriguing bits and pieces to play around with, I had never felt more stimulated and inspired. Finally, I had become more than a spectator of fashion, more even than a reporter of fashion. As editor-in-chief, my perspective on each season really mattered. It was a joy to report back to the team on my return from a collections week, letting them know the mood of the moment, describing what would be coming down the pipes in the coming months, and suggesting ways we could spin it all into the rich fabric of *FQ*. Dreaming up the fashion shoots with Michael and the art team was especially thrilling, because Michael and I really clicked creatively and never failed to spur each other on. "Let's go dream the dream, darling," he'd say to me as we began to conceptualize each issue. It was all very magical. We were making things happen, not just following what others put out there.

There were two editorial shoots in that inaugural issue. The first was the elegant art deco fantasy we staged at the Carlu. And then there was its virtual opposite, a "walk on the wild side" shoot that I convinced a friend, the German-born photographer André Rau, to undertake. For this photo fantasy, we took a model to Times Square in New York and dressed her in a series of trench coats (the trench had made a big comeback that season) with ultra-sexy lingerie underneath. The story was called "Out of the Trenches, into the Streets," and it caused quite a stir as we were shooting it. We hired a little Winnebago and parked it on one of the streets just off Broadway. And every time our gorgeous model emerged, clad in a different dramatic trench and flashing that fancy underwear, the crowds went wild. We even managed to get the Naked Cowboy to interact with our model in one of the shots. (He's the legendary busker who has been performing in nothing more than a cowboy hat, boots, and skivvies in Times Square for years.) The shoot was outlandish, energetic, gritty, and glamorous. My *Fashion Television* camera was on hand too, capturing all the urban craziness, with scores of onlookers both excited and mesmerized by what was going down. Having masterminded this outrageous fantasy, I was on a total high, choosing clothes, working with the stylist to dress the model, and helping to direct André.

Back in Toronto, our deco shoot at the Carlu, which we called "The Women," loosely basing it on the iconic 1939 movie, turned into its own mini drama. We had booked the New York model-turned-actress Michele Hicks to be our "leading lady," with the Somalia-born, Toronto-based model Yasmin Warsame in a strong supporting role. We were also planning to shoot Michele for our important first cover. As a model, Michele had been around for a while, and she was desperately trying to spread her wings into the acting world. That was something we liked: We wanted our subjects, and especially our cover girl, to be multi-dimensional. Michele also had a strong, sophisticated, dramatic look that we thought would work well on our cover, setting us apart from other fashion magazines, especially in the Canadian market, that were catering to a younger demographic.

I had known Michele for years and had interviewed her numerous times. Besides being a sensational model, she had intelligence and spunk. But for some reason, her attitude on set that day at the Carlu was off. She had flown in from New York and seemed a little world-weary, and she didn't appear to be drawing any joy from the project. And while the shots she delivered were pretty fabulous—she was a great model, after all—there were no warm and fuzzy feelings between her and the rest of the crew. Yasmin, meanwhile, was also delivering some amazing shots, but with none of the drama that we were seeing with Michele. The crew was charmed by her work ethic, warmth, and down-to-earth personality. When our star subject had to leave to catch a flight, we decided to give Yasmin a shot at the cover. We decked her out in a stunning black-and-white Dior gown, dynamic red platform shoes, and a vintage red-and-black deco necklace. And as Michael and I watched her pose and drank in her exquisite, exotic beauty, we instinctively knew we had our crucial first cover long before we saw any of the resulting shots. The fact that Yasmin was black, and black models conventionally and controversially rarely make it onto magazine covers, didn't even figure in our decision. We were after artistry and beauty, plain and simple.

We launched *FQ* on the opening night of the 2003 Toronto International Film Festival, at a gala party in a space that was still under construction—the restaurant and lobby of a hip new boutique hotel, Le Germain. Our party became one of the hottest tickets at the festival, and we managed to attract many of the filmmakers who were in town, including the Oscar-winning Quebec director Denys Arcand. I wore an ultra-sexy little black Gucci dress to the event, and spoke to the crowd about the sensibility behind the magazine and why we were all so proud to be associated with it. People were blown away by the oversized format and the edgy photography, and everybody told me they couldn't wait to go home to devour this new baby of ours. It seemed as if a whole new era was beginning in Canadian fashion—not just for us, but for everyone who loved high style.

As it turned out, my duties at *Fashion Television* didn't change at all. I continued to juggle my hosting and producing responsibilities in my own signature fashion, always getting the assigned work done, as well as maintaining the level of creative input I had been contributing to the show since its inception. Call me a workhorse, but this is something I prided myself in—always have, and always will. I've always found both the time and the energy for the projects I've undertaken. And I have never missed a deadline. The idea of finding a younger co-host to work with me was eventually abandoned, and I simply carried on, albeit at a fraction of my old salary. Happily, the opportunity to throw myself into this magazine venture made up for any bitterness I may have felt towards the powers that be at CHUM. Ironically, my own brand just grew stronger as my profile and credibility expanded. And then, in 2006, CHUM Television, which produced and aired my series, was taken over by Canada's major TV network, CTV. It seems that the folks who ran CTV appreciated me, believed in the strength of my personal brand, and understood what it could do for the network. My former salary was reinstated, and the new regime realized my value and got me involved in more of their programming. The old adage had come true for me once again: What doesn't kill you makes you stronger. I embraced my position with renewed optimism and passion, grateful to the gods for again helping me to find my way.

MATURATION DATE

I SOMETIMES CATCH MYSELF looking in hotel room mirrors, and I'm astounded by the fifty-eight-year-old face looking back at me. I can't believe how many lines I've earned, how tired I look, how the once-taught skin on my neck is now a bit crepe-like, how my eyelids aren't showing as much as I think they should, how bland I look with no makeup at all. "What do you expect?" I reason to myself. "You've had a big life, a ginormous life. You've put on a lot of mileage. You've lived and loved and lost and learned how to survive like a true pro." Anyway, what choice do I have? Cosmetic surgery is always an option, I suppose, though one I'm constantly trying to talk myself out of. "You may have succumbed to pressure and had an eye-job way back, before you turned forty," I reflect. "And yes, dear Dr. Trevor Born shoots you up with Botox a few times a year, just to ease the grooves a bit, to soften the furrows and relax those lines. But you've never gone all the way—never had a facelift. Hmm. Is it time?" I sometimes wonder.

Once in a while, I get carried away and playfully pull my face back a bit to see what I would look like sans the sagging. While I would certainly look more rested and refreshed, I usually end up laughing at myself. I'll never say never, but I just can't imagine doing something as drastic at this point as taking a knife to my face. Still, as we all know, this is a bona fide crazy-making business that I'm in—a business that has an uncanny way of persuading people to subscribe to fantasies about the possibility of eternal youth. If only we work at it hard enough, exercise enough, diet enough, wear the right clothes, and use the right beauty products, no one will ever guess our real age! But honestly, I've never tried to hide my age. As long as I'm feeling good and have my health, I'm proud to be the age I am—grateful for what I've managed to accomplish and happy about the woman I've become, warts and all. Usually I feel like I'm still seventeen. But I certainly don't long to be seventeen again! Or twenty-seven or thirty-seven or forty-seven ... or even fifty-seven, for that matter. I've got an amazing life to reflect on, and the optimist in me still believes the best is yet to come. Sure, I may need more of Dr. Born's help as I get a little further down the road. But right now—today—I'm totally at peace with how I've aged thus far.

Back in the early days of *Fashion Television*, around 1986, Anouk Aimée, the elegant French actress who had been the muse of Emanuel Ungaro for years, came to Toronto to help promote the designer's label at Creeds, the chic (now defunct) Bloor Street clothier. We cozied up on a couch at the store and talked about the meaning of style. I asked Anouk what she loved about fashion, and without hesitating, she told me that fashion and its ever-changing nature is the one thing that can keep you young and "plugged in." I decided then and there that I would be forever young, since I was passionate about fashion and reporting on it was my new trade.

Whenever I start feeling a bit long in the tooth, I flash back to that cozy chat and think how lucky I am to be working in this arena. And even though I often have to dance as fast as I can just to keep up, I wholeheartedly believe that this is a business that keeps you young, socially informed, and "with it," no matter what your age. As a matter of fact, the people who have been in fashion the longest are often the ones who garner the most respect. They're the ones with the broadest frames of reference, the most savvy, and the most experience in general. And in a business like fashion, which owes so much to history and mentorship, those who have been around a long time are revered, celebrated, and applauded for both hanging in and keeping up.

Coincidentally (or perhaps not), it was at an Ungaro show in Paris in 2004, nearly two decades after that chat with Anouk Aimée, that the problem of ageism really struck me for the first time. There I was, as fit and feisty as ever at fifty-two, backstage at a grand salon of the Carrousel du Louvre, waiting to speak with the talented young Italian who had taken over from Emanuel Ungaro when the master retired. Giambattista Valli, a class act and true gentleman (to say nothing of his extraordinary design abilities), was conducting interviews with a small number of camera crews, and everyone was patiently waiting their turn. Suddenly, a haughty young redhead, probably no more than twenty-two, came into view, and I saw her telling the PR woman that she wanted to go next.

"Excuse me," I piped up, "but I believe we're next."

The redhead was from a rival fashion program, *FTV Paris*—or *Fashion Television Paris*. This is a fashion channel that was started in 1997, twelve years after our Toronto-based *Fashion Television* had been established. (The similarity between their name and ours initially caused some confusion in the industry.) And here was this young *FTV* reporter trying to butt in, and I wasn't having any of it.

"Everybody's waiting," she told me.

"But there's an order," I replied.

"But I've been here for a while," she insisted, venom in her eyes.

I was incensed by the challenge. "You haven't been here for twenty years," I told her, which was just about how long our show had been on the air.

"Hopefully, not. Maybe that's why I have better skin," she said sarcastically, playfully stroking her face. I was aghast. "You know," she continued, "there are some young people coming up."

I couldn't believe my ears, and turned to my cameraman, who was diligently and wisely rolling on the whole ugly exchange. At that moment, Giambattista wrapped with the person he was talking to and immediately acknowledged me. We launched into our brief interview, but I was shaking with anger throughout.

When my chat with Giambattista ended, I thanked him and turned to the camera. "Could you actually believe all that?" I asked, wide-eyed. I needed some kind of reassurance that this bizarre encounter with the *FTV* reporter was, as I felt, nothing short of lunacy. Actually, it was such a rude and tactless bit of behaviour that it was almost funny. But I wasn't laughing. My field producer and cameraman, both as shocked as I was, tried to comfort me. They dismissed the young reporter as an arrogant and ignorant two-bit amateur, but I had been bitterly stung. What kind of mother brought up this young woman? I thought. What disrespect! I tried to pull myself together and stoically went out front to take my seat. But for whatever reason—call it thin skin, a sense of injustice, or maybe just overtiredness—the tears started to roll down my cheeks. And I just couldn't stop crying.

I thought of all the years I'd spent in these trenches, working my butt off, going where no TV reporter had gone before, carving out a niche that would appeal to a whole generation of fashion lovers. And then the insecurity set in. Did I actually look horrible and wrinkly and dumpy and grotesque? Despite how hard I'd tried to look attractive, maybe I was really a hoary old bag who was hanging on to an illusion. Was it time to give up and make way for a new generation? Had Anouk Aimée been wrong all those years ago? Was fashion no longer keeping me young, relevant, and vital?

The lights went down, and the presentation began. The beauty of Giambattista's romantic garments soothed me, and I slowly began to take heart. The rudeness of the young reporter was deplorable, but I began to see that it was based on nothing but ignorance and blind jealousy. Shame on her! I made up my mind to turn this negative into a positive: I would make sure this hideous instance of ageism would be exposed as part of our coverage of the Ungaro collection. Thankfully, our camera had captured all the nastiness. This would make for great television, even as it revealed an enlightening, if unsavoury, slice of human behaviour.

Back in Toronto, my creative and crafty producer, Howard Brull, a man who adores the absurd and unexpected, had a field day with our story. Happy to let the *FTV* reporter "really have it," he cut the video in a way that made this heartless young woman look like a little witch, padding the audio track with cat yowls as she dissed me. He even had whiskers and a pair of cat ears drawn on the girl's head! It was a little over the top, but still hysterically funny. I'd got my revenge.

The segment aired to much fanfare, and the reaction from our viewers was extremely heartening. Everyone agreed that the young reporter was a creep, and no one could believe that I'd been subjected to such mean rubbish. To this day, people still talk about the segment. I only wish the reporter had seen herself acting so crassly, and being so rightfully condemned. Actually, since our show airs in close to one hundred countries, maybe she did eventually see it. If so, I wonder what she thought. Or more important, I wonder what her mother thought. Still, while her rudeness initially threw me, it ended up reminding me of how pleased I am to be my age. Happily, aging has made me better, not bitter. And like Anouk Aimée, I credit fashion with keeping me stylishly poised on my fifty-something-year-old toes.

EXOTICA

FOR YEARS, I had heard people say how their trip to India had transformed them, raised their consciousness, and resulted in a profound spiritual experience. I knew that one day, I'd make it my business to get to India. But that would be in the far-off future. For the time being, the country was not at the top of my must-visit list. Maybe I was scared of what it would be like to witness all that squalor and gut-wrenching poverty I'd heard about, scared of how it all might affect me.

Then, in the spring of 2006, Michael King struck up a connection with the Indian tourist board and began making plans for both *FQ* and *SIR*, our new men's magazine, to produce two fashion spreads in Jaipur. The trip would begin with half our team—Michael; Abel Muñoz, the associate art director; Hayley Atkin, now the associate fashion editor; and me—journeying to the northeastern Assam region, to Kaziranga National Park, for a two-day elephant safari. Evidently, my time had come to travel to these most exotic places. Suddenly, I was enthralled by the idea. And while I was a bit apprehensive at the prospect of seeing the kind of impoverished living conditions I'd heard so much about, I knew I was ready for some life-transforming experiences.

It was night when we entered the gates of Kaziranga National Park, and though the long drive from Guwahati had been exhausting, our excitement was mounting. We continued on to the remote Bonhabi Resort, a modest hotel with fourteen unremarkable guest rooms. A few minutes after I was shown to my room, the electricity went down. I panicked and screamed in the pitch darkness. I'd never felt more vulnerable. It was as though this mini blackout was some kind of signal of the beginning of my spiritual journey. Moments later, the lights came on again as the generator kicked in. I noticed a small painting of the Arc de Triomphe hanging over one of the beds and marvelled at what a world away I was from my beloved Paris. As I unpacked my things, I started worrying that my mother and the girls wouldn't know how to reach me—cellphones had no reception out here, in the middle of nowhere. The fact that no one would be able to find me was at once scary and liberating.

At 4:30 the next morning, there was a knock at my door: time for our elephant safari. My excitement mounted as I donned my cherished Ganesh pendant, which I had bought at a St. Germain boutique the season John Galliano riffed on Bollywood. Ganesh, the Hindu god of protection, has an elephant's head. I figured that since I was going to be riding an elephant in search of white rhinos and a Bengal tiger (for which the park is famous), I'd need all the protection I could get.

The mist was surreal, and the sun was barely up when we arrived at the departure area in the park. I was filled with wonder as a dozen large elephants came into view, all saddled up and ready to go. Most could accommodate three passengers, but some of the larger ones would carry up to five, with some people riding sidesaddle. There were three adorable baby elephants milling around beneath their mothers, some nursing from time to time as we set out across the misty plain. Soon we were seeing deer, wild boar, and many of the mighty white rhinos, which looked prehistoric with their leathery, armour-like skin. All the while, I was enchanted by the three baby elephants obediently walking beside their working mums, scooping bunches of tall grass as they made their way through the sunny fields. The light was ethereal, and everyone was stone silent as we watched for the next amazing beast. The next couple of hours felt like a totally mystical experience.

Back at the resort, we downed a hearty breakfast, returning to the park at 8:00 a.m. for an open-Jeep safari ride. This time, it was the rare Bengal tiger we were trying to spot. Eighty-six of them lived in the park, but sightings were extremely rare. Seven of us packed into the tiny Jeep, with a park security guard armed with a rifle riding on the back. We held on to the metal bars for dear life as we bounced merrily along the bumpy, winding road through the lush jungle. The birdlife was stupendous, with brilliant blue kingfishers, cranes, flying storks, and eagles perched in trees. There were sightings of more rhinos, several water buffalo, and more elephants. Every time a creature was spotted, the guard on the back of our Jeep yelled out: "Rhino!" Or, "Buffalo!" Or, "Elephant!" Or, "Deer!" Or, "Monkey!" At one point he called out, "Butterflies!" I turned to see a delicate cloud of tiny white wings disperse into yet another field of dreams.

Two days later, I had fallen hopelessly in love with the gentle people and beautiful culture of the region. But it was time to leave this Shangri-La and make our way back to Delhi to prepare for our big fashion shoot. As we drove along the highway, I was awestruck as I watched rural life unfold outside the car window. It seemed that it was mostly women, many dressed rather beautifully, who toiled in the fields and the rice paddies. Meanwhile, their men were out on the main drag, doing their business at stores that served as village gathering places. Once in a while, I would see a man sitting at a sewing machine—a tailor, perhaps—right in the doorway of his shop. At other open shops, I saw barbers giving men shaves and mechanics working on auto parts. Outside many of these shop doors, the garbage was heaped up, but no one seemed to mind. I couldn't believe that it was okay to be living with all this filth and disarray around, yet the women were so beautifully made up, dressed so impeccably in gorgeous traditional apparel. There was something about the strange culture here that I just couldn't comprehend.

One bustling town, Nagin, left us all speechless. We gazed out the windows, shocked by the terrible poverty and the sight of goats and cows wandering aimlessly about, the bicycles and motorcycles and tricycle rickshaws, the chaos and filth. There was also the ubiquitous rancid stench. But ultimately, it was the exquisite colour of life that touched us. On the outskirts of town stood a big plaster Ganesh, like some kind of grand circus fixture watching over this outrageous carnival of human existence.

After a night in Delhi, we hired an old air-conditioned bus to transport us to Jaipur for our fashion shoots. Such luxury, at such a low price! From the cool comfort of our private, privileged conveyance, we bid adieu to the big city and watched the abysmal outskirts pass by the bus windows. But even in these depressing surroundings, among old buildings reduced to rubble, there was a kind of poetry: A handsome young man sat on a curb, selling garlands of marigolds. There was a lot of construction going on—hope for India's future—but the conditions the men were working in seemed horrendous: Their world was so dirty and dusty. We saw dozens of workers crammed into dilapidated trucks and buses. One pickup truck carried men in the cab upfront, while a handful of women, their heads covered, were crammed into the open back. Grimy-faced children with irresistible dark eyes relentlessly appealed to us from the roadside. At one point, Michael opened the bus window and threw out a few rupees, but unfortunately, only one kid caught the money, and a scuffle ensued.

All along the highway, I saw men bathing in square concrete tubs; some were even squatting, defecating right out in the open. I was shocked at this total disregard for privacy and propriety. Here were humans reduced to a crass, animal state! As we journeyed farther south, the northern lushness slowly began to dissipate, and then suddenly, the terrain was very desert-like. The style of dress changed as well: Colours remained vibrant, but the women's saris took on a Middle Eastern aspect. All heads were covered as the intense heat escalated. Long lines of camels loaded down with huge bundles of hay slowly trekked down the sides of the highway. There were communities of tents situated in open fields, the temporary homes of nomadic people. Other men and women lived in crude makeshift shacks by the side of the road, all extremely filthy. How couldn't this make for a wretched existence?

We stopped for gas, and a trio of gorgeous, colourfully dressed young children carrying big brass urns on their heads approached our bus, smiling and waving. They didn't ask us for money, but on my way to the loo, I forked over twenty rupees to each of them. They were wildly delighted and readily posed for our photographer. These adorable urchins were so picture perfect, so happy. Their infectious energy lifted our spirits.

Our destination was the four-hundred-year-old Samode Palace, which was located about thirty minutes outside Jaipur. This would be our base for the next three days. The palace was located in the sparsely populated village of Samode. Most of the male villagers were employed at the palace, which had been functioning as a five-star hotel since 1987, though the Prince of Samode still resided in one section.

When we arrived at the palace gates, we disembarked from the bus and entered the grounds on foot, incredulous at the majesty that awaited us. The palace grounds were impeccably manicured, with fuchsia bougainvillea lining the pink gravel pathway to the grand staircase. Monkeys swung from trees, adding to the full-out exoticism of the experience. The ancient palace was staggeringly beautiful, with numerous inner courtyards, one hosting a puppet theatre. There were countless terraces, a huge swimming pool, and mammoth rooms featuring intricately hand-painted walls. Each of the twenty-four hotel rooms was exquisite. I was assigned to a grand suite with blue drapery, marble floors, woven rugs, and two ornately carved antique beds. This had to be the most amazingly sumptuous hotel room I had ever occupied—the level of luxury was staggering. The contrasts I was witnessing in India were simply incomprehensible.

Our two fashion shoots were the stuff that dreams are made of. In the first, our striking red-haired model, the Toronto-based Lisa Coté, portrayed a jet-setting Westerner and mistress of the breathtaking palace. Lisa looked incredibly beautiful in every shot—one taken in front of the palace stairs, another in a fabulous painted living room, yet another in my very own suite. Hayley had brought a diverse assortment of European and Canadian designer clothing from Toronto, and our Mumbai-based producer sourced some local Indian garments, making for an intriguing global mix. The second layout we were producing was for *SIR*, our men's magazine, and starred Nick, a handsome male model from Mumbai. The fantasy story we concocted cast our model in the role of a cool and stylish photographer on safari, and his co-star was an elephant we hired from Jaipur. While that town was only thirty minutes away by car, it took the elephant about ten hours to walk to our location at the Samode Bagh, a garden that was originally the royal retreat but had begun operating as a hotel, with tents for rooms.

There was a bit of a production crisis when we arrived at the garden. Our lovely elephant was all decked out with colourful flags hanging from his ears and an opulent red-and-gold saddle, as if he were going to take part in some celebratory holiday procession. This obviously was not the look we were going after, and we had to break it to the owner that his beast had been cast as a safari elephant and was just a tad overdressed!

Once that hiccup was resolved, the day proceeded wonderfully, and we got some terrific shots, all with a very different feel from those we had taken at the palace. Lisa had wrapped all her shooting, but she came along for the fun, clad in sexy, tiny shorts. When she got off the bus, a group of young boys who'd been hanging around began to howl with laughter. The sight of this six-foot-tall glamazon with the alabaster skin must have been strange enough. But those totally exposed legs that went on forever were a true sight to behold for these kids, who had never seen anything quite like that before. The laughter continued until Lisa modestly donned a sarong. Still, the kids' curiosity had been piqued, and they swarmed around her. For the rest of the afternoon, a never-ending parade of local kids came by to check out the excitement. It was heart-rending to see them so shabbily dressed. They all kept asking for pens or chocolates or rupees, but they didn't seem miffed that we had none to give them. "Helloooooo!" they kept saying, sweetly greeting us. "What's your name?" That was about all the English they knew. They were so excited to have us there in their midst. And I wanted to rescue them all. But from what? The profound poverty, I supposed. Yet all these kids seemed so totally carefree and happy, just glad to be living in the moment.

For one of our last shots, at dusk, our producer, Katisha, wrangled a group of local female dancers, all garbed in colourful red-and-yellow saris. Nick pretended to photograph them with a vintage camera as they danced in a field. Unfortunately, the field was rife with brambles, and the barefoot dancers weren't having an easy time at all. Passionate about getting just the right shot, our photographer, Colston Julian, kept screaming, "Okay, girls—dance!" And then, "Faster … faster!" The dancers obediently whirled and twirled while our spirited photographer kept barking orders, constantly snapping away. It was rather comical at first, but we soon realized that some of the girls were really in pain. Michael and I wanted to call it a wrap, but these dancers were troopers, and they giggled on despite the physical misery they may have been experiencing. I was awed by their commitment to the project, and we finally got our amazing shot. Suffering for fashion never looked so good!

On our last day in India, we headed to Jaipur for some last-minute power shopping. As soon as we arrived, we realized our bus was far too large to navigate through the busy, narrow streets. So we hired a few of the three-wheel bicycle rickshaws and their drivers to pedal us around. Although the day was steamy, these earnest young guys were unfazed and energetically rode us through the bustling city. Traffic was utterly chaotic, with horns blasting, motorcycles cutting in front of us, and cars and trucks competing for road space. The stench, the smog, the dirt, and the filth—and the stench, the stench, the stench!—joined with the noise, the colour, the characters, and the lively shops to make a wild assault on the senses. It was one of the most exhilarating rides I have ever been on, and I don't think I have ever felt so alive. Still, the squalor was totally wretched and utterly stupefying.

We didn't have much time, so we hurriedly did our haggling at a handful of shops and market stalls, and I came away with some choice treasures, including antique jewellery, assorted textiles, embroidered pillowcases, and a small silver elephant. Then it was back on the bus to the Rambagh Palace Hotel for a quick lunch before heading to Delhi and the long trip home. The sheer magnificence of the plush palace took our breath away. It was situated on the most elegant grounds, surrounded by pristine manicured lawns and flowering trees. This was luxury to the max, and the tremendous disparity between this and the crass and colourful inner city was too much to fathom. But perhaps it's this very juxtaposition—this poignant heaven-and-hell reality—that ultimately is India, and is precisely what makes this remarkable country so incredible. It's all a metaphor for the absolute agony and ecstasy of the human condition, and a powerful reminder of the depths to which we can sink and the heights to which we can soar.

AT HOME

As passionate as I am about my work, and as much as
I bask in the rewards it brings me, heart and home are
the true centre of my life. The romantic, domestic me
struggles to get that right, knowing that without love
and my strong sense of family, my glamorous career
would be lacklustre and meaningless. And so, as part of
my juggling act this past decade, I kept an open mind
as I searched for love, all the while making sure I was
there for the people who meant the most to me. Making
a home for my growing girls, being there for my aging
mother, and still taking care of my own emotional needs
as a woman wasn't easy. But I was determined to have it
all, even though I sometimes broke my heart trying.

BACK ON TRACK

AS THE WEEKS and months after my marriage breakup passed, I began to see myself and my two daughters as a loving trio, an invincible little team that was growing stronger and more independent in the aftermath of what had happened. I was hell-bent on learning to love life again, on savouring all the good things I still had and being receptive to the positive opportunities that I felt confident would be heading my way.

That summer, I took the girls to Martha's Vineyard to visit family friends. We had a magical time, spending lazy afternoons on the beach, having sunset picnics, going to great parties, and even sailing on a hundred-year-old wooden boat. I was feeling physically fit, thanks to a new workout regime, and most important, I was seeing that even though worlds come crashing down and situations change dramatically, life goes on. I even had a brief romance with an old high school pal—someone I normally would never have got involved with. But one especially lonely night, I was out at a restaurant with my girlfriend Jackie Feldman and we met up with this unlikely suitor, someone from high school, whom neither of us had seen in years. When he learned I was newly single, he playfully put his hand on my butt for a moment, and something went off inside me: I knew instantly that I was ready for my first post-breakup fling.

Unfortunately, the dalliance ended miserably after only a couple of months, and he proved to be a bona fide cad. It served me right for having been so impulsive! My shrink summed it up beautifully. It was, he said, as though I had been hit by a truck and was in need of medical attention, so I just went to the closest emergency department. The attention I got was totally substandard. But at least now I could limp away and try to find a better hospital.

Though this romantic misadventure ended up being a bit of an embarrassment, the old boy had indulged me with countless bouquets of flowers and syrupy love letters. And for a few fleeting weeks, I got my mojo back. Now that the ice was broken, I was ripe for my next big relationship—the one that would truly get me back on track, help heal me, teach me to trust in others and believe in myself once again.

My mother and my girls and I were out having Sunday brunch when we ran into Jack Steckel, a strapping fifty-something guy who was an old family friend. Jack and his dear mother, Sophie, had been in our lives ever since I could remember. He was an only child, about the same age as my sister, and Sophie had raised him as a single mum. My parents had befriended Sophie in Lodz, Poland, just after the war and shortly before Jack was born. Eventually, my parents lost touch with the Steckels. But they all ended up immigrating to Canada in the late 1940s, and by the early 1950s, they'd managed to reconnect. Sophie and Jack immediately became part of our extended family.

Jack was very good-looking—tall, dark, and handsome—and the light of his mother's life. As we got older, Jack grew into a real ladies' man, and I would sometimes hear of his playboy exploits from my sister. But Jack was six years older than me, and although I worked for him one summer selling waffles at the Canadian National Exhibition when I was sixteen and he was a twenty-two-year-old university student with his own little seasonal business, I didn't have much in common with him. Jack went on to become a successful advertising and marketing executive, and the proud poppa of five kids. In the late 1980s, before my dad died, Jack and his second wife bought my dad's slipper business. My family was forever grateful to Jack for "saving the day," since my father was quite distraught at the thought of having to dissolve the company he had worked so hard to build. Jack became a bit of a hero in our eyes. The last time I had seen him was at his mother's shiva in the early 1990s.

That Sunday at brunch, Jack approached our table, excited to see us after so many years. He asked how I was doing, and I told him that I was all right, even though my marriage had broken up earlier that year. He was sympathetic, and told me he and his second wife had split a couple of years earlier. He suggested that we get together and commiserate over lunch sometime. I readily gave him my number, pleased by the prospect of spending some time in the company of such a handsome guy—someone who, because of our pasts, knew where I was coming from, and even felt like a relative of sorts.

Within a week or so, Jack called asking if I'd like to go for lunch. I donned a little black dress and a pair of leopard stilettos. I had rediscovered myself, and was feeling upbeat and relatively attractive again. We went to a lovely French restaurant, Bistro 990, and had a wonderful time catching up and reminiscing about our various experiences. But I remember looking across the table at him and thinking that this guy was so "not me." He was wearing a beautifully tailored pinstriped Ralph Lauren suit and a Hermès tie, but I just kept thinking that I'd never gone out with a conservative businessman before. And then I'd think about all that baggage: the two ex-wives and a whopping five kids. Nah, not for me, I mused. He had also suffered some business setbacks a couple of years earlier and was just slowly building his professional life back up to what it had once been.

After lunch, Jack walked me to the parking lot. I guess we were both trying to leave the ball in each other's court, because we simultaneously blurted out something like "Call me!" as we were saying goodbye. I didn't think I would ever hear from him again. And maybe I wouldn't have. But a couple of weeks later, I was feeling a little lonely and decided that a dinner out with a good-looking "straight" man would be just the fix I needed. So I got up my nerve and dialled Jack's number. He seemed happy to hear from me, and when I told him I was feeling a bit down, he immediately suggested that he take me to dinner.

This time we went to an Italian restaurant, Giancarlo's, and once again, I had a lovely time, though I still felt as if we were both just treading water and not really going anywhere. Still, at the end of the evening, I asked him if he would mind accompanying me to a benefit I was hosting at the museum later that week. He said he would be delighted.

At the museum event, I was pleasantly surprised by how self-sufficient Jack was, encouraging me to go off and do my thing as he worked the room for his own purposes. The evening wrapped up with us going out for a nightcap. And then he drove me home, walked me to the door, and gave me the dreamiest goodnight kiss I could ever imagine. I hadn't been kissed that way since I was a teenager! We looked at each other, surprised by the magic that had just transpired. "Old family friends, eh?" he said softly. Maybe so. But who said friends can't become lovers?

And so, my relationship with Jack shifted into high gear. I was swept away. I had been feeling so lonely for so long, and had been craving a meaningful connection with someone so badly, that I plunged headlong into this new relationship, not caring whether Jack was totally right for me. We were both ambitious, had adventurous spirits, and shared the same family values. So what if we didn't really see the world in the same way? Suddenly, I had this big macho guy telling me how much he loved me, assuring me that he would always watch out for me and take care of me and make sure nothing bad would ever happen to me again. I believed him with every bit of my heart.

Jack and I went away on romantic weekends together. He regularly brought me bouquets of red roses and showered me with the most beautiful baubles I'd ever received. The best part was bringing our families together. We revelled in how well everybody got along, in a "Brady Bunch" kind of way. I could see that my kids were happy, not because I had someone new in my life, but because we all felt part of something bigger—this raucous, joyful family. Suddenly, there were people there to celebrate holidays with. Jack was adamant about being a great father, and because he was so experienced and had been through so much with his kids already, I knew I could turn to him for wise child-rearing advice. He encouraged me to get a big dog, buy my country place, and send my career in myriad directions. Jack adored travelling, and we went on lots of exotic, fun vacations together, to Bali, Israel, and Las Vegas. We piled all the kids into a van and drove to Montreal. We skied in Colorado and swooned through Provence. And he was always more than happy to accompany me on work trips, to New York or Paris, the Bahamas or Hong Kong. Jack was determined to squeeze every last drop out of life, and he inspired me to do the same. He was my biggest cheerleader. He thrived on the glamour of my world and constantly urged me on, thinking up new marketing ideas that would garner me a higher profile and hopefully make me more money. He began to negotiate my contracts, and I depended on him for business advice. I felt cherished for the first time in many, many years. Jack was just what the doctor had ordered. I couldn't help loving him.

I had for a while been toying with the idea of creating a simple line of travel basics—a no-nonsense, practical approach to dressing that would be easy and carefree. I wanted to give women some focus in the blur of options that came with the end of 1990s minimalism. When Eaton's, the legendary Canadian department store chain, expressed an interest in teaming up with me for just such a project in 2001, it all made perfect sense.

The partnership with Eaton's was especially appealing, since the company had played an important part in my past. Throughout the 1950s and 1960s, the biggest and most glamorous client of my father's small manufacturing company was Eaton's. Every time he got a big order from the revered retailer, he would treat himself to a celebratory shot of his special Crown Royal whisky. And I can remember working with my mother to type his shipping labels at home on our tiny portable typewriter, so proud to be addressing our packages to the mighty "T. Eaton Co." in such far-flung places as Moose Jaw and Fredericton. I was impressed that my hard-working dad had placed our humble product in all those fancy, important stores across Canada. Now, the grand old chain, which had risen from the ashes under new Sears ownership, was asking me to edit an exclusive collection for them. Talk about a fantasy! But even more thrilling than the prestige of working with Eaton's was the opportunity to share my style sensibility and the wardrobe solutions I had discovered over the years. How do you go from morning to night when there's no time to go home and change? What do you pack for a three-day business trip when you just want to take one carry-on bag? How do you sit on a plane for hours, then go directly to a meeting as soon as you land, without your clothes looking like a wrinkled mess? What were the basics, the staples—the perfect T's and sweaters and pants and skirts and jackets—that we would keep coming back to, that we could mix with our fabulous designer pieces, that would make us feel chic and confident and together? To add to the challenge of bringing these items together in one comprehensive collection, we would also have to deliver these high-quality, timeless pieces at an affordable price.

It was important to bring an objective eye to our work, an experienced party that could help shape my brand, understood what I was all about, and knew how to make image jibe with product. I hooked up with the Mimran Group, the remarkable team that had given us the successful Alfred Sung and Club Monaco brands. Again, my past was coming into play: I had known Joe and Saul, the Mimran brothers, since high school. Again, it felt right.

From the get-go, I was adamant that I was to be an editor, not a designer. I may have learned a lot about fashion through sheer osmosis over the years, but I had too much respect for designers and the complexity of their craft to ever fancy myself one. I saw myself as a real woman who happened to have this amazing career that allowed her to hobnob with some of the greatest style-meisters on the planet. I was a single mother of two leading a hectic, multi-faceted life. I worked and played extremely hard. Most of us did. We had enough to worry about. I wanted to make dressing fun and easy.

Eaton's assembled a brilliant team from the merchandising and marketing departments, under the guidance of the merchandising whiz Ed Matier. With the help of a talented fashion co-coordinator named Cyndi Howard, we spent weeks gathering fabric swatches and clothing samples from a wide variety of manufacturers. I tried on everything that appealed to me, deciding first if I loved it enough to have it in my wardrobe and then how I would change or adapt it. Of course, every garment also had to make sense for the collection. How would it work with the other pieces I had chosen? Was it redundant? Was it timeless? How did it feel? Would the style be appropriate for a variety of body types? Would it work for travel? Was the quality high enough? Would the retail price be fair? What about the fabric, the colour, the buttons, the zippers, the pockets, the collars, the slits, the seams? I never realized how much a designer agonizes over every little detail. Once a garment has been made and gets out there, it's at the customer's mercy. She will be the acid test of its beauty, desirability, and validity. I had to justify each item in my collection. And since my name would appear on the label of every piece, the task was especially daunting. I even had to worry about what the label and the hang tag looked like.

Then there were all those other elements to consider—the advertising, merchandising, promotion, and publicity. The whole process was both edifying and exhilarating. And I was scared. As confident as I was about the collection we had come up with, I knew I might be judged harshly. I was also afraid that some might feel I had deserted other Canadian designers by developing my own line. Of course, I would never abandon fabulous designer clothes—especially those by Canada's own bright talents. Designer collections always will be in a league of their own. I was simply offering some of the nuts and bolts that were needed to fill in the gaps, the basics that wouldn't break the bank. The world's couturiers had nothing to worry about. I wasn't giving up my day job.

Happily, the Jeanne Beker Collection was well received, and the first season was a great success. I toured the country, visiting the seven Eaton's stores and meeting fans. My perspective on fashion, made real in this easy-to-wear line, resonated with all kinds of women who were looking for practical wardrobe solutions. We enthusiastically launched into the next season, putting together an appealing spring collection that also proved to be a hit. But by mid-February 2002, the dream was over: Sears, Eaton's parent company, announced that it would be converting all seven Eaton's stores to the Sears brand. The 133-year-old retail icon was being eliminated from the Canadian marketplace.

As successful as my clothing line had been, and as much promise as it had shown, it was deemed too pricey for the more downscale Sears market. And since it had essentially been created as a private label for Eaton's, it was over. I considered coming up with a new line, at a lower price point, with Sears in mind—but the idea just didn't appeal to me.

Still, I had learned quite a bit about the retailing business, and I wasn't ready to abandon the notion of having some sort of label. Besides, I had just started getting my feet wet. And since I have learned that the best way to deal with disappointment is to throw myself into a new project, that's just what I did. Wertex, a Toronto-based hosiery company that had been around since the 1940s and had an impressive factory in Montreal, approached me about doing a line of stockings. I mentioned it to Jack, and the cogs started turning. We met with the Wertex owners—the charming Werner family—and started bouncing ideas around.

The Werners, a father-and-son team, were Orthodox Jews. They may not have been progressive in terms of their marketing skills, but they did have a factory filled with impressive state-of-the-art equipment that could spin out wonderful, good-quality seamless garments. Since working out and yoga had become such a big part of so many women's lives, and Wertex had the ability to manufacture this kind of line, I started toying with the idea of doing a hip, colourful, no-nonsense "underwear as outerwear" collection: simple garments you could wear to the gym or the yoga studio or as underpinnings. There would even be some seamless underwear in the mix—all with great cuts and in fashion-forward colours. We decided to call the collection "Inside Out by Jeanne Beker."

Jack was instrumental in my deal with the Werners. Sears agreed to carry the collection, and for a couple of seasons, everything went along fine. Of course, this type of humble collection paled in comparison to the major line I had done with Eaton's. And as much as I enjoyed my dealings with the Werners (just imagine talking thong underwear with a Hasidic Jew!), I didn't feel the company had the marketing vision, savvy, or funds to promote the line the way it needed to be promoted. No matter how good the product was, how reasonably it was priced, and how timely it was, Jack and I instinctively knew this company would not be able to take it to the next level. So we amicably dissolved the partnership with Wertex and abandoned the notion of another collection—for the time being.

I never for a moment thought of either of my clothing lines as a failure. Both were successful while they lasted. I was lucky to have all that hands-on experience, to get an up-close look at the shmatte business, warts and all. It was only a taste of the daunting challenges so many designers and fashion houses have to go through to get their products out there. But for me it was a real eye-opener, a personally enriching experience, and good fun to boot. Some things just aren't meant to last.

My relationship with Jack ended in May 2006. We spent seven and a half years together, and it was a wonderful ride. But as much as Jack had been there to help to heal my broken heart and support my independence as a single working mum, there was still a big hole in my life. I wasn't ready to settle, and I longed for a different kind of love.

THE CASE OF THE MISSING MOON BOOTS

OF ALL THE JOYS and challenges that have come my way, few can compare with those I've encountered raising my girls. Bringing them up to be kind, compassionate, and creative young women has been one of my life's sweetest and most trying adventures, as well as my most blessed accomplishment. Bekky was ten and Joey was eight when Denny left in 1998. I was in the throes of this monstrous career of mine when our world was blown apart. While I can't say I would have opted to raise them as a single parent if given the choice, I got through a lot of tough stuff these past thirteen years, and I'm proud to still be standing alongside my two remarkable beauties, who are poised to take on the world.

Any working mother—especially one obligated to travel so much for her job—will tell you that there can be a tendency to overcompensate for the pangs of guilt brought on by separation. My heart always went out to the girls when I had to be away, and I often tried to make up for my absences with little gifts. Sometimes, when I had the time to shop, these were exotic treasures. But usually, the presents were nothing more than token Beanie Babies picked up at an airport terminal. However humble these wee gifts were, the girls were eternally appreciative that I'd brought back a bit of "the road" for them. Denny thought I was spoiling them terribly. "Look at how many Beanie Babies these girls have!" he said disdainfully shortly before he moved out. I had to admit that their burgeoning collections were impressive. But how could I deny my children something they took such delight in? How much longer would I be able to win their hearts with such meagre purchases? I didn't think for a moment that I was spoiling them.

When Denny did leave, I felt horrendously guilty. It was as if I had failed the girls in my inability to hang on to their dad, in becoming so utterly undesirable that he felt forced to tear himself away from them. Some parents may have fought to conceal their pain, to put on a brave face and not let their children witness their heartache. But my girls were everything to me, and I needed them to know that I was crushed, that my dreams, as well as theirs, were being smashed.

The hardest thing for them to understand was why their father, who loved them so much, was leaving home. We would talk about it just before bedtime, up in Joey's room. I explained that this wasn't about them. Daddy adored them, I said. It was all my fault: He just didn't love me anymore, and that was making him unhappy. "He does so love you, Mum!" Joey would insist, desperately trying to make me feel better. And then the ever-astute Bekky would chime in, trying to make sense of the wretched situation for Joey, for all of us. "No, he doesn't love her anymore, Joey!" she'd say fiercely. And that, of course, would make Joey cry. And I would cry. And this went on for days and weeks and months, until we all slowly began to learn to live with this sudden void in our lives.

My writing became a welcome therapy for me. I had always shared so much with readers in my regular *Flare* magazine columns, which I began writing in 1994. But in 1999, I had the opportunity to share even more with all those who had grown up watching me when I was given a weekly syndicated column in the Southam chain of newspapers. The columns could be about anything I chose to write about. Often, they reflected the stories I was working on for *Fashion Television*. But sometimes, I would write about my personal life—about the trials and tribulations of raising my girls, and my observations about this rollercoaster existence I was leading as a mother, daughter, career woman, and impassioned fashionista.

I adored the time I spent writing, especially when it was in my office on the second floor of our house. When I wasn't pulled away by travelling assignments, I tried to spend as many hours as possible at home with the girls, helping them with homework or cuddling up in blankets on the big comfy couch with our dog, Beau, watching old movies. The most luxurious time for me was when I'd tucked them safely and snugly into bed in their third-floor rooms and then headed downstairs to my office sanctuary with a giant mug of tea, lit a fire in the small fireplace, and wrote into the wee hours. The opportunity to review the accomplishments, setbacks, and insights that crowded my life in this focused, concentrated way always filled me with awe. The columns I wrote about the girls seemed to garner the most attention. Bekky and Joey were intrigued to know which of them—or which particular trial—would become the subject of a column, and they never really winced too much when they saw our personal stories in print. Often, they seemed rather proud, if a little surprised, to think that our family travails were captivating readers of my columns. I had evidently struck a chord with parents who were raising adolescents. I always wrote from the heart—and while I did have to censor myself to some degree, I took pride in the fact that I was as candid as I could be. Initially, the girls were a little uneasy about all this, but as time went on, they accepted my judgment about what I chose to share with readers. The positive feedback we got was always fun and very welcome. It was heartening to know that I wasn't alone. There were countless parents out there struggling to figure things out, get it right, carry on a rich and meaningful relationship with their kids.

I began writing my column for the *National Post* in 2001. Then I switched to *The Globe and Mail* in 2003, when we launched *FQ*, which was distributed by that paper. Some columns resonated more loudly than others, and I revelled in gauging which stories mattered most by the quantity of reader mail that came my way. The column about my struggle with the girls over their messy bedrooms was a hit. My artist friend Vivian Reiss finally convinced me that we waste too much precious time arguing with our kids over minor issues. So instead of abhorring the tornado-like conditions on the third floor, I learned to embrace the chaos by viewing it not as a disaster but as a kind of art installation—an ode to the girls' unbridled energy.

The column that described my shock at seeing Bekky's first tattoo also made an impact. Dozens of parents across the country could really relate to that one. But one of the most popular columns I have ever written—one that people still talk about today—dealt with the issue of entitlement and the theft of a pair of Bekky's boots at a New Year's Eve party in 2005. "The Case of the Missing Moon Boots" was told in two instalments, and it taught me a lot about the necessity of speaking up for justice, no matter how banal an episode may appear.

It all started at a New Year's Eve bash at the home of our young pal Ben Brill, who lived around the corner. Ben's annual party customarily attracted large groups of private school kids and university freshmen. Eighteen-year-old Bekky had come home from school in Montreal for the holidays, and she had borrowed a pair of my black suede stiletto booties to wear to the party. But because it was a snowy night, she carried them with her as she made the trek over to Ben's in her brand-new white Moon Boots—those mega-cozy clodhoppers that first surfaced in the 1970s but had made a trendy comeback that winter. The Moon Boots were a cherished Christmas gift from her dad, who bought them to keep her tootsies toasty in the frozen wasteland of Montreal.

When Bekky woke up on New Year's Day, I asked her about the party. She was dismayed to tell me that the evening had ended badly. "My Moon Boots got stolen!" she glumly reported. She then explained that while no one had 'fessed up, she had heard that one girl had been searching for her own boots at the end of the party, and when she couldn't find them, she simply put Bekky's boots on and left. I asked Bekky if she knew who the girl was. She said that she didn't but there were some kids who did, and these kids had volunteered to help Bekky find her. I doubted these kids would be diligent in their search, especially on New Year's Day. Bekky was slated to go back to school in Montreal the next morning, and she needed those warm boots. The mother in me was determined to pursue the matter, even though I knew Bekky would kill me. And so the sleuthing began.

I called Ben, and he gave me a name: J.Y., a grade-twelve student at the neighbouring ritzy girls' school. Apparently, Ben's friend Mike had seen J.Y. scrounging around for her own boots and then finally leaving the party with big white Moon Boots on her feet. I was incensed that a young lady from such an upscale school would do such a thing. Did she think that no one would notice, or that she was beyond reproach?

If justice was to be done, I would need a witness. I called Mike, who confirmed that J.Y. had indeed left the party in the Moon Boots. Mike didn't have her number, but he said that Ben knew her best friend's boyfriend. I got back to Ben, who, after some time on MSN, managed to get me the contact info for J.Y.'s friend.

"Hi. Happy New Year. This is Bekky O'Neil's mum," I began, feeling at once apprehensive and a little like a lioness looking out for her cub. "I was wondering if you knew anything about your friend J.Y. leaving Ben's party in my daughter's Moon Boots last night?"

The girl was very sweet, and she began apologizing profusely for her friend.

"She couldn't find her own boots and was freaking out because she had to get home and pack for a trip. So she just put the Moon Boots on and wore them home," she explained.

"Right," I said. "Well, maybe we can just call her and get them back."

"Uh, actually, J.Y. left for Mexico early this morning," said the friend. "She won't be back til next week. I'm sure she didn't mean any harm by it," she continued. "You know how it is at these parties—everybody's always taking everybody else's shoes."

This did not console me. I was enraged that this J.Y. girl seemed to think that because someone had stolen her boots, she was somehow entitled to steal Bekky's.

"Do you know where in Mexico J.Y. is staying?" I asked, feeling more like Nancy Drew by the minute.

"I think it's someplace called Palace ... in Playa del Carmen," she replied.

I was on a mission only a mad mum could relate to, and I started ringing every hotel in Mexico with the word "Palace" in its name, looking for the Y. family. Finally, I struck gold.

"Mr. Y., sorry to bother you on your vacation, but do you have a daughter named J.?"

"Yes," he replied.

I proceeded to tell him the sordid tale, explaining not only that those boots had sentimental value for Bekky—they were a Christmas present from her dad—but also that she was leaving for Montreal in the morning and all the shops were closed, so we couldn't buy her a pair of new ones if we wanted to. He told me to hang on a minute, and then came back on the phone a few minutes later.

"Well, does your daughter know where J.'s boots are?" he queried.

"No!" I snapped. Was he insinuating that Bekky had taken them?

Unfortunately, he explained, there was no one who could access their Toronto home to retrieve the boots, but he'd "try to have them sent over in a few days." As it turned out, the girl had worn those honking Moon Boots all the way to Mexico, and we had to wait for the family's return to get them back.

I was amazed at the reader response to this story. It evidently struck a chord with people—mostly mothers—who seethed over the injustice of it all. And then there were those who were just happy to see another mum go to battle for her kid. I was thrilled that I had mustered the nerve to take a stand and speak up. And even Bekky seemed impressed. I hope I showed her that the squeaky wheel often does get the grease— or in this case, the Moon Boots.

True to his word, the father did bring the boots back to our Toronto home about a week later, but there was not even a note of apology from the girl who had committed the crime in the first place. As I drove across town to take those darned boots over to a friend of Bekky's who was travelling to Montreal, I prayed that my daughter appreciated all the hassle I had gone to in the name of justice, and of course, motherly love.

FAMILY VACATIONS

IN FALL 2000, I got carried away at a charity auction and bid on something wildly extravagant: a week's stay at a magnificent house in the Irish countryside, generously donated by its owners. I had taken possession of our farm that past summer, but my affinity for the Emerald Isle got the better of me. In the summer of 1998, when I was just crawling out of my post-breakup depression, I took a trip to Ireland to visit my close friend, the Irish designer Louise Kennedy. That adventure helped heal me, and got me to believe in magic and poetry again. Since then, I had fantasized about one day taking my daughters—both O'Neils—to the enchanting land that was so instrumental in my recovery. So when this sojourn at a grand five-bedroom home outside of Galway, on the shores of Lough Corrib, was offered, I just couldn't resist. Besides the satisfaction of knowing the money would be going to a worthy cause, I knew this special house—dubbed Cappagarriff—would provide the perfect end-of-summer getaway, the calm before the inevitable craziness of fall. Bekky and Joey, then thirteen and eleven, respectively, had never been to Europe, and I wanted to initiate them in a way that wouldn't feel "touristy."

Our adventure started off in Dublin, at Louise's swish digs. She lives atop her divine boutique—a restored Georgian rowhouse in historic Merrion Square. Louise had just returned from a jaunt to London, and she filled us in on Elton John's annual "tiara" party, which attracted a dazzling array of luminaries, from Mick Jagger and Naomi Campbell to Elle Macpherson, Hugh Grant, Kevin Spacey, and Fergie. The girls and I lapped up the celebrity dish, but not before the *Irish Independent* newspaper showed up to snap us for their Saturday society column. *Fashion Television* had been on the airwaves in Ireland for years, and apparently, I had a strong following there. We couldn't get over how down-to-earth and friendly everyone was, and we were especially charmed by the cabbies. That night, we dined at the fabulous loft of Louise's sister, Caroline. By the end of the evening, we were all dancing around the living room to the Chieftains' *Long Black Veil* CD in a fit of true Irish passion.

The next day, on a small plane to Galway, I read stories to Joey from a little Irish folklore book. She firmly believed in faeries at the time, and I did what I could to encourage her, speculating that it was highly likely there'd be at least a few of them living on the shores of Lough Corrib. It was an unusually clear day as we flew across the country, and the girls and I marvelled at the lush and varied shades of green beneath us.

My first big test as the fearless family leader was getting behind the wheel of the rental car at Galway airport. I was terrified of driving on the "wrong" side of the road. With Bekky acting as the navigator, and keeping me in line with sporadic shrieks, we headed out on the highway. It took every ounce of nerve I could muster. I kept telling myself that our lives were up to me now—there was no man to fall back on. It was nerve-racking and empowering at the same time. And even though I dreaded every roundabout we came across, since I was never 100 percent sure how to navigate those suckers, I ended up managing respectably (even though I did almost drive into oncoming traffic on my first turn out of the airport).

We eventually found our way to the bustling little village of Oughterard, where we met up with Cappagarriff's cheerful caretaker at the Boat Inn, the community's preferred watering hole. Outside the pub in the sunshine, people of all ages were sitting at long wooden tables, having early dinners and knocking back pints. We followed our leader five kilometres down the narrow, windy Glan Road. On the way, a weathered man in a tattered hat who looked like he'd just stepped out of a travel poster crossed the road with a small herd of cows. The girls were charmed to witness this surreal slice of Irish country life.

Cappagarriff took our breath away. The sprawling pale yellow stucco house featured numerous white-framed windows, French doors, stone patios, and old stone walls and walkways. The beautifully landscaped gardens boasted beds of lavender and black-eyed Susans, and the grandest violet-blue hydrangeas on the planet. Inside, the vast rooms were irresistibly homey, with large fireplaces and antiques everywhere. The yellow-and-vermillion walls were lined with folk art—including some by the famed Nova Scotia artist Maud Lewis—and the entire place was hung with colourful handmade quilts and hooked rugs and yards of patterned drapery. There was a state-of-the-art kitchen with an antique harvest table and an enormous hearth. The sun-drenched conservatory was filled with white wicker. Through the glass, the rambling lawns gave new meaning to the word "green" and a heartachingly beautiful view of Lough Corrib. We knew we were blessed to have discovered such an amazing place. As night fell, our dear New York friends Carol Leggett and Tony Gardner arrived with their six-year-old son, Marley, to share the magic.

In the morning, the kids paid a visit to Rosie and Daisy, the two donkeys penned up on the property. We drove to the picturesque village to shop for hand-knit sweaters and tweed salt-and-pepper caps. The girls looked like they'd hopped off the pages of a fall fashion editorial as we strolled down the quaint streets. We dropped by the Boat Inn for chips and smoked salmon, then headed back to Cappagarriff to build a faerie house out of twigs and twine. And so it went. Each exquisite day presented itself as a gift filled with poetry, adventure, and wonder. And as we kicked back by the fire each night, waiting for the faeries to come, I patted myself on the back, proud as punch that this single mum had the guts to pick herself up, dust herself off, and with her two gorgeous girls in tow, experience the kind of cozy family fantasy she thought had escaped her life forever.

Heartened by our successful and rewarding trip to Ireland, we opted for a very different kind of getaway in March of the following year. I was about to turn fifty, and I longed to be reminded of life's exotic possibilities. The girls and I thought Mexico might be fun, but we were determined to think outside the box and steer clear of package deals to conventional beach resorts. I had heard of a charming town, San Miguel de Allende, nestled in the mountains three hours outside of Mexico City. My artist friends Marion Perlet and Toller Cranston, the celebrated skater-turned-painter, had moved there in the early 1990s. And I had just read *On Mexican Time*, a wonderful book by the Los Angeles writer Tony Cohan about his life-transforming sojourn in San Miguel. By all accounts, San Miguel was mystical, romantic, and inspiring. I could see it, smell it, feel it, and I was certain it would awaken the artist in me. I booked our tickets and searched the Internet for just the right house to rent.

The gods were with us, and the small casa we found was perfect: two bedrooms filled with antiques and local artisanal furniture, with an outdoor living room and a tropical landscaped courtyard, just three blocks from the main square. So that we could share a sense of purpose, and not just spend our days hanging out, resting, shopping, and sampling salsa, I decided art classes were in order for the three of us. Marion put us in touch with a handsome local artist, Gerardo Ruiz, who had a studio on the edge of town, and each day, the girls and I would taxi to his place and spend a few hours painting and printmaking. I worked on a couple of timely self-portraits: one of a glamorous me thrusting a birthday cake and a chicken into the air, and the other of me gingerly walking across a tightrope, parasol in hand—a statement about the delicate balance I have always been obliged to strike.

We scoured the market for just the right straw cowboy hats and carried our precious art supplies in cheap plastic tote bags emblazoned with the faces of Frida Kahlo and Catrina, the famous skeleton lady. I cruised the dusty cobblestoned streets in my faded jeans and fancy green-and-black cowboy boots, while Joey made the radical fashion statement of a twelve-year-old in flannel Paul Frank pyjama bottoms, and Bekky opted for Boho Chic, with vintage silk scarves and the romantic peasant blouse I had bought for her in Paris. But beyond the fun we were having with fashion, each of us took great delight in getting into the Mexican groove and, above all, savouring our sense of family.

Because we missed all our friends back home, we frequented the local Internet café. The girls were intrigued to think that they were communicating from this exotic locale to their girlfriends' boring bedrooms. Joey ordered nothing but *leche con chocolate, frio*, while Bekky became addicted to a soft drink called Squirt and I became a margarita maven. We spent our afternoons having long, lazy lunches in courtyard cafés resplendent with bougainvillea, discussing art and life and just which little souvenirs to purchase. Marion was our guide, an elegant vision in white linen and a straw fedora, swaggering down the skinny sidewalks like she owned the place. She has become a highly successful artist in San Miguel these past few years, and I thought back to the days she struggled in Toronto, living in a basement and subsidizing her income by working in a bar. I started collecting her striking figurative paintings in the early 1980s, and my girls had grown up with them on the walls of our home. It meant so much for the girls to finally get to know her.

Most evenings were spent in the bustling main square, which hosted tiny parades and vendors selling balloons and toys on sticks and ice cream and cups of corn—a mecca for mariachis and artists and lovers and little kids who get to stay up late and old people simply content with watching the world go by. You could lose yourself in that square. And some nights I did, savouring each and every joyous moment.

Then there was the flamboyant Toller, my old confidant and original style icon, one of the first true artistes I had ever befriended. We had lost touch over the years, and it was bliss to rediscover him in his little Shangri-La. Toller's San Miguel estate comprised a magnificent four-house garden compound hidden behind great wooden doors, complete with a glass-walled studio filled with enormous, vibrant, and lyrical canvases. To celebrate my big 5-0, he hosted a simple yet lively Champagne-and-pizza dinner for us in his studio. The highlight was the birthday surprise he'd arranged with my sister, Marilyn, in L.A.: In the middle of dinner, a nine-member mariachi band, all dressed in gleaming white suits, strolled into the garden and up the studio stairs. "Any requests?" they asked. I didn't know any Spanish songs and thought for a minute. "How about 'My Way'?" I asked. To our delight, the band launched into a Spanish rendition of that classic corny tune. And I, Champagne flute in hand, drank in every last word.

But few trips I have taken with my beautiful girls can compare to our enigmatic but memorable time in Paris. The passion I feel for the City of Light dates back to 1974, when I spent a joyous few months there as an aspiring young artiste intent on mastering mime. I often think it's because I get to travel to Paris four times a year (covering the two prêt-à-porter and two haute couture collections) that I stay in this business. The inspiration I glean each time I stroll along the Seine, pull up at the Place Vendôme, see the Eiffel Tower, or sip a café au lait at a corner bistro is unfathomable. It's what feeds my spirit and soothes my soul.

For years as my girls were growing up, I dreamed of taking them to Paris to witness all the fantastic things that I had been telling them about, and to share those passions that run so deep in me. I wanted them to see the art and the architecture, taste the croissants and the crêpes, see the style on the streets, hear the music of the language, and experience the sheer joy of bearing witness to all that ubiquitous beauty. But regrettably, for me, Paris and work are synonymous, and with my days spent running around from shows to ateliers to interviews, there was never enough time to deal with the girls. Besides, between school and summer camp, their schedules were too harried to coordinate.

In July 2006, when Bekky was nineteen and Joey sixteen, and summer camp was no longer a factor, I felt that my chance to show them Paris had finally arrived. I would be working the first few days of the trip, of course, covering the fall couture collections. And I would have a cameraman in tow. But I figured these young ladies were now old enough to amuse themselves. And I would try to finagle some tickets for them to at least one of the shows, so they could witness the splendour of the runway and see me in action. They seemed pumped for the trip, and I was certain that my fondest fantasies were about to be realized.

Paris in the sweltering heat is not ideal, but with the temperature in the thirty-degree range the day we arrived, we just had to sweat and bear it. In the cab on the way from the airport, I anticipated my daughters' "oohs" and "ahhs" as the city unfolded, remembering so vividly what it was like for me the first time I saw Paris. But then I got my first rude awakening. "Feels like Montreal to me," sniffed Bekky. "I think I like Florence better," added Joey, getting nostalgic for the school trip she had taken the previous year. Complaints about the stifling heat dissipated as we neared the hotel. I had booked them an extra room at the Odéon Hôtel, the charming little St. Germain hideaway where I had been staying for almost a decade. Happily, they were charmed by the neighbourhood and the accommodations, though the tiny elevator to the sixth floor gave Bekky a case of claustrophobia. There was a view of the Eiffel Tower from both rooms, and the girls were delighted with that. It was decided that Joey would bunk in with me, however, so the volatile Bekky could luxuriate in the privacy of her own little room, which the writer in her saw as quite garret-like.

We crossed the Carrefour de l'Odéon for our first meal, choosing to lunch at one of my regular haunts, Les Éditeurs. It was then the real bickering began. I dismissed it as jet lag and tried to lose myself in a glass of Chardonnay. A plate of frites later, an exhausted Joey returned to her room, leaving Bekky and me on our own to savour St. Germain. I showed her all my favourite shops and cafés, and she seemed to be lapping it all up. But she did proclaim her disappointment at the way women were dressed. "I thought Parisian women were supposed to have such style," she mused. "I can't see it at all." I sort of understood where she was coming from: The women on Bloor Street in Toronto dressed just as chicly. I knew it would take Bekky a while longer to realize that great style goes far beyond the superficiality of what people wear.

Just when Bekky was ready to crash, Joey got up and was ready to rock. So I took her to the opening of the new avenue Montaigne Chrome Hearts boutique. Decked out in funky plaid pants, a studded belt with a skull buckle, and an old Doors T-shirt, she fit right in. The label's cool co-designer, Richard Stark, struck up a conversation with her. I stood back and watched as Joey—my baby—got into the Paris groove, proud as punch that she was holding her own.

The next morning, I took off for the shows while the girls went exploring with my cameraman's lovely girlfriend. We met up at the end of day, and they told me about riding the giant Ferris wheel and the carousel at the Trocadéro, while I regaled them with stories of Cher at Armani and Mischa Barton, Drew Barrymore, and Liv Tyler at Dior. Bekky was zapped once more, so she napped while I took Joey to Valentino. I hoped it was as much a fantasy for her as it was for me, rubbing shoulders backstage with the likes of Liz Hurley and Martha Stewart. I even introduced her to Valentino himself.

As the week progressed, the city's romantic and adventurous spirit overcame us in spurts. In between fashion shows and all the bickering, we went on mini shopping sprees. I had been shopping for Bekky and Joey for years, trying to guess what might appeal to them. Now, it was exhilarating to see them make their own choices. The adventure continued as I sneaked them into the Christian Lacroix show and taught them the art of scamming a seat. (Wait til the last minute and nonchalantly ease your way in. If the rightful owner shows up, make a quick exit.) Watching the brilliant Lacroix collection cruise down the catwalk from the front row was a dream come true. "The dresses look like Fabergé eggs, Mum," Joey astutely noted.

In the days that followed, sporadic squabbling was *de rigueur*, and complaints about everything from the way the milk tasted to the flavour of the coffee were constant. I grew to appreciate the girls' iPods, which allowed them to escape into their own little worlds and gave my aching ears a rest. Joey made her way through the Musée d'Orsay listening to Death Cab for Cutie, while Bekky was tuned to classic Kinks. At Shakespeare and Company, the famous St. Germain bookstore, Bekky went for James Joyce's *Ulysses*, while Joey opted for Sartre's *Nausea*— more welcome distractions to keep the bickering at bay.

Excitement ensued one morning when Bekky bravely took a Hemingway walking tour and met a nice young man from B.C. She made plans to meet him at the Louvre the next day. I occupied Joey by taking her to Angelina's for hot chocolate and then to the Balenciaga exhibit at the Musée de la Mode. Unfortunately, we learned that Bekky's "date" was a no-show (perhaps because she got to the Louvre fifteen minutes late). But my heart really broke for Bek the night we went to the cinema to see *Marie Antoinette*. There was a torrential downpour, and Bekky had left her hotel room windows open. When she got back, she discovered that her precious journal, in which she had been keeping copious notes, was totally drenched—a sopping, smudged disaster! I worried that the bleak episode might mar our entire trip.

By the end of the week, I was exhausted from trying to give them the time of their lives so they'd fall in love with Paris as I had done so many years ago. I finally realized something: You can't expect your children to be inspired by the same things that moved you. Nor can you instil in someone the same kind of passion just because you feel it. There were many times on the trip when I felt I was jamming square pegs into round holes, and several occasions when I wondered why I had even bothered trying to realize this fantasy of mine. But finally, on our last night, sitting under the stars at Café Ruc, both girls made it all worthwhile when they thanked me for bringing them to Paris. Bekky even ventured to say that perhaps she'd move to Paris one day. And when I asked them to write a few paragraphs each for *The Globe and Mail*, so I could add their observations to the end of the story I was writing—just to give readers an idea of what their take on the week was—I was blown away by how inspired their comments were, how sensitive they really had been to things I assumed had gone unnoticed, and how grateful they were finally to have been in the eye of this ultra-fashionable storm I had grown to love. So that's one more lesson learned, I suppose: Never underestimate your kids.

TENNESSEE STUD

GETTING IT RIGHT often takes time. Seasons come and go, fashions change, and remaining true to yourself is often painfully trying. Sometimes staying fashionable is about following your head. And sometimes, it's about following your heart. The most successful collections—and the most successful designers—are those that manage to walk the line between practicality and fantasy, a very precarious place to be. Sometimes, a designer will strike out with a collection and get panned by the critics. But that kind of failure rarely heralds the end of a career. The following season, the same designer can come back stronger than ever. What's important is experimenting with new directions. After all, no guts, no glory.

When my relationship with Jack ended, I yearned to find someone who saw the world the way I did—a kindred creative spirit who could read the poetry in every line of life. Someone who got the music, who could always make me laugh. I longed for such a complete about-face in my personal life because the last few years had been so inexplicably lonely for me. I was on a mission to find Mr. Right.

You might imagine that being in the public eye has some advantages when it comes to meeting people—after all, you're constantly "out there" in a variety of social situations. But in my experience, "out there" can be a rather wretched place. First of all, as a woman who has achieved a degree of public success, you can be intimidating to men who would rather have the spotlight to themselves. Then there are those guys who are put off by all the attention that comes with being a well-known face. They prefer anonymity and resent the constant scrutiny that comes with the territory. I should have known my marriage was in trouble when I first heard Denny tell someone that being out with me was like "being with a neon sign." I had worked for so long to build my visibility, but now it seemed like some kind of curse.

I had several girlfriends who were meeting men online—but that was something I could never feel comfortable doing. Too many people knew me, or at least thought they knew me. It would just be too embarrassing to put myself out there like that. And while you might suppose that the social aspect of my work would make it a cinch to meet all sorts of interesting guys, any woman who works in fashion will tell you that about 98 percent of the men she meets play for the other team. I never gave up hoping that the man of my dreams might be around the next corner, but I started thinking that a little divine intervention might be in order if I didn't want to be alone for the rest of my life. All my friends were aware that I was eager to meet someone, and that I might be willing to entertain a blind date. The problem was, there was a shortage of straight, single, age-appropriate guys around. I would just have to be patient.

In September 2006, four months after my relationship with Jack ended, I was in New York covering the spring collections when my friend Deenah Mollin called.

"Jeanne, do you remember H.?" she asked.

H. was a Nashville musician and record producer who had worked with one of America's legendary country stars for years. And he was a dear friend of Deenah's ex, who was also a musician. I recalled meeting H. about five years earlier at a dinner in Toronto, when he had just left his long-suffering wife for some aspiring young starlet, a Jewish girl who had moved to Nashville from Upstate New York, changed her name, and desperately wanted a recording contract. I tried not to be

In the immediate aftermath of 9/11, I was slated to fly across Canada to launch my new Jeanne Beker clothing line for Eaton's. The collection was inspired by my jet-set lifestyle, and the ads showed me, ironically considering the timing, posing beside an airport luggage carousel. (DAN COUTO)

LEFT: For her sixtieth birthday, the incomparable Betsey Johnson hosted a huge fairy-tale themed fashion extravaganza at her home in the Hamptons. I brought my daughter Joey along to share the fantasy.

RIGHT: With iconic Canadian supermodel Linda Evangelista backstage at New York Fashion Week in the early '90s.
(COURTESY OF CTV)

LEFT: I first interviewed Bono with U2 in the early '80s. In 2004, we featured him on the pages of *FQ* magazine, and Michael King and the team celebrated the launch of the issue at a private dinner at Toronto's Celestin restaurant.

LEFT: With legendary Italian film star Gina Lollobrigida at Valentino's forty-fifth anniversary dinner party at the Parco dei Daini of the Villa Borghese in Rome.

RIGHT: My relationship with Valentino goes back to the mid '80s, when *Fashion Television* first visited his couture atelier in Rome.

LEFT: With the indefatigable Pierre Cardin at his Paris office in October 2010.

TOP: Backstage with John Galliano, after Dior's fall couture presentation in July 2006. Dior initiated proceedings to have him fired in March 2011 after complaints were made that he had uttered racial slurs in a Paris restaurant. (ROBYN BIGUÉ)

LEFT AND RIGHT: Interviewing Jean-Paul Gaultier in November 2010 about his 2011 retrospective at Montreal's Musée des Beaux-Arts and in spring 2010 (right) at his Paris headquarters.

TOP: I never fail to glean inspiration from interviewing the brilliant and enigmatic Karl Lagerfeld. We're pictured here at the Chanel 2009 fall couture show. (ROBYN BIGUÉ)

LEFT: Running into Paul McCartney backstage at his daughter Stella's shows has become a regular, much-anticipated affair. When Joey accompanied me to Paris for her twenty-first birthday on October 4, 2010, I had the privilege of introducing her to Sir Paul. Needless to say, it made for a most memorable birthday fantasy. (STEVE WOOD)

TOP: Hosting the launch of Sarah Jessica Parker's first fragrance, Lovely, at the Toronto Eaton Centre in 2005.

RIGHT: Backstage in New York with Calvin Klein, who was a fixture on *Fashion Television* until his retirement in 2003.

LEFT: Backstage with Andy Summers of the Police after the group's Toronto concert in the summer of 2007.

BOTTOM: I first interviewed Andy Summers in a bathtub on *The New Music* circa 1980. It was fun to get into a tub with him for another interview when he came to Toronto in 2007. Little did we know that the candles would provide some additional excitement!

The eccentic and incomparable Isabella Blow at the Paris couture shows shortly after the launch of *SIR* magazine in 2005. Two years later, her tragic suicide rocked the fashion world. (FOC KAN/WIREIMAGE/GETTY IMAGES)

judgmental at the time, though the thought of it all made me cringe. But H. seemed to be a really nice guy, and while he was a little older than me and a tad rough around the edges, I remembered him as hip, witty, and charming as all get-out. He kept teasing me about being a "fashionista." And when he uttered the word in his thick southern drawl, it struck me as outrageously funny. We had got along like a house on fire. Little did I know that H. was about to literally set my house on fire! But I'm getting ahead of myself.

"Sure, I remember him," I said. "Why, what's up?"

"Well," said Deenah, "he was really attracted to you when he first met you, and he always asks about you. I was talking to him the other day, and he said he was in New York. When I told him you were also in New York, he said he would love to meet you for a drink. Interested?" she asked.

"Whatever happened to the young girlfriend?" I asked. Deenah informed me he wasn't with her anymore. My schedule was jam-packed, and I was running around to the shows at my usual hectic pace. But hey! If H. was up for a late-night rendezvous, I figured it might be fun to catch up. "Sure," I said, excited to actually be going on a date. "Tell him to call me."

The next day, the drawl on the phone was unmistakable, and H. had me laughing within seconds. I suggested he come by my hotel bar for drinks at around ten that night, once the last show we were covering was over. When I got back to my hotel, I slithered into my best pair of skinny jeans and the cool new Isabella Fiore boots I had just bought in L.A., which had "Faith, Hope, and Love" embroidered on them. Maybe they'd bring me luck. I went downstairs to the lobby to wait.

Minutes later, a tall, lanky guy sporting a Kangol cap, wire-frame spectacles, an oversized plaid wool shirt, faded blue jeans, and Frye boots moseyed into the lobby carrying a very unfashionable big plastic bag. It was raining, and he was a little wet. "Hi, baby!" H. said as soon as he saw me. He looked much craggier than I remembered him, but there was something so loose and relaxed about his manner that he seemed like a breath of fresh air.

We headed for the bar, and I asked him what was in the bag. He told me it contained some of his personal effects, the last few things he had left at his ex-girlfriend's apartment. Apparently, the aspiring starlet was living in the Big Apple now as a Broadway chorus girl.

"Whoa, that was frightful," he drawled. "I need a drink." H. ordered a Jack Daniels and proceeded to tell me that he had just come from his ex's place, and she had given him a really hard time. I wasn't sure what he meant, but I chose to ignore the drama and try to get to know him better.

We sat in the bar for a good couple of hours, totally engrossed in our conversation, me regaling him with tales of my old rock-and-roll days, him making me laugh out loud with his hilarious perceptions of the fashion world and his endearingly self-deprecating ways. He talked about how proud he was of his two beautiful grown daughters. And he also shared the pain and sadness he felt because of his severely mentally and physically disabled son. His love for that special child—his eldest— was particularly profound. That explained why there was something so world-weary about this guy, a kind of inner sadness. My heart went out to him, and I sensed that this aspect of his life had made him a bigger, more compassionate person. But H. kept coming back to the lighter side of life, and with his witty observations, constant wisecracks, and huge guffaws, he had me laughing more than I had laughed in a very long time. I was amazed how refreshingly different this guy was from anyone I had known.

Round about midnight, we decided to stroll through Times Square and get an ice cream. I was a little unnerved at first when he grabbed my hand, but soon I was merrily trying to keep up with his big, long strides. This was fun, I thought. New York took on a new complexion, miles away from anything to do with fashion. H.'s cellphone kept buzzing, and he constantly checked the text messages that were pouring in, complaining it was his ex, distraught over his departure. "I told her I was meeting you for a drink. She's probably all jealous now," he said. "But I'm not breaking down!" he added, with fierce determination. Again, I chose to ignore the shenanigans going on between these two and just be happy that I had found a cool new friend.

It was 2:00 a.m. by the time H. walked me back to my hotel. We said our goodnights, and he left me with a CD of his music to listen to. As soon as I got back to my room, I put it on, crawled under the covers, and savoured every last note of his wonderful bluesy style. About a half hour later, he called to say goodnight, asked me how I liked the CD, and told me how pumped he was about reconnecting with me. I told him he would have to come to Toronto and pay a visit to my farm.

In the days and weeks that followed, my life became a blur of entertaining emails and late-night calls from H. Our conversations often lasted for hours, sometimes until four or five in the morning. We talked about everything: art, religion, politics, human nature, our families, our histories, our hopes, our dreams. I discovered that he was well educated, a devout Christian, and a dedicated father. The downside was that while he had achieved success in the past, he had fallen on hard times in the present and scarcely had two cents to rub together. But his sense of humour was so profound and his insights so brilliant (I thought) that it didn't matter to me. I was falling for this crazy guy, hook, line, and sinker. He told me he had to see me again, and about a month after our fateful New York rendezvous, right after I had returned home from covering the next round of Paris collections, he was on his way to Toronto.

I met him at the airport and was a little shaken by his far-from-suave appearance. But I quickly erased that thought as the charm surfaced. I couldn't wait to take him to the farmhouse, where I could cook for him and we could spend a cozy couple of days listening to great music, watching old movies, and getting to know each other better.

Before I continue, I want to say that now, in retrospect, telling this story as honestly as possible, the whole thing seems unsavoury and wrong to me. I suppose I was so desperate to reinvent myself, to go for what I thought I wanted, to get a cool new boyfriend and recapture a kind of long-lost passion that I threw myself into this relationship with reckless abandon. I know it happens to people all the time. I'm just incredulous at how sadly desperate I must have been.

H. and I and my dog, Beau, made the short trek out to the farm. It was that glorious time of year when the fall colours were peaking. We sat on the couch for hours, quietly listening to some CDs he had made for me, so many of the great old tunes I'd grown up with—a fabulous compilation of rock and pop and R&B. He understood it all so well: which riffs were genius, which lyrics were amazing, the brilliance of each production. Finally, I had found someone who "got the music"! I felt honestly happy and wildly content for the first time in years.

All day, H. had been religiously tending to the living-room fireplace, taking a kind of macho pride in the sizeable fire he had built—one that raged more intensely than any fire that small hearth had ever seen. At around 1:00 a.m., as we were nodding off on the couch watching *Charade*, I detected smoke. I went over to the fireplace and saw a small curl of smoke that seemed to be coming out of the floor behind it. "Oh, no!" I said. "Looks like we may have some sort of chimney fire!" H. got up to investigate and told me that maybe we should call the fire department. I called 911, telling the woman who answered that we may have a small chimney fire and asking her to please dispatch someone to help us. Because it was so late, and we had only a volunteer fire department in the area, I was worried that it might take a while for someone to get there. But there was nothing we could do to hurry them along. I went over to the fireplace again. The curl of smoke was still there, but now it seemed to be coming from the gap between the floorboard and the hearth. I dashed to the kitchen and opened the trap door leading downstairs. The entire basement was engulfed in smoke!

I made another call to 911 for more urgent attention, while H. grabbed his laptop and barked orders to get the dog and leave the house immediately. Incredulous over what was happening, I chased Beau out of the house and followed suit. The smoke was getting thicker. I looked through the basement windows and saw raging orange flames! Through the glass door, I could see that the main floor of my beloved little farmhouse was totally engulfed in smoke. The tiny, perfect haven I'd worked so hard for, which was so emblematic of my independence and my sense of myself, was going up in smoke! I felt totally helpless. I just kept talking to God, praying harder than I ever had for my little house to be saved. And then I heard the sirens coming up the long road towards the driveway—music to my ears!

There were three trucks of volunteer firemen. By now, it was almost two in the morning. They had all been woken up from their sleep and hopped immediately to the call of duty. A few of the men were local farmers I had met before. They seemed happy to see me, though they must have wondered about this mysterious new man with the exotic southern drawl. H. sat on the hammock and looked on as the firemen rolled out their hoses, opened the door to the basement, and went down to see what was going on. I suppose we were just so relieved that help had arrived that we started getting a little giddy, with H. joking about how I had tried to kill him. He actually managed to make me laugh in the midst of this potential disaster!

Finally, after a good couple of hours, the fire was extinguished. We were told to stay awake for another couple of hours to make sure there wasn't any further flare-up. Apparently, because the initial fire H. built was so large, a flying spark had fallen through the crack in the floor-boards and ignited one of the 150-year-old beams in the basement. Luckily, the basement was totally empty (a flood down there some years back had forced me to get rid of everything), and that was what saved the building. If there had been something like an old couch down there, it would have caught fire in seconds, and the whole house would have been toast. I thought it was nothing less than an act of God that my precious farmhouse had not burned down, and also that H. and I had survived the fire. After all, we could have fallen asleep and not woken up in time. I installed smoke alarms the next morning. And the romantic in me naively interpreted the whole misadventure as a symbol of the burning passion H. and I shared, and as proof that if we could survive that, we would survive anything. Stupid, or what?

The romance continued for several months after that, with more phone calls that lasted long into the night. I flew down to Nashville to meet his lovely family and his two dogs; stayed in his rather squalid apartment; cooked pots of my chicken curry for him, leaving them in his freezer so he would have food for weeks. He even introduced me to his minister. (By this point I had invested in a copy of the New Testament, which I kept by my bedside and tried to digest each night because I knew the Scriptures were a cornerstone of H.'s life.) I'll never forget the prayer circle at his minister's house, which I joined on my final day there. Everybody prayed that I would be protected on all my exotic travels. Let me tell you, it was quite the send-off, considering that my next trip was to see Karl Lagerfeld in Monaco!

My life had definitely taken on a bizarrely comedic complexion. I was thrilled by H.'s late-night calls and melted just about every time I heard that deep-voiced drawl greeting me with that irresistible "Hey, baby!" H. and I had a couple of rendezvous in New York, and he flew to Toronto again, with me more than happy to cash in my frequent flyer points to get him here. I worried about him because he told me he rarely ate properly, except for the frozen curried chicken I had left him with and the tacos he regularly made for himself. I even sent him care packages of food from a local Nashville delicatessen on several occasions. Then there were the beautiful shirts and sweaters I bought him in Paris—delighting in how much he appreciated my generosity. I was seriously hooked on this guy, and when he came to see me just before Christmas, I hosted a big party at my house so my mum and all my friends could meet him. Not surprisingly, he charmed every last one of them. And though my girls seemed a bit cynical about the whole thing, they were glad to see me so happy at last. I would listen in the car to the compilation CDs he made for me, with the volume full blast. It was as though he had brought music back into my life. The pièce de résistance was when he wrote me a song for Christmas. Called "Jeanne, Come Home," it was inspired by all the time I spent in airplanes, running around the world, when he knew full well that for me, there really was no place like home.

While his forte for the past couple of decades had been producing the music of other artists, H. was a wonderful performer in his own right, and I strongly encouraged him to get out there and start playing, something he hadn't done in years. Shortly after Christmas, he told me the great news: He was going to play a small club in New York in January, just for one night. He was eager to see if he could start playing regularly again. I was thrilled that he was going to take this plunge, and enthusiastically made arrangements to be there for him. At first, he seemed excited that I would be present. But a couple of weeks before his gig, he mysteriously changed his tune and started suggesting that perhaps I should just let him test the waters on his own this first time out. It was suspicious behaviour to be sure, but I gave him the benefit of the doubt. I thought he was just feeling so much pressure that he was a little nervous about having me there. It broke my heart to have to stay in Toronto on the weekend I knew he was performing in New York, but I acquiesced. Shortly after his performance, he sheepishly admitted that his ex-girlfriend had shown up at the club, just to be supportive. I was bitterly stung but tried to be mature, stoically soldiering on when I should have been heeding the alarms.

I had become friendly with H.'s two beautiful twenty-something daughters. The youngest lived in New York, and it was her fondest wish to tag along with me to a couple of shows at Fashion Week that February. H. apologized that he wouldn't be able to meet me in New York that week—he had some important business to attend to in Nashville—but he said he was thrilled I would be showing his daughter around. We planned a fabulous day, and I took the dear young woman with me for an interview I was conducting with Norma Kamali, as well as taking her backstage to meet Betsey Johnston at her Bryant Park show. I took pride in introducing her to everyone as "my new boyfriend's daughter," and we had a blast. Several times that day, we tried calling H. on his cell, eager to share all the fun we were having. But we could never reach him, and he didn't return any of our messages. We both thought it was peculiar that he seemed to be missing in action.

At the end of the day, H.'s daughter went home, and I couldn't wait to talk to H. and tell him what a great day we had spent together. But he never called that night, and all my messages went unanswered. Now I was getting worried. The next morning, there was still no call. I was homeward bound, waiting for my plane in the lounge at LaGuardia, when my phone rang. It was H., apologizing profusely, saying he had been severely bummed out and completely tied up with something very heavy that was going down. He promised to explain everything to me when he came to Toronto that weekend. I was still worried and puzzled, but I had faith that it would all eventually make sense. I imagined that one of his business deals had gone south, or that he was in some kind of serious financial trouble, or maybe, God forbid, that something was wrong with his health. It was unnerving, and I couldn't wait to get the story.

H. showed up in Toronto a couple of days later (thanks again to my air miles, of course), and he seemed a little antsy. I begged him to tell me what "heavy" thing had gone down, but he said he didn't want to talk about it right away, assuring me that he would tell me everything once we got to the farm. I couldn't begin to imagine what all the mystery was about.

We finally got to Chanteclair, but H. was still delaying the big "reveal," saying he wanted to relax and watch a movie. Finally fed up, I insisted on hearing what his big "news" was. He took a deep breath.

"Well, you know when you were in New York this past week?" he began. "I was there too. But I couldn't see you, or even talk to you, because I was with my ex."

My heart plummeted.

"I was staying with her, but it isn't what you think!" He scrambled to find the words to mollify me. "I swear I never slept with her. I just had to go there and get some things straight with her, make sure she knew it was really over between us," he said.

My jaw dropped as I listened to this crock. Obviously, he wasn't ready to let go of the old girlfriend. How dare he!

"How dare you!" I screamed, as the painful memory of Denny's betrayal came rushing back. "There's one thing I can't stand, and that's a liar!" I roared.

"Well, I never lied to you! I never told you where I was exactly," he said feebly, trying to save his sorry ass.

I was sickened at the thought of having been so deceived.

"Why couldn't you just have told me you still had issues with her?" I asked.

"Because then I knew I wouldn't have her anymore, and I wouldn't have you. I didn't think you'd accept that."

"You should have tried me!" I shot back. I was livid.

But as incensed as I was, I didn't have the heart to throw him out of the farmhouse. It was a freezing February night, and we were in the middle of nowhere, after all. So I just sucked up my anger and wrote him off forever. What a jerk he was! And what a vulnerable fool I'd been! I was deeply ashamed of myself, and realized how empty and lonely I must have been to have allowed myself to be drawn into this dark, hurtful situation. Still, in retrospect, I suppose I can't be angry with myself for having an open heart, and for giving someone the benefit of the doubt. It's just unfortunate that sometimes we do get taken advantage of—especially when we're needy. I made up my mind to get over H. *tout de suite* and concentrate on refining my survival skills as a soloist for a while.

By early December, ten months after my H. fiasco, I was relishing my life—footloose and fancy free. Surprisingly, a whole new spate of suitors had miraculously surfaced. I was dating and feeling confident once again when I got an email from H. His beloved son had died suddenly. I knew H. must have been beside himself with grief, and my heart went out to him. I decided to reach out and gave him a call. He was happy to hear from me and wept openly over his loss. He said he would love my input on the eulogy he had written for the funeral the next day. I told him to send it, and I would go over it for him. I could only imagine the depth of H.'s agony, since I knew how profoundly his special needs son had affected his life. In my heart, I forgave H. for treating me so badly, but I still wanted no part of him in my life.

After his son's funeral, H. contacted me a few times, asking if he could come to Toronto for a post-Christmas visit. My answer was a resounding no. That chapter was over, baby. I had definitely moved on.

A MOTHER'S COURAGE

MY MOTHER is one of the great loves of my live, and I thank God every day that I still have her to share in my joys and success, to inspire me, and to comfort me with her unconditional love. Unfortunately, though, since my sister, Marilyn, has lived in Los Angeles since the early 1980s, I'm the only child my mother has close by (even though she's about a forty-five-minute drive away, which makes it seem not nearly close enough most days). I speak to my mother every single day, no matter where in the world I am, and I try to see her for dinner or an outing at least once a week. Sometimes, she spends the weekend with me at the farm. Once in a while, she comes out to see me host a fashion show or speak at an event. It's those times I particularly cherish, so grateful that she was able to see her "little Jeanne" grow up to live the dream.

Naturally, like all of us with aging parents, I am concerned about her physical well-being. Both my sister and I were especially worried when, in April 2007, my eighty-six-year-old mother started complaining about getting fatigued after just walking a block or so. She was also experiencing pain in her left arm. My dad had been the one with heart problems. My mother's malady was Parkinson's, which had been diagnosed a couple of years earlier. We all assumed that her Parkinson's was to blame for her sudden fatigue. We never thought that my mother's heart might be in trouble too.

Still, at the suggestion of my mother's doctor, I took her to see a cardiologist. Within minutes, this specialist told us he suspected she had a major blockage in her heart, and he urged us to get her to the hospital immediately for observation. And so it began. Within days, we learned that my mother had two major artery blockages that were so severe, she wasn't even a candidate for angioplasty. A double bypass was her only hope. Trouble is, there aren't too many surgeons willing to do open-heart surgery on eighty-six-year-olds with Parkinson's.

We were all in shock. How could our vibrant, Energizer Bunny of a mum be in this much peril? And after all she had been through, would she even be willing to entertain the option of surgery, assuming we could find someone who would take the chance and operate on her? My sister and I were terrified. My mother was in disbelief and seemed unwilling to make such a grave decision. "I'll do whatever you want," she told us from her hospital bed. "I can't decide for myself." My sister and I were sick with indecision. But we knew it was up to us.

On April 17, Bekky's twentieth birthday, Marilyn, Bekky, and I spent a couple of agonizing hours in my mother's room at North York General Hospital, trying to decide whether she should "go for it" and have the risky double bypass. Marilyn was against it at first. She believed it would be too much for my mother. Even though my mother was walking on eggshells, her heart capable of giving out at any minute, Marilyn was understandably worried about subjecting her to such an invasive and potentially dangerous operation. My sister had a valid point.

"What would you do if it were you?" my mum asked me.

"Well, Mummy," I said, choosing my words carefully, "I guess I always thought of myself as a risk-taker. If there's a chance—any chance at all—to make something better, I think I would probably go for it."

My mother closed her eyes, digesting what I'd said. And then, much to the surprise of all of us in that stressful meeting, she bravely told us that she had made her decision.

"I'm going to try to have the operation," she told us. "As long as I have you to live for, I think I should try to do it."

It was an announcement that was at once scary and inspiring. The tears ran down my cheeks as I silently applauded my dear, sweet mum—this amazing woman who had already been to hell and back— for having the courage to take such a daunting risk at such a vulnerable stage of her life. I was reminded of what had made her such a survivor in the first place.

We relayed the news to her cardiologist, who was impressed by her decision. Now the task would be to find someone who was willing to do the surgery. The surgeons the cardiologist usually worked with had flat out refused to operate. But some things are meant to happen. Miraculously, my friend Kate Alexander Daniels offered to help. She was friends with a brilliant young Toronto heart surgeon named Vivek Rao, and he kindly agreed to see my mother.

"I'll be brutally honest with you," he told me over the phone. "I'll know right away, as soon as I meet her, whether I think she can endure this type of surgery. I won't beat around the bush." I was pleased with Dr. Rao's straightforwardness, and started praying as hard as I could that my mum would pass the audition.

Dr. Rao showed up at my mother's hospital room the next day. I was both surprised by and impressed with how young he was, and I could sense his great bedside manner immediately. He asked my mother to squeeze his hand, and he told her how great she looked, like someone in her seventies. My mother acted a bit shy, like a little girl. I suppose she was hoping to make a good impression. After all, her life depended on it.

Within a couple of minutes, Dr. Rao gave us the good news: He was confident he could perform surgery on my mother. And the sooner the better. But he warned us that the recovery wouldn't be easy. It would be difficult enough for her to get her physical strength back—but the true healing hinged on her attitude and stamina. It would be up to me and my sister to encourage her through the whole process. The prospect of my mother's undergoing this major ordeal was frightening. But our main focus had to be the fact that my mum was being given a second chance. My father's old motto—Don't be afraid, and never give up!—had never resonated so loudly with me. We made arrangements to have my mother moved downtown, to Toronto General Hospital, and started gearing up for the big operation, which was scheduled to take place a few days later.

The hours my sister and I spent in that hospital waiting room were the longest and scariest of my life. I don't recall ever praying so hard. It seemed painfully unfair that after all my mother had lived through—the hell of the Holocaust, as well as my father's long illness and eventual death—she was fighting for her life in some operating theatre.

It was anticipated that the surgery would take about three hours. But it was an agonizing five-hour wait before Dr. Rao came into the room to tell us that while my mother had come through the initial operation, they'd had to take her back into surgery and open her up again because she was having a bleeding problem. Another frightening couple of hours passed. Finally, Dr. Rao reappeared. The heroic doctor told us he had held his thumbs over my mother's breastbone for about twenty minutes to finally stop the bleeding. She was okay now. The next twenty-four hours would be crucial, he said, but he felt she would be just fine. I was overwhelmed with relief.

I spent the next six weeks in a blur of hospital visits, determined to be there for my mum in any way possible. Eventually, my sister had to get back to L.A., so it was up to me to attend to things. Luckily, my team at the magazine could fill in for me, although I had to cancel a couple of exotic location shoots. It was just too risky to leave town while my mother was in recovery mode. After about two weeks, she moved into a wonderful convalescence hospital and slowly began to get her strength back. Her spirits were phenomenal. She charmed everyone she met, and everyone who cared for her. The optimism she displayed during that long recovery period—a kind of positive perseverance I hadn't ever detected in my mum before—saw her through. Today, my mother wears the scar on her chest proudly, a testament to her tenacity. The survivor in her had endured once again. I was wildly inspired by her courage, and thankful that she dared to take a risk at an age when others might have given up.

FAME

As a kid, I always entertained the notion of becoming famous when I grew up. But I've paid a lot of attention to the nature of fame over the years, and I've had the chance to see what that monster we call celebrity can do—or not do—to people. However lustrous it seems, fame has a very dark side, and those who play into that can be lost forever. The stars I have met who can handle the heat usually use their celebrity status for higher purposes, and they never fail to inspire me.

LES GIRLS

A BUSINESS so consumed with appearances can make you crazy. It's what I both love and hate about fashion. Over the twenty-five years that I have covered this industry, surrounded by some of the most extraordinary physical beauties on the planet, I have learned more than I ever wanted to know about how thin physical beauty can wear when sensitivity and intelligence are in short supply. I have also learned a lot about the fleeting nature of beauty—and not just because we weather and age, earn a few lines, and gain a few pounds. Our own perceptions of what or who is truly beautiful can often turn on a dime. Something is revealed, someone shows her true colours, and suddenly the gorgeous image shatters, the glow subsides, the light is extinguished forever. Of course, there are those beauties who constantly work on their inner selves: cultivating their talents and their compassion, nourishing their spirit by feeding on the positive, and basking in gratitude for what they have, not wallowing in resentment for what they don't have. Those are the real timeless beauties, the girls who grow up to become great women—women who endlessly inspire me, and whom I support every step of the way.

When it comes to models, I have been lucky to have met many of the industry's true beauties over the years—including the elegant Carmen Dell'Orefice, who was photographed by such legendary photographers as Horst P. Horst and Cecil Beaton in the 1940s; the indefatigable Twiggy, one of my original 1960s icons; the spectacular and exotic Iman, who broke through social barriers to become one of the highest-paid models of the 1970s; the fabulous supermodels of the 1980s, like Linda Evangelista, Naomi Campbell, Christy Turlington, Cindy Crawford, Elle Macpherson, Claudia Schiffer, and Helena Christensen, who really punched up high glamour; and the rash of exquisite, disparate girls who took the 1990s by storm, like Amber Valletta, Shalom Harlow, Kate Moss, Erin O'Connor, Karen Elson, and Alek Wek. By the millennium, Brazilian Giselle Bündchen had resurrected the notion of the super-model, and after my first conversation with her, I completely understood why. Giselle could light up a catwalk with her personality alone. The fact that she is stunningly beautiful is merely a bonus. And then there's the arresting, quirky charm of Irina Lazareanu, the Romanian-born Canadian model who helped inspire the artist in some of the world's most creative designers, including the mighty Karl Lagerfeld, Yohji Yamamoto, and Balenciaga's Nicolas Ghesquière. Another Canadian sensation, the Polish-born beauty Daria Werbowy, is both gorgeous and remarkably grounded. More recent runway sensations, like the charming Vancouver native Coco Rocha and the captivating St. Louis–raised Karlie Kloss, add to my faith that personal charisma and intelligence are as important as physical beauty in today's modelling arena.

Models are unquestionably the scene's most electrifying and enigmatic players. They have the potential to make or break the image of a fashion house, yet often they are treated like cattle, mere manne-quins hired to strut a designer's vision. Some are vital muses for a house. Some are doggedly determined to use the scene as a stepping stone to greater heights, and wisely hone additional skills and work their connections to reinvent themselves once the modelling assign-ments begin to wane. I've often said that while I may have helped to propagate some unfortunate myths about modelling by the very fact that *Fashion Television* often casts a glamorous light on the fashion world, I would never encourage my own daughters to pursue a career in the business. Yes, modelling can and does open many doors for girls who might otherwise never have the chance to travel and meet interesting people. And yes, modelling can be very lucrative. But that's like winning the lottery. Only a precious few really make it out there; only the ultra strong survive.

My involvement as a judge on the popular TV series *Canada's Next Top Model*—a show that I was cast in back in 2006, and that ran for three seasons—was a bit of roller-coaster ride, to say the least. Because the show dealt with a world I'm so passionate about, and because it did involve groups of beautiful, sensitive, flesh-and-blood girls—some of whom reminded me of my own daughters—emotions ran high. I realized what a powerful position the judges were in: We had the ability to change—at least to a degree—a girl's life. That being said, I have always maintained that if a girl really has what it takes to make it as a model, and she's prepared to work very hard, she doesn't need to subject herself to the brutal trial of a reality television series. Still, there are those who want fame at any price. And if they're willing to endure the gruelling tests that a show of this nature puts its contestants through ... well, they will get the attention they crave, without a doubt. Trouble is, not everyone is psychologically ready for what can happen.

Most people realize by now that when it comes to television, where programs are produced in a limited time frame and are made to be dramatic and entertaining, few things can ever be that "real." Still, this series, which is produced in different countries around the world, does reveal a lot about the machinations of the fashion world, and just how judged, scrutinized, and objectified models really are. Being tough with these impressionable, often naive young girls was rather gut-wrenching, and many nights, after hours of deliberations (most of which was never aired), I would go home quite depressed. I admit that there were times when I regretted decisions I made or conclusions I came to about some of the girls. But you have to realize that we judges were never allowed to know what really went on in the house the girls occupied. We were asked to judge solely on the work the girls produced, their behaviour on photo shoots and before the judging panel, and the odd personal encounter we had with them. I was often shocked by what I saw watching episodes when the show was broadcast, and I came to the realization that sometimes I had assessed these hopefuls without having seen the whole picture. Then again, in real life, models are constantly judged on the basis of limited encounters. That's just the way the business operates, and if a girl can't get her head around that and accept it, modelling is not the career for her.

The first cycle of *Canada's Next Top Model* was shot in Victoria, British Columbia. We were on location for almost a month, and because it was the first time we had done the show, we were all a little green. I was particularly idealistic, and I allowed myself to fall in love just a little with most of these young women. Of course, we judges saw the girls only when they were on their best behaviour, and in retrospect, we had no idea who they really were.

When the *Canada's Next Top Model*—or *CNTM*—judges first met one particular nineteen-year-old hopeful, we were astonished at how implausible a candidate she seemed. You've got to be kidding! I thought, the moment her waif-like frame came into view. Clad in the most un-chic getup imaginable—complete with passé pedal-pushers, bad shoes, and a poor-boy cap—this skinny red-haired girl struck us as the epitome of geek-dom. I was astonished that this mere slip of a girl—vulnerability personified—had made it into the top ten.

But we romantic fashion arbiters do tend to encourage seemingly impossible dreams sometimes. This contestant talked about why she was so intent on winning the competition, and our hearts melted. "I just want to get back at all those people who made fun of me growing up, who said that I looked like a beast," she said. This young lady had undergone numerous dental operations to fix her unsightly smile. There was no doubt she had suffered as a kid, and while we judges suggested that she let go of all the bitterness she still harboured, we knew she felt she had something to prove. Right or wrong, it's that passion that often spurs us on to miraculous heights.

This candidate had an unmistakable fire in that petite belly of hers, and over the next few weeks, we delighted in seeing her beauty and bravado blossom. Her photos were exceptionally strong, and we were enchanted by her range and her ability to transform herself as the occasion demanded. Over the course of the competition, this girl became emblematic of fashion's inherent magic. Like a natural, she knew how to turn it on for the camera lens and bring fantasies to life. Of course, we hadn't a clue about the goings-on at the model house. We had no idea that this aspiring young model, who wore her heart on her sleeve so flagrantly, also hoarded suitcases filled with candy under her bed and cried like clockwork. We also eventually discovered something else about her—something that would have disqualified her from the competition immediately. But the sad truth wasn't revealed until it was too late.

All of us judges were concerned from the get-go that this contestant might have an eating disorder. She was exceptionally thin. And while her frame did translate well in photographs, we thought that perhaps she wasn't eating properly. But she swore that it was a matter of genetics, that her whole family was ultra thin, and that she had no eating disorder. We demanded to see a doctor's letter, and we did. The girl's family doctor assured us that she was in good physical health, and we believed him.

Still, the title was no slam dunk. The other remaining finalist was pretty fabulous as well, though in a different way. She was also nineteen, but she was much more the girl-next-door type—lovely and grounded, although her potential as a high-fashion model was doubtful. Did we go with the quirky redhead or the more mainstream, athletic-looking contestant? At the eleventh hour, our judging panel was divided. When all was said and done, it was up to me to cast the deciding vote.

It was agonizing having to choose between the two. In the end, after hours of gruelling deliberation, I came to the conclusion that it was our quirky redhead who exuded that star quality. Her chameleon-like ways were captivating. And besides, she had perfect bones—all mouth, naturally clothes-hanger thin, with a penetrating gaze. When she was announced as the winner, she was overjoyed, and she promised us that she would work as hard as she could and make us all proud of her. It was exciting to see this Cinderella story play out, and for a few weeks, before the final episode aired and the winner was announced to the nation, I was inspired by this intriguing young lady who had been transformed before our very eyes. Most important, I was convinced she would have a modelling career.

Once the winner was announced, it was time for her to step forward. I urged my editor at *The Globe and Mail* to feature her in a fashion spread, and I felt proud when I heard that she had done a good job. She readily jumped into the spotlight and dutifully began doing interviews with a number of media outlets. I was at home one evening when the publicist at my TV station called to say that there was an item about to be broadcast on *ET Canada* that I might find upsetting. Apparently, our new Top Model had said some disparaging things about me. So I tuned in to the program.

The report featured quotes from an interview the girl had done for an upcoming issue of *Inside Entertainment* magazine. Our Top Model's disturbing words were up there on the screen for the whole country to see. She called me a "workaholic with two failed marriages," and compared me to the Meryl Streep character in *The Devil Wears Prada*! I was flabbergasted as I watched the report, which went on to say that she'd hated all the judges, and that we had only done the show "to be famous." I was distraught that she had spoken about my personal life in this hurtful way. It especially stung when I flashed back to how I had cast the deciding vote in her favour. I was dumbfounded, enraged, and just plain hurt.

A few minutes after the segment aired, my phone rang. It was the girl, beside herself, apologizing profusely for what had just been reported. She said that her comments had been taken out of context, and that she was so nervous during the interview she didn't really know what she was saying. "I've never even seen *The Devil Wears Prada*!" she protested. I told her how hurt and disappointed I was, and while I wanted to give her the benefit of the doubt, I had a sinking feeling that maybe I had horribly misjudged our winner.

A producer at *ET Canada* offered me the opportunity to go on the program to defend myself, but I declined. I was assured that the interview was on tape, that the girl's comments had not been taken out of context, and that she had not been coerced in any way. I was crestfallen that we had made such a grave error. It is possible to speculate about what would make a person behave so unpredictably and irrationally, and so clearly against her own best interests. Obviously, one explanation is nervousness in the face of intense media attention.

As it turned out, my friends in the industry were just as upset as I was, and I guess a lot of people simply wrote her off. Several months later, I heard that she was throwing in the towel and abandoning the modelling world. She also publicly admitted that she had been anorexic all along. I was shocked and saddened by the whole experience. And I felt sorry for this naive young woman who had lost what might have been a golden opportunity.

THE BATHTUB CAPER

EVER SINCE I was a teenager, the notion of walking on the wild side has held great appeal. While I was never a major rebel, I certainly indulged in my share of sex, drugs, and rock and roll growing up. But evidently, I had an inherent moralistic sense of moderation, because I never went too far, and thankfully, I never got into any big trouble. Certain moments of my impetuous youth have remained with me to this day, however. In the summer of 1969, for example, when I was seventeen and attending the Toronto Pop Festival, I jumped onstage in a yellow pompom-trimmed bikini top for an impromptu dance with the legendary rocker Ronnie Hawkins. A large photo of this suburban kid—and I was identified by name—boogying her brains out as the Hawk did his mean rendition of "Hey! Bo Diddley" appeared in the *Toronto Telegram* the next day. Of course, my mother was mortified, but I was proud as punch. The whole experience was downright exhilarating, and it unquestionably contributed greatly to who I am today.

But a certain modesty comes with age. While I have always applauded the playful audacity of those in the fashion world—from the late Alexander McQueen, who dropped his jeans to reveal American flag–decorated boxer shorts when he took his runway bow in spring

2000, to the inimitable Betsey Johnson and her risqué cartwheels—I sensed that my own days of succumbing to unbridled outrageous behaviour were over. Then, in October 2005, the *FQ* team and I went on a photo shoot to the five-hundred-year-old seaside town of Cartagena, Colombia. To add to the excitement, we were accompanied by a documentary crew from *Cover Stories*, a reality TV series about the making of our magazine, which I was co-executive producing. Though we'd been warned about the potential perils in that part of the world, from kidnappings to drug cartels, we also knew that Colombia was full of gorgeous geographical and architectural settings, to say nothing of the country's incredibly beautiful people. It was all too much to resist.

Our first day was spent shooting on the cobblestone streets and bustling squares of the old walled city. From the lively craftspeople selling their wares to the glamorous designer boutiques and restaurants, we quickly fell in love with this magical place. Crowds gathered to watch our stunning models, clad in local and international designer clothing, joyously camping it up for our photographer, Paul Wright. We even enlisted some colourful local characters to join in the fun, including a group of amiable musicians and an elegant woman carrying a basket of fruit on her head. After each setup, the intrigued onlookers burst into wild applause. By the time I got back to my hotel to change for dinner, I was jubilant: Our first exotic holiday spread for *FQ* was going to be utterly exquisite. And watching my creative team in action was a pure joy. In the trenches of the fashion magazine world, it doesn't get much better than that.

We had been invited to the swank home of a prominent and gracious Colombian woman for dinner. I was debating what to wear when my BlackBerry buzzed with a message from my sister. "Today is International Very Good Looking, Damn Smart Women's Day," it read, "so please send this message to someone you think fits this description. And remember this motto to live by: Life should not be a journey to the grave with the intention of arriving safely in an attractive and well-preserved body, but rather to skid in sideways, chocolate in one hand, wine in the other, body thoroughly used up, worn out, and screaming, 'Woo hoo! What a ride!'"

Inspired by this spirited statement, and feeling almost svelte in comparison to the corpulent Fernando Botero statue I had just seen in Santo Domingo Square, I donned a skin-tight, cherry-red cocktail outfit by the Canadian label Zenobia. Sucking in my stomach, I made my way to the lobby to meet my colleagues, and for a precious few seconds, I actually did feel "very good looking" and "damn smart."

Our hostess's home was truly spectacular: an ancient building transformed into a deluxe modern palazzo, complete with an indoor swimming pool. There were about twenty of us altogether, and as we sat on the rooftop, drinking delicious mango cocktails, I felt unspeakably privileged to be feted in such an opulent manner, in such wildly exotic climes.

Downstairs, we took our seats at a beautifully set table next to the pool. Dinner included a rich bouillabaisse imaginatively served in coconut shells. Just as we were finishing our scrumptious desserts, a lively band of musicians marched into the house and began playing some steamy Latin tunes. Within minutes, we had all kicked off our shoes and were dancing our hearts out. We might have known that the pool would be too tempting on such a hot and humid night. Suddenly, guests began jumping in in all their finery. It was one of the most surreal scenes I had ever experienced! Twisting and turning to the Latin rhythms in that cool blue water, laughing madly with my pals, I was amazed that this South American fever was so infectious. The fact that I was wearing skin-tight jersey was fortuitous, as my sopping wet outfit fared much better than some of the chiffon numbers several other women wore. Still, I'll never forget how beautiful everyone looked, and how little it mattered what anyone was wearing. This was so beautifully beyond fashion: It was about losing ourselves in the moment. The whole outrageous escapade somehow felt totally natural, and all I kept thinking was "Woo hoo! What a ride!"

Maybe it's the Pisces in me, but I seem to have an affinity for water. Take my memorable interview with the guitarist extraordinaire Andy Summers, of the hot 1980s rock band the Police. There are precious few ways to add years to one's life, but one of the most effective has to be getting into a bathtub with a rock star.

I first met Andy back in 1980, just after the release of the Police's third album, *Zenyattà Mondatta*. The band was touring western Canada to promote the record, and as the host of *The New Music*, I was invited to Regina, Saskatchewan, to do a story on the group. I was hugely charmed by all of them. A few months later, the Police came to Toronto, and I was granted a one-on-one with Andy. Always the imp, and playfully adamant about pushing the boundaries of television propriety, he naughtily suggested that he hop into the bathtub for the interview—sans pants. Sitting on the tub's edge, attempting to conduct my "serious interview," I could hardly contain my laughter as the bath bubbles began to dissipate and Andy nervously tried to cover himself up. It all made for great TV, and to this day, it's remembered by a generation of *The New Music* fans as a music television "classic."

Fast-forward to the summer of 2007. More than a quarter of a century later, Andy, who always had a penchant for photography and took delight in documenting those hedonistic early days in his life as a rock star, had just released *I'll Be Watching You*, a beautiful book of his old photographs. Because the art of photography had always been a staple on *Fashion Television*, we decided it would be very cool to profile Andy and his new book. My office called to see if he would be up for a segment with me. Happily, he had fond memories of our old bathtub romp for *The New Music* and readily agreed to be interviewed the day after the Police played the Air Canada Centre. He also suggested that we do something as outrageous for the TV camera as we had all those years ago. "Maybe this time, I'll get in the tub with him!" I joked to my producer, Christopher Sherman. Christopher mentioned the idea to Andy's management. Apparently they loved it. I was offered tickets to the show and provided with a backstage pass to see the boys both before and after the concert. It was starting to feel like the old days all over again.

It had been many years since I'd seen the guys, but Sting recognized me immediately and was as amicable and gracious as ever. Andy was happy to see me too, and we began plotting our shoot the next day.

"So you're thinking of getting into the tub with me this time?" he asked.

"Well, if I can talk myself into it, sure," I said, laughing.

"I've got it all planned," said Andy with a twinkle in his eye. "I'm going to take this rich brocade fabric that's draped all over my dressing room and decorate the bathroom with it. And I'm going to put candles all around the tub ... Rather exotic and mystical, don't you think?"

"I'll bring the bubble bath," I laughed. I said I couldn't wait, but secretly I wondered what the heck I'd got myself into.

The Police concert was astoundingly good. The guys sounded as amazing as ever, and I was blown away by their talent, energy, and overall stage appeal after all those years—almost better than I had remembered. I couldn't wait to get my up-close interview with Andy the next day. With his approval, I asked the Toronto photographer Paul Alexander to document our interview so I could use the stills in *SIR*—the men's magazine we'd launched in 2005—alongside the transcript. With the *FT* camera crew capturing it all in motion, this was promising to be a sublime multimedia experience.

The next morning, readying myself for the bathtub encounter at the Windsor Arms Hotel, I agonized over whether I should be packing a bathing suit—and if so, one piece or two—and whether I should even be entertaining the notion of getting into a tub with Andy at all. After all, I was a fifty-five-year-old mother of two! I had told my own mother about the possibility of doing this bathtub interview, and she was shocked that I would even consider such a thing.

I rummaged through my drawers for my old black bikini with the leopard trim and quickly stuffed it into my purse just before I left the house. I'm taking it just in case, I told myself, though I honestly didn't think I would have the nerve to wear it. On the way to the hotel, I stopped at the drugstore to buy a big bottle of Mr. Bubble. Couldn't take any chances with dissipating bubbles this time around! I arrived at the hotel in a little black dress, still not sure exactly what I would be wearing for the interview.

Andy was sitting in the living room of his suite, picking away at an acoustic guitar, when I arrived. We set up a laptop and popped in a DVD of the original 1980 bathtub interview. He was transfixed as he watched the folly unfold. We had a good laugh, and when the segment was over, it was time to get down to business. Andy disappeared into the bedroom and donned a T-shirt emblazoned with the American flag and a drawing of a two-fingered 1960s peace sign. This time, though, his maturity showed: He put on a pair of plaid boxer shorts, evidently shy of the kind of exposure he'd toyed with in his youth.

I disappeared into the bathroom, and was charmed to see that Andy had arranged the exotic brocade fabric from his dressing room, as promised, and had placed an assortment of candles around the edge of the tub. This was bikini time! I quickly put it on, wondering all the while where this unfathomable chutzpah could possibly be coming from. Trust me, I was faking any confidence I may have exuded: I was totally freaked by the whole experience! Still, I wrapped myself up in the terrycloth bathrobe that was hanging on the door, put my hair up with a clip, removed all my jewellery, and took a very deep breath—as ready for my closeup as I would ever be. I emerged from the bathroom, and the crew crowded in—my cameraman, Jeff Brinkert; his assistant; and Paul, the photographer. The boys were impressed that I was actually going through with the wacky plan. I was feeling at once encouraged and crazy.

Andy entered the room and turned on the taps. The big moment was approaching. I got my pink bottle of Mr. Bubble and started pouring. As the sudsy clouds erupted, Andy gingerly entered the tub. "You coming?" he asked. Suddenly, the diminutive sixty-four-year-old rock star looked like a little boy. With every ounce of cool I could muster, I sucked in my gut and disrobed. The guys cheered me on. It was all so thoroughly outrageous that I could only laugh. Hurriedly stepping into the tub, I prayed that my body would become instantly invisible. Right on cue, the cosmopolitans we had ordered from room service arrived. I definitely needed a drink.

"Just don't drop the mic," warned Jeff. "And try to hold it way above the suds." This wireless microphone was much hipper than the old hard-wired mic I had used for my first Andy-in-the-tub encounter. Andy rested his cosmo on the edge of the tub and produced a joint, which he proceeded to light as the camera started rolling and Paul started snapping. Our giddiness soon gave way to a surprisingly comfortable feeling. This was by far the most intimate setting I had ever conducted an interview in, and strangely, it felt like the most natural, relaxing, cozy place to be. Andy took a toke as I launched in to my first question. I was luxuriating in the heady conversation and pressing Andy about what he had learned about himself from his whole 1980s rise to fame. "To be an artist of any kind, you have to operate in a raw, bleeding way," he told me between sips of his cocktail. "You have to be vulnerable and creative in any sphere. You have to go to a place that's open … It's a balancing act to walk that tightrope of keeping on an even keel, yet remaining emotionally vulnerable so you can be creative."

Somewhere in his opining about the meaning of art and the meaning of life, Andy threw his head back for a second. When he brought it back up, I screamed with horror: Flames were dancing on top of his head! His hair had caught fire from the candle! I panicked, dropped the mic, and forgetting my modesty, immediately jumped up to help. "His hair's on fire!" I yelled. Two seconds later, before Andy even knew what hit him, the fire had been put out, and my invincible subject just kept on talking, while I had flashes of Michael Jackson's horrific misadventure on that infamous Pepsi commercial shoot. Fortunately, Jeff kept his cool the entire time and kept on rolling, which resulted in YouTube gold—a video watched by thousands.

By the end of our interview, Andy and I and the crew knew that what had just transpired was magic—an intimate, intelligent, and animated interview with a bona fide rock star, conducted in a preposterous setting, with a totally unexpected drama cropping up in the middle. The fact that I'd had the guts to don a bikini—and actually allowed the cameras to capture me wearing it—was the icing on the cake, and certainly won me the "good sport" award with everyone present. On a more personal note, though, although I knew I was bound to cringe when I saw the resulting images, I felt as though I'd risen to the occasion, abandoned ego, and thrown myself wholeheartedly into the moment. I had walked on the wild side once again! It made me proud to know I was still very much in touch with my inner teen.

BROKEN PROMISES

HIGH SARTORIAL STYLE and good manners do not necessarily go hand in hand. I'm not sure at what stage of life a person can afford to be so self-involved that others simply don't matter. But sometimes, the unimaginable happens, and those of us who want to believe in the best in people are in for a very rude awakening. Case in point: Sean Combs, the former Puff Daddy, now commonly known as Diddy. But I still call him Puffy.

I first met Puffy in November 1998, when the entrepreneurial rapper/producer/actor turned his talents to design and launched a small men's hip-hop clothing line called Sean John. The line, at that time, consisted of little more than a group of oversized shirts, some with a Hawaiian-style motif. My cameraman and I had an appointment to meet Puffy at his West Twenty-first Street eatery, Justin's (named after one of his sons). Almost two hours into our wait, our main man sashayed in with his posse. I remember being a little agitated at how late he was, but he was such a striking figure that I knew our wait was worth it. He was dressed to the nines, complete with white satin tie, like some old-time movie star—as sartorially suave and debonair a subject as I had ever encountered.

I may not have been that impressed by his clothes line back then, but I remember thinking that this guy was scary smart in terms of knowing his fans and understanding the market he was going after. This ostentatious man had swaggered in to romance the urban jungle, and he made no bones about the powerfully glamorous vibe he projected. He was unquestionably poised to make his mark in fashion.

"Big business—that's what I would like to think I specialize in," he told me. "Presentation is everything, you know, from the way your phone is answered, the way your cards look, the lawyer you have behind you, your accountant. The way you present yourself to the world is the most important thing ... There's nobody who can represent you like you, and [nobody who can] take you where you got to go but you."

Puffy's business observations were sage. I asked him where he'd learned all that.

"A lot of this stuff is just in my head, you know what I'm sayin'? I'm just bursting with information. Like God truly blessed me," he answered.

He was blessed all right. Two years later, the clothing label he'd founded scored over $100 million in sales. And he was adamant about giving credit where credit was due. In February 2001, at his big Bryant Park Fashion Week show, he actually conducted a mini prayer session backstage for his hunky models just before they hit the runway. I suspected it may have been partly for the benefit of the cameras, but you can't blame a guy for trying to set an example.

"I mean, to be honest," he said to me, "I had to put different priorities in my life, and God is definitely first, you know. It's important for people to know that, 'cause without God, we would not be here. You would not even be talking to me. And sometimes, we're moving so fast, we take that for granted. So we have to slow it down and give Him His praise."

Puffy needed God's help more than ever that season: He was on trial for illegal gun possession and bribery, charges that had been laid following a Manhattan nightclub shooting. If convicted, Puffy was facing up to fifteen years in the slammer. But he had retained the famed attorney Johnnie Cochran, and everybody—media and fans alike—was giving Puffy the benefit of the doubt and praying that this icon would be able to carry on. So with his trial looming, Puffy wanted to stage a brash, sexy, and in-yer-face show in New York, and he arranged for it to be broadcast live on *E!* in the U.S. Besides the ghetto-fabulous collection he was presenting—which was packed with over-the-top stud-wear like mink-lined ostrich trench coats, lynx-tail scarves, and coyote stoles—Sean Combs had a spiritual message to impart: Be proud. Be tough. Fight back. Make your voice heard. And above all, don't ever give up.

The attitude on the runway was militant, with some rapper ranting and raving about "motherfuckers" every two seconds. Then Michael Jackson's old hit "Don't Stop 'Til You Get Enough" started blaring. And as models strutted in the opulent clothing, some in Che Guevera T-shirts and others with bare chests emblazoned with "Black Power" slogans, a frenetic video played, spewing images of Malcolm X and Martin Luther King, disturbing documentary footage of race riots, and a healthy helping of Puffy's ex, the babe-acious J.Lo, thrown in for good measure. (The show was dedicated to her.) The finale was a poignant quotation from Maya Angelou, the great poet and activist, about fighting back against lies and oppression.

Then out walked a subdued Puffy, looking more like a college student than a bad-boy pop star, to the tune of Elton John's "I'm Still Standing." It may have seemed like bullshit to some, but I liked Puffy and found the personal theatrics rather inspirational.

Backstage, Puffy seemed as earnest as ever. "We know you for your music, and your flash, and your own personal sense of style," I said to him, "but what would you want to be most remembered for?"

"Hopefully ... I'll be known as being a great entertainer, [a] child of God, and a nice human being. It's a long road to get to that point. But you know, I'm up for the journey," he said. God must have been on his side, because a few weeks later, a jury found him not guilty on all charges.

By July of that year, Puffy was tripping the light fantastic once again, this time in Paris during couture week. It was moments before the Versace show at the Théâtre National de Chaillot, and Puffy made his grand entrance with date Emma Heming (now Mrs. Bruce Willis) in tow, enveloped by an entourage of security heavies. Shutters clicked, bulbs flashed, and I made a beeline for Puffy, microphone in hand. But it was impossible to get to him. He was being guarded like royalty, or some precious, paranoid politician. I had a post-show invite, however, to a party he and Donatella were hosting for a couple of hundred people at Cabaret, the newly opened Paris nightspot at the Place du Palais-Royale. Maybe I'd see Puffy there.

Cabaret was a basement club that felt like a glam 1970s rec room. The space was decorated with countless twinkling votives and huge roses. Donatella's brother Santos was sitting at a table near the door with some beautiful blonde. The Champagne flowed. The Hilton sisters were cruising. I was munching caviar canapés when I noticed Puffy sitting at the back of the room with Donatella, Rupert Everett, Kevin Spacey, and Naomi Campbell. All the models and stylists and other assorted fashion types were crowded in front of the table, gawking at the celebs. Heath Ledger walked by. Chloë Sevigny posed for pictures. When Puffy got up from the table, I tapped him on the shoulder. He looked happy to see me and grabbed my hand. We did a little jive to the funky music, and then Puffy went over to start deejay duty. My pal Tim Blanks, the *Fashion File* host, and I started dancing like crazy with Amber Valletta and Shalom Harlow. It was a million degrees in the club, and we were all dripping with sweat. Puffy was on the mic, urging everyone to "have another shot of tequila" and "take your clothes off and get naked." It was another one of those hedonistic moments that will stay with me forever.

I started running into Puffy more and more in the years that followed. In 2004, around the time he won the coveted Council of Fashion Designers of America award for best menswear collection, Puffy and his "Sean John" company bought a 50 percent interest in Zac Posen's label. Zac was a young designer whom *Fashion Television* had followed from the very beginning of his career, just after he graduated from Central Saint Martins. Because Zac was always so grateful for my support, I was treated with great respect at his shows, and Puffy seemed especially pleased to see me backstage. No matter how many crews were fighting to get to him—the mood was electric whenever he entered the space—he always came directly towards us and never failed to give us great sound bites, forever thanking me on camera for being the first to recognize him as a design force to be reckoned with.

In February 2008, I managed to secure an intimate one-on-one interview with Puffy to be used for both *SIR*, the men's magazine I was editing, and *Fashion Television*. Puffy was relaxed and eloquent, with the controlled chat taking place in his large studio space. His design team was readying the fall/winter Sean John collection for its impending Fashion Week presentation, the first big show he had staged in five years, on the tenth anniversary of his label.

Puffy's income had been estimated at $346 million a couple of years earlier, making him one of the richest men in hip hop. Now, with all his successes and a new huge billboard towering over Times Square, he admitted that he felt as though he was living a dream. "I wish we all could," he told me, characteristically conscious of the countless fans who'd helped him make it. "I worked hard to get to this point," he said. "I want to keep living it. I want to keep dreaming." He had carved out his role as an urban folk hero, and I was impressed to see that as grandiose as his persona had become, he still stayed focused on his goal. "I'm not just doing this for myself," I remember him telling me ten years earlier. "My motivation is that I'm trying to make history. I'm just doing things that show younger people what you can do if you keep your eye on the prize and you have fun with your life." Now, Puffy was advocating social change. He was very much behind the power of the youth vote and was committed to helping get Barack Obama elected. He credited his past with preparing him for his success. "Growing up in Harlem," he said, "growing up without a father, watching my mother and grandmother work multiple jobs to make sure I could go to college, I grew up watching a certain type of work ethic. And it makes me a person that really believes he can achieve whatever he puts his mind to, because that's how my mother brought me up. Failing, for me, is not an option."

That September, I was thrilled to hear that my network, CTV, had booked Puffy to play at a big, splashy party we were hosting for the

Toronto International Film Festival. He would be performing live on a grand stage to be erected in the CTV building's Queen Street West parking lot, as part of what promised to be the hottest ticket in town. We asked if Puffy might swing by our studio just before or after his afternoon sound check for a live-to-tape interview before a live audience, which we could then package and broadcast as a special. His office agreed, and we hurriedly made arrangements to pull the show together.

I was excited by the prospect of sitting down with Puffy again, and especially pleased that about one hundred of his fans would get the chance to hear him speak in this intimate setting. Most of this select group of fans had won tickets to watch this exclusive interview, and everyone who arrived at the studio that afternoon was pumped at the thought of seeing their hero at such a close vantage point. We didn't have an exact time for Puffy's arrival, but we wanted to be ready for him. So we assembled the crew and the audience at least an hour in advance. The studio was buzzing with anticipation as we all practised our welcome, cheering loudly and applauding wildly. The hour passed. But there was no sign of Puffy.

I entertained the patient audience by recounting stories about my encounters with their hero over the years and answering any questions I could. A producer came by to tell us they had just got word that Puffy was on his way to do the sound check. Instead of doing the interview before the sound check, however, he would do it afterwards. We were all relieved to hear that at least he was on his way to the building. We would just have to be a little more patient.

Another hour passed. It was as though we were waiting for Godot. But eventually a producer assured us that Puffy had finally arrived and was in the parking lot, doing his check. Another few minutes and he would be all ours. I refreshed my makeup, readying myself for our big welcome. When another half hour had passed and there was still no sign of Puffy, I decided to go out to the parking lot myself to see what the holdup was.

"Well, where is he?" I asked a small group of producers and technicians who were huddled with what appeared to be some of Puffy's people.

One of the producers looked me and humbly said, "Well, he was here. But he just left."

"What!?" I shot back. "We've got a studio full of fans who have been waiting close to three hours. When's he coming back?"

"I don't think he'll be back until right before he has to go on tonight," the producer sheepishly explained.

I was appalled. "Can I talk to one of his people?" I asked.

A young woman came up to me and introduced herself as Puffy's assistant. "I'm so sorry," she told me, "but Puffy was really wiped out. He had to go back to the hotel to brush his teeth."

I couldn't believe what I was hearing. It was almost funny.

"Are you serious? We've been waiting for so long … He's coming right back, isn't he?"

"Well, actually, I'm not sure that he is. I'm so, so sorry. Nothing I can do about it," she said, evidently a little mortified that her boss had pulled such a stunt.

I went back to the studio and announced to the audience that Puffy wouldn't be showing up after all.

"Sorry," I said. "It's probably one of the most outrageous things I've ever seen in over thirty years in the business. But he's gone back to his hotel, and he's not coming back until he does his performance tonight. That's showbiz, I guess."

The fans were crestfallen, and I just wished that Puffy could have seen the disappointed looks on their faces. We tried to make things better by offering everyone a wristband to get into the concert in the parking lot that night. But many were so disillusioned that they just went home. I wondered how they would regard their hero now.

I never heard from Puffy after that—no explanation from his office, no note of apology, nothing. I never even saw him backstage at Zac Posen's show the following season—though if I had, I had made up my mind to pass him by. Forget about the professional impropriety Puffy had committed against me after all those years of support—I just can't imagine any excuse for the total disregard with which he treated his fans that day. Any notion I had ever had that this man was a style icon went up in a great big "puff" of smoke.

HEELS ON
THE GROUND

WITH THE HYPE and hysteria around celebrities, we frequently assume that they're all egomaniacal misfits. While I've certainly met my share of self-important, arrogant divas, there have been a few mega-stars who have wowed me with their kindness and humility. I'm always inspired by those who remain real and down-to-earth, and aren't caught up in the superficial trappings of their celebrity status.

I'll never forget interviewing Sarah Jessica Parker at the Eaton Centre in Toronto in 2005 when she launched her first fragrance, Lovely. I'd had several encounters over the years with the talented star of *Sex and the City*, and I always found her to be affable and generous. But these exchanges were brief and usually took place on the fly, at various fashion shows and on a number of red carpets. Our first sit-down Toronto chat was on a small stage inside the busy downtown mall, at lunchtime, in front of about five thousand adoring fans. After our interview wrapped, the diminutive star sat at a table for about an hour and a half, meeting fans who diligently stood in line to get autographs. Many who came up to her were in tears, overwhelmed at getting the chance to meet their heroine—*Sex and the City*'s Carrie Bradshaw—up close and personal. Whenever these fans started gushing over how much they related to Carrie, and how much she had meant to them, Sarah Jessica was quick to point out that it was the talented team of writers on the show who'd created this compelling character.

When it came time for the actress to leave, she held back, determined to sign as many autographs as possible. The security team had to practically drag her out of there! She was evidently moved by her fans, and she knew how much meeting her or getting a quick scribble from her would mean to them. She tried to indulge as many as she could. This was one star who knew on which side her bread was buttered. The mutual respect I witnessed that day was inspiring.

"It's very hard to not be aware of why I have an opportunity," Sarah Jessica told me when she came to Toronto in 2010 to launch her Halston Heritage clothing line. "I know that if I hadn't been part of *Sex and the City*, I certainly wouldn't be here today, talking to you about this particular job at Halston. I certainly wouldn't have come to Toronto a few years ago to launch a fragrance ... The audience of *Sex and the City* is the most important part of the equation," she said. "So if I'm not willing to spend time with the people that are really responsible for the privileges that I have in my life ... I should be looking to do something else." The much-loved actress agreed that all the hobnobbing with fans was a lot of hard work. But it's work she takes on voluntarily.

Not all stars are as comfortable meeting their fans face to face. For some, the media melees that develop whenever they make a public appearance are nothing short of frightening. And I've learned that sometimes a star's unwillingness to stop and chat is based not on snobbery but on fear. Take the inimitable Olsen Twins, for example. The front-row frenzy that erupts whenever the duo walks into a fashion show is among the most extreme I have witnessed. The twenty-something sisters, who began their acting careers on the hit TV series *Full House* when they were only nine months old, have grown up to become bona fide style icons, and now, with their own clothing lines, "The Row" and "Elizabeth and James," they are among fashion's most powerful players. Their irreverent approach to dressing—a kind of effortless chic—has won them respect as trendsetters for a whole new generation.

I have watched Mary-Kate and Ashley Olsen through a particularly loving lens since 1995, when they were in Toronto shooting *It Takes Two*, a comedic romp that co-starred Steve Guttenberg and Kirstie Alley. Bekky and Joey, my own girls, about eight and six at the time, were diehard fans of the twins, so I took them on set with me when I interviewed Mary-Kate and Ashley, who were then nine. The young movie stars were delightfully personable towards my girls. The film's unit publicist, Prudence Emery, told me they were off to Muskoka that weekend to shoot—coincidentally on the same lake our cottage was on. I enthusiastically extended an invitation for a boat ride, sincerely hoping—but not really expecting—that the twins would take me up on it.

To my great delight, the Olsens contacted us at the cottage that weekend and told us they were staying at the Deerhurst Inn, which was just minutes away. Thinking they would get a kick out of our 1939 Shepherd, a vintage mahogany boat that my husband, Denny, had restored with loving care, I gathered a few spare lifejackets and we all piled into the impressive craft for the quick trip across the lake. We pulled up to the dock of Deerhurst, where Mary-Kate and Ashley; their older brother, Trent; their little sister, Lizzy; their dad; and a young woman who appeared to be a nanny or assistant were all waiting, eager to get on board. The kids got into their life jackets, but much to our chagrin, when we tried to start the old boat up again, she simply died. The engine had conked out, as it often did, and Denny couldn't get it started again. Both sets of little girls—our Bekky and Joey and the twins—didn't seem too upset, and they all waited patiently while we called a neighbour to come and get Denny so he could return to Deerhurst with our other, more reliable speedboat.

Finally back at our cottage, we had a delightful time relaxing on the dock and taking the Olsens on tube rides around the lake— something they had never done before. I was completely taken with the twins, charmed at how down-to-earth and unspoiled they seemed, especially for kids who had grown up in the public eye. At one point, I saw the four little girls—who had really bonded that afternoon—all go into the bathroom together. Years later, when the *Hollywood Reporter* dubbed Mary-Kate and Ashley "The Most Powerful Young Women in Hollywood," I joked to my girls that they had had the honour of peeing with "The Most Powerful Young Women in Hollywood"! It was a real, if dubious, claim to fame.

The Olsens went on to build a substantial empire for themselves, and by 2006, they had reached number five on *Forbes* magazine's list of the top twenty earners under the age of twenty-five. I interviewed them again when they launched their kids' clothing line for Walmart in 2001, but I had seen them only fleetingly in the past few years, at the Paris and New York fashion weeks, when they would make a much-ballyhooed appearance at the odd show. While I occasionally made eye contact with them, they never spoke to me and never responded to questions I threw their way. The Olsens were constantly surrounded by security types and throngs of press and paparazzi, and they were always escorted directly to their seats, never stopping for a moment to acknowledge anyone. I often wondered what they were thinking, and what kinds of young women these "little girls" grew up to be.

In August 2009, Mary-Kate and Ashley came to Toronto to launch their "Elizabeth and James" collection at Holt Renfrew, and I was granted an exclusive TV interview with them. I was enchanted to discover that not only had the sisters managed to plough through the muck and mire of celebrity culture, tenaciously forging their way to the top, but they also were still as sweet and down-to-earth as that day we went tubing on Penn Lake. They had fond memories of that afternoon, and were eager to know what Bekky and Joey were up to after all these years. When I asked them how they felt to be called two of "the most powerful players in the fashion world," they both laughed.

"Those are just words," said Mary-Kate. "I think you just have to stay grounded. Maybe that's powerful."

"And stay true to yourself," piped up Ashley.

I asked the twins how difficult it was to be in the public eye all these years.

"It was important to learn early on that you really couldn't pay attention to the noise," explained Ashley. "That would really be the biggest distraction, paying attention to whatever is getting written about you, and just all that noise. It's the most distracting thing. We don't pay attention to it. We don't read it."

I told them that whenever I had seen them at fashion shows, I couldn't get near for all the craziness. "I wonder what goes through your minds," I said, "when you're sitting there, in the front row, and the paparazzi are going nuts, and you've just got to keep 'grounded,' as you say. Because it doesn't look enjoyable."

"I turn white," said Ashley, "and—"

"Shake!" laughed Mary-Kate, finishing her sister's sentence.

"And my palms start sweating, my legs start shaking," Ashley continued.

"I think you just sort of black out for ten minutes, and then it's over," interjected Mary-Kate.

"There's nothing about the whole experience that's normal or natural, or anything that's very fun about it for me, except the few minutes of the show," confided Ashley. "I think that's why we don't go to very many shows, based on that other, negative side," she explained.

It suddenly became crystal clear to me why the twins never utter a word to the reporters who clamour after them in those preposterous situations. I was a little ashamed of myself for ever thinking that fame and fortune had corrupted them. Nothing could have been further from the truth. I gave them each a big hug, and they asked me to say hi to Bekky and Joey for them. I told them that I most certainly would, and that I would be looking forward to seeing them out there in the trenches. If they didn't acknowledge me, I'd totally understand why.

ENDINGS

In fashion, as in life, change is the only constant. It's an exhilarating concept, one that always keeps me on my toes, ready for the next big wave—whatever that may be. Sometimes, though, it makes for heart-rending situations, and the pain of letting go is something you never get used to. Over the past twenty-five years, the fashion world has lost some incredible people—a few of whom I had managed to make a profound personal connection with. Losing these bright lights certainly makes the world a darker place. It also makes me realize just how fleeting everything is, and how blessed I have been to have known such extraordinary individuals.

MISTRESS OF ILLUSION

THE WORLD is filled with illusions, especially in the fashion arena, where so much importance is placed on image and appearances, and things are so often not what they seem to be. One of fashion's most fearless and flamboyant icons, the late Isabella Blow, was also one of the saddest and most tragic figures I've ever encountered. As revered as her sharp eye for fashion talent was—she discovered the brilliant Irish milliner Philip Treacy and the inimitable Alexander McQueen, as well as the models Sophie Dahl and Stella Tennant—and as much of an inspiration as she was to designers, acting as a muse to several, this ultra-talented fashion editor was terrifyingly insecure and shockingly vulnerable.

For years, I had watched Blow at fashion shows, always making a grand entrance, often clad in wildly eccentric and expensive designer gear. One afternoon, she dazzled photographers as she swept across a Paris courtyard in an outlandishly dramatic creation from a young Japanese designer that looked as though it was made from ballooning plastic garbage bags. I asked her what had inspired her to wear it. "'Cause you think it's going to be some fun for the day," she told me matter-of-factly. A seasoned stylist, she was often backstage, helping a favourite designer with last-minute details or just being there for moral support. Or she'd be sitting front row centre, hobnobbing with all the hip fashion cognoscenti, dressed to the nines, frequently in amazing vintage clothing or original couture pieces that had been designed especially for her. A fashion show just didn't seem worthwhile unless "Issie" was in the house.

It never occurred to me that she would be an especially friendly person. She just seemed a little too eccentric, offbeat, and intimidating to be personable too. But it was Issie who first approached me, backstage at a Philip Treacy show, complimenting me on the pink eye shadow I was wearing. Our next little chat came just after McQueen had shown his first Givenchy collection in 1997. She must have known that I had a special relationship with McQueen, and she was sympathetic to the preposterous situation in which he was finding himself: a true artiste having to follow the dictates of a big commercial fashion house. "The artistry has totally gone out of fashion!" she wailed at the end of McQueen's Givenchy debut. McQueen himself told American *Vogue* later that year that he knew the collection was "crap." But by the end of his tenure at Givenchy, three years later, he had certainly redeemed himself. Still, Issie seemed to see the writing on the wall: Fashion had become big business, and the days of unbridled artistic expression, with no regard for commercial viability, might very well be numbered. "Globalization has destroyed the designers," she declared.

In the years that followed, I would regularly run into Issie at Paris shows, and I always took delight in her unabashed critiques. There were times when she was so totally unimpressed by a collection, however, that she wouldn't comment at all. But even getting turned down by Issie made for good TV. We were such big fans, we just wanted her on our show, in all her sartorial splendour, whether she gave us a sound bite or not.

For our spring 2004 issue of *FQ*, we decided to go with an "Artistry in Fashion" theme, and I felt that the perfect designer item to feature on the cover was a Philip Treacy hat. I called Philip, who said he would be delighted to participate and suggested we use as a model his and Issie's newest discovery, twenty-one-year-old Lady Eloise Anson. The daughter of the society photographer Lord Lichfield, niece of the Duke of Westminster, and goddaughter of Princess Anne, Anson was destined to become London's new "It girl." Philip also suggested that Issie be on hand to help style the shoot. We were thrilled! I had wanted to do a proper sit-down interview with her for some time now and figured this would be the perfect opportunity.

When my crew and I arrived at the studio for our cover shoot, Philip apologized and said that Issie couldn't be there—she was off doing her own editorial shoot for *Tatler* magazine, for which she was fashion director. I asked if I could take my crew to where she was shooting and grab something with her there. Philip gave Issie a call, and she said we could drop by anytime. So once our cover shoot with Lady Eloise was done, my cameraman and I scooted over to the *Tatler* shoot. We met Issie in a large trailer filled with models and clothes. The pictures were being taken right out on the street.

Issie was dressed in a white mink coat that set off her signature red lips. She was sitting in the trailer with a young man—an aspiring photographer—whom she introduced as the son of the rock star Bryan Ferry. She was affable, but confessed right off the bat that she was feeling out of sorts, quite depressed, actually. She told me that so many of the people she had discovered—people she had helped promote— were abandoning her. She had also recently lost her consultancy gig with Swarovski. She had been working with the Austrian crystal company for quite a while, helping team them up with designers and inspiring designers to use crystals in their collections. But now that Swarovski had established themselves, they had no need for Issie's services anymore. "That really represented a lot of my income," she confided. "I don't know what I'm going to do." I was surprised to think that this iconic figure, who was so extraordinarily well connected and so talented, was freaked out about her finances. I tried to make her feel better, telling her that she was so respected that she would surely find more work to make up for what she had lost. But she kept saying that she was overwhelmed and everybody was abandoning her.

She asked me if I had kids. I told her about my two girls. "You're so lucky!" she said. "I wish I had children." Then she said again how depressed she was. I told her I had gone through a bout of depression a few years before, when my marriage ended, but happily had come out of it.

"How?" she asked, with an air of desperation.

"You've just got to hold on to your sense of yourself. Believe in yourself. Your situation will change. Things will get better. You have to have faith," I told her. I added that I had written a book in which I described some of what I had gone through. I said I would be happy to send her a copy.

"Oh, yes, please do!" she said. "I would love to read it!"

So the next day, I sent her *Jeanne Unbottled: Adventures in High Style*, feeling both proud that Issie wanted to read it and a little insecure that my humble fashion adventures would seem pretty measly compared to hers.

A couple of months later, I ran into Issie at a show in Paris. She was dressed elegantly in a chic, edgy suit and dynamite stilettos—the very picture of haute style.

"I absolutely loved your book!" she said. "Thanks so much for sending it."

I asked her if she was feeling any better.

"Oh, no. I'm worse. Totally depressed. And my marriage is falling apart. I should probably just end it all now. No one would even care."

"Don't say that!" I said, trying to comfort her. "You always look amazing. You're an inspiration to all of us! We need you in this world!"

She looked at me incredulously and told me how horrid she felt she looked. She confided that she had lost her drive. "You don't get paid for this, you know … And the boys have drained Mummy."

I gathered she was referring to those designers who she felt didn't need her anymore. My heart went out to her. There she was: a bona fide fashion icon, flitting about the Paris shows, hobnobbing with all the A-listers, looking like the total queen of the scene. Who could have known that she was so torn up inside, gasping for breath and doubting herself every step of the way?

About a year later, in 2005, shortly after Kate Moss was featured doing cocaine on the cover of London's *Daily Mirror*, we did a story on

TOP: With *FQ*'s dashing creative director, Michael King, on the beach at Cannes in 2004. We travelled to the Cannes Film Festival for an ultra-glamorous shoot with supermodel Eva Herzigova.

RIGHT: As the executive editor for *FQ*, the lovely Kate McDonald was my right-hand woman. We were all shocked when she took her life in the spring of 2004.

FQ MAGAZINE|PREMIERE ISSUE FALL 2003
CANADA'S INTERNATIONAL MAGAZINE OF STYLE

DIVINE DECO DRAMA

by marian fowler

BEHIND THE SCENES AT
PARIS HAUTE COUTURE
WITH JEANNE BEKER

ISAAC MIZRAHI'S COMEBACK

THE ABSOLUTELY FABULOUS
JEAN PAUL GAULTIER
BY GODFREY DEENY

THE TRENCH GOES UNDERCOVER

DRESS OUR PAPER DOLL
IN FALL'S HOTTEST TRENDS

INVASION OF CANADIAN
ACTOR MARIE-JOSEE CROZE

plus: *Elton John, Hugh Grant, Trudie Styler,
Nelson Mandela, Tom Ford, Naomi Campbell*
and more...

DISPLAY UNTIL NOV. 14/03 $4.95

33

0 63399 70483 2

LEFT: The inaugural issue of *FQ* in the fall of 2003 was dramatically oversized, and featured Somalian-born Canadian model Yasmin Warsame.

ABOVE: Partying in 2005 at the swish Cartagena digs of a gracious Colombian socialite, Consuelo Zuluaga (second from left), ended with a spirited, fully-clad post-dinner dip in the pool. Colombian Trade Commissioner Rodolfo Moseres (pictured above Michael King in the centre of the photo) arranged the trip for *FQ*, which resulted in a beautiful editoral shot by photographer Paul Wright, far right.

RIGHT: Travelling to India for a shoot with *FQ* in the spring of 2006 was an eye-opening experience, providing some of the most disturbing and beautiful imagery I'd ever seen. (SABU PHOTOGRAPHY)

RIGHT: Celebrating the twentieth anniversary of *Fashion Television* with producer Jay Levine and supervising producer Marcia Martin in 2005.
(GEORGE PIMENTEL)

BOTTOM: *Canada's Next Top Model* judges for Cycle 3: Mike Ruiz, me, Jay Manuel, Yasmin Warsame, and Nole Marin.
(COURTESY OF CTV)

LEFT: In San Miguel de Allende on New Year's Eve 2010 with my original style mentor, old friend, painter, and former Olympic skater, Toller Cranston.

BOTTOM: Dancing to the mariachi beat on my fiftieth birthday in San Miguel de Allende at Toller's studio.

RIGHT: Being entertained by the prime minister's wife, Laureen Harper, at 24 Sussex Drive in Ottawa in 2007 was a privilege for both my mother and me.

BOTTOM: The honour of carrying the Olympic torch in Ladner, B.C., in February 2010 made for one of my proudest moments!

(THE CANADIAN PRESS/DARRYL DYCK)

LEFT: Taking Joey and Bekky to the couture shows in Paris in July of 2006 was both a trial and a fantasy.
(ROBYN BIGUÉ)

BOTTOM: At a Toronto luncheon for the G20 wives in June 2010 with Michelle Obama. Laureen Harper had invited a handful of distinguished Canadian women to the lunch at the CN Tower, and I was honoured to be included.

RIGHT: With Canadian actor Barry Flatman at the Canada's Walk of Fame celebration in Toronto in 2009.

BOTTOM: At my home office in Toronto, where I spin many of my stories and reflect on the extra-ordinary life I lead.

drug use in the fashion industry, and I questioned a variety of movers and shakers about the subject at Paris Fashion Week. When I asked Issie, she readily admitted that she needed medication just to be able to cope with everything that was going on around her, and she asserted that most people in her situation would as well. I cringed at her painfully truthful response.

The next year, Issie was diagnosed with ovarian cancer. With her celebrity status on the wane, her depression escalated, and she attempted suicide by taking an overdose of sleeping pills. Later that year, she jumped off the Hammersmith Flyover Bridge, breaking both her ankles. I remember talking to Philip Treacy, who told me that Issie was despondent, and that most of her friends had indeed abandoned her. In 2007, she tried to take her life several times again, eventually succeeding by drinking a bottle of weedkiller. She was forty-eight years old. My heart sank when I heard the news. I knew the scene would never be the same to me again.

"She's the spice in the stew," the designer Michael Kors once told me. Issie's relentless passion for fashion ran deep, and her philosophy will always resonate with me. "It's about emotions," she once reflected. "It's about love."

BITTERSWEET

PURE, UNADULTERATED GLAMOUR is something I have always craved: to be swept away, to see the world through rose-coloured glasses, to be titillated by beauty and excited by life's endless possibilities. This brand of glamour happily comes my way quite often, though my appetite for it is never completely satisfied. But glamour at its most alluring isn't necessarily black and white. Sometimes, glamour possesses a contradictory nature—a kind of bittersweet taste that speaks of heart, struggle, and passion. And perhaps that is why, for me, the personification of true glamour has always been the great Valentino Garavani.

Valentino, who retired to much fanfare in 2008, remains one of the kindest and classiest gentlemen I have ever met. I often ran into him backstage, sometimes just minutes before showtime, as he was tending to some last-minute detail. He always took the time to say hello, and often would stop what he was doing, if only for a few moments, to talk about what he was up to or ask me what I thought of the clothes hanging on the backstage racks. Sometimes, his business partner, Giancarlo Giametti—another extraordinarily kind and caring individual—would get a little frustrated as he tried to get Valentino back on track so the show could get under way. But as tense as things would sometimes get at his shows—as they do at all shows—Valentino never ignored me. He always indulged me and my TV camera, if only for a few fleeting moments.

I first met Valentino in the late 1980s. He came to Toronto for a fragrance launch, and I found him to be the personification of elegance and charm. The next year, I visited him at his Rome atelier, and once again was taken with how personable and warm he was. We talked about how confusing the times were for women, in terms of style. Never before had they been offered so many options, and Valentino was sensitive to their dilemmas. "Often today, a woman doesn't know on which foot to dance," he said. That vivid image has stayed with me.

As the years passed, I had the pleasure of attending countless Valentino shows, and I had several opportunities to interview the master. He never failed to inspire me with his romantic vision and perfectionist nature. Valentino always knew what he wanted, and he was fiercely proud of the exquisite creations his Rome atelier turned out. In 2007, ownership of his venerable house changed hands, but he still seemed determined to hang on to his position as creative head of his label. That spring, he invited me to a fitting at his Paris atelier just days before presenting his spring couture collection.

When we arrived, he was perched on an overstuffed chair—looking like a country gent in a brown tweed jacket, striped tie, and chinos— in the stately Place Vendôme showroom. Two of his beloved pugs, Maude and Milton, were dancing at his feet as a lithe and lovely model emerged, wearing a black-and-white suit. The model fixed her eyes on the designer and confidently strutted towards him down a narrow cream carpet that ran the length of the huge room. Valentino smiled, and the handful of seamstresses standing by broke into applause. And so it went, with Valentino carefully assessing each outfit that emerged, generally pleased with how his ideas had so beautifully materialized. "Nice dress, ah?" he called out to me from across the room, always looking for approval but knowing full well that he had another hit with this Hollywood-inspired collection. I gave him a nod, amazed that at seventy-something, this guy was actually getting better.

"I myself want glamour," he told me that day. "I want beautiful women. I want sensational things. I always want to have girls that look unbelievable dressed in my designs."

I asked him if his idea of beauty had changed over the years.

"I've always had blinders on," he told me. "I just follow my own path. When fashion was upside down, in turmoil, I never really fell into that because that's not what my vision was. My dream was never to see a woman looking like a poor girl who's just come out of a convent, so I never followed that minimalist movement," he said. "Many people weren't so crazy about my way of thinking, but all my clients, all of my women—my admirers—loved my things. So it's been important for me to work with a kind of consistency, without changing too much, without any kind of big revolutions."

Valentino's focus had been unwavering. But the rumour mill continued to speculate that his days in fashion were numbered. In July 2007, on the occasion of his forty-fifth year in the business, the seventy-five-year-old Valentino hosted a three-day extravaganza in Rome, inviting the movers and shakers of the international fashion scene, along with a galaxy of stars, to join him. First on the agenda was the opening of a retrospective at the Richard Meier–designed Ara Pacis Museum, a stunning year-old structure built around a two-thousand-year-old Roman peace altar. Featuring three hundred dresses and rare archival material, the impressive exhibit was a testament to Valentino's prolific genius.

I was lucky enough to be one of the first people Valentino and his long-time business partner, Giancarlo Giametti, saw when they came through the door at the media preview. They made a beeline for me, and I told them how moved I was by the whole experience of coming to Rome, not only to see this retrospective but also to witness Valentino's first couture show in the city in seventeen years. For the sake of business, the Italian had religiously presented his couture collections in Paris. Now, as an act of gratitude to the city that gave him his start, Valentino paid homage to Rome. "The only thing I ever wanted to do was make women look and feel beautiful," he told me. "I'm so proud and happy to see my life's work all together in this special city that I love so much. It really is an emotional moment for me."

"I just find him to be such an inspiration," mused a statuesque and stunning Uma Thurman on her way into the museum. She was wearing a simple white column gown, flat sandals, and gold embroidered shawl. "And more than being this brilliant creative artist, he's also a good friend."

Many of the stars who came out revealed that their relationship with the designer was more than merely professional: They had learned a lot about style from the legend. "We often holiday together," said Liz Hurley, clad in a sexy white beaded Valentino. "And I have to be careful what I pack. He notices every little detail of what I'm wearing!"

Sarah Jessica Parker, decked out in a gold brocade vintage Valentino suit, said, "He's taught me the beauty of ultra-feminine style, and the meaning of grace and charm. Besides, his clothes just feel so good to wear!"

Other luminaries on hand included Anne Hathaway, Claire Danes, Jennifer Hudson, Eva Mendes, Claudia Schiffer, Elle Macpherson, Princess Caroline of Monaco, Princess Marie-Chantal of Greece, and a sprinkling of world-class designers. Tom Ford claimed that beyond the inspiration Valentino had given him, the two had become close friends. Diane von Furstenberg and Carolina Herrera also sang the designer's praises, and Zac Posen commented on Valentino's technical genius. "His dresses seem so light of hand, but there's so much work that goes into them. That's the sign of a great couturier."

What was most astounding about Valentino was his longevity in the business, and his constant red-carpet appeal. Downstairs, there was a collection of creations that had been worn on an assortment of red carpets by some of the biggest luminaries of our time. From a white beaded number that Liz Taylor wore to the Oscars back in the 1960s and Jackie Kennedy's black velvet ruffles to a black-sequined lace gown worn by Sophia Loren and a white tulle dress originally worn by Audrey Hepburn, Valentino seemed to be saying there wasn't anyone he hadn't dressed. The display also included memorable dresses worn by the younger Hollywood set, such as Gwyneth Paltrow's black lace-and-mesh gown; the black-and-white vintage gown that Julia Roberts wore for her Oscar win; another "Oscar win" dress, worn by Cate Blanchett, in yellow; Penélope Cruz's big flower-print ball gown; and the white tulle fantasy Cameron Diaz wore to the Oscars. And the list went on. Beside each dress was a small screen showing video footage and press coverage of the stars in their Valentinos. We all waxed nostalgic as we remembered the impact these dresses had had on us. But what impressed me most was that any of these dresses would work as well today as they did when they first debuted. It was that timelessness that explained the master's extraordinary longevity.

After the official opening of the exhibition, Valentino and Giancarlo Giametti hosted an exclusive outdoor dinner party at the historic Temple of Venus, on a mammoth terrazzo facing the Colosseum. The event was staged by Dante Ferretti, one of the world's leading scenographers, the creator of sets for the likes of Fellini and Scorsese. Eight hundred guests, including Karl Lagerfeld, the shoe god Manolo Blahnik, and Philip Treacey, along with most of the luminaries who had attended the exhibit launch, dined on a sumptuous buffet dinner and drank countless glasses of Champagne, all in awesome surroundings. Just past midnight, an aerial dance show began. To the strains of opera, artists clad in flowing Valentino gowns sailed through the night sky. The performance culminated in a seemingly endless display of fireworks. This was over-the-top beauty at its most spectacular, a dream that only Valentino could have masterminded, and many were rendered speechless. It reminded us all of why we stay in a business that at times can seem so tough, heartless, and shallow.

"I think every designer should learn from Valentino how to make dresses!" Karl Lagerfeld told me the next day. The Chanel designer, whom I have rarely seen at another designer's show, was joined by Donatella Versace, Carolina Herrera, Giorgio Armani, and a host of other celebs from the night before to soak up the splendour of Valentino's special anniversary collection. Valentino retraced his past for this presentation, serving up a kind of "greatest hits" package, with iconic looks from every era reinterpreted with renewed gusto.

"That's precisely what I intended to do because there are so many young people now who don't know my clothes," said the designer. "This collection will help people understand the scope of what I've done through the years." The eclecticism of the silhouettes, attitudes, fabrics, detailing, and construction techniques was astounding. There wasn't a dry eye in the house as a white-suited Valentino took his walk down the ultra-long runway, with music from *Tosca* punching up the passion of his life. He got a well-deserved standing ovation, not only for his efforts here but for a lifetime of creativity. It was an incredibly emotional moment for us all. Backstage, Valentino and Giametti were jubilant that their elaborate presentation had been so well received. "It was absolutely flawless," Lagerfeld raved. And coming from that calibre of critic, the praise doesn't get any higher. "I'm so proud, so emotional," Valentino told me. "Now I know I must go on!"

The final stop on the Valentino party circuit was a sit-down dinner for one thousand at the Parco dei Daini of the Villa Borghese, a masterpiece of Italian garden architecture. My camera wasn't allowed into the party—it was being shot exclusively for Matt Tyrnauer's documentary, *The Last Emperor*. But I was honoured to have received a personal invitation to this event, even though it felt a little strange going on my own. Actually, it was a tad intimidating, and pretty lonely, walking through the exquisite villa and out into the gardens, where a big tent had been erected. But at the same time, I knew I was amazingly blessed to be bearing witness to this high-fashion fantasy. With legends like Gina Lollobrigida, Joan Collins, and Mick Jagger joining the other stars that came to celebrate the memorable weekend, the festivities reached new heights of glamour. The celebs mingled in the red-draped dining room before taking their seats, and dinner began with a video presentation of Valentino at work in his atelier. At dessert, Annie Lennox performed, and we all marvelled at Valentino and Giametti's staggering attention to detail. The weekend's festivities were more than just a salute to a couturier's career—they were a celebration of haute fashion itself. This was, quite possibly, the party of the century.

Three months later, on September 4, Valentino announced his retirement. I immediately phoned my long-time friend Carlos Souza, Valentino's right-hand man and devoted PR honcho, and asked if we could get a TV interview with the designer. The dashing Carlos promised me an exclusive, just as soon as Valentino was ready to talk. I was sitting in Café de Flore in Paris about a month later when Carlos, true to his word, called me on my cellphone to say that Valentino would grant me an interview. I contacted my cameraman and another crew I had on standby, and within a couple of hours, we were back at Valentino's Place Vendôme showroom, where he was preparing his Fashion Week collection.

Valentino was wearing a blue crocodile blazer and looked handsome, relaxed, and at peace with the decision he had finally made—a decision that must have been excruciatingly difficult, given how incredibly passionate he had always been about his métier. We sat on a couch and had a cozy chat. I told him I would miss him. He told me not to worry—he wasn't totally disappearing. He was sure our paths would cross again. Of course they did, at his final runway show later that week, and at his final couture show that January. I saw him again after that—at the house's spring couture presentation in January 2009, when his former accessory designers, Pier Paolo Piccioli and Maria Grazia Chiuri, took over the label. Valentino pulled me aside backstage after the show and told me he was going to be designing costumes for the Bolshoi Ballet. It was exciting for him, no question. But I couldn't help thinking how much he must be missing what he always loved to do most—creating beautiful clothes for some of the world's most elegant and glamorous women—and just how bittersweet this new phase of his life might be.

DESIGNERS
I HAVE LOVED

ONE OF THE BEST THINGS going for us as a team at *Fashion Television* is our longevity: After a quarter of a century covering fashionable goings-on around the world—profiling designers, reporting on collections, and introducing diverse new perspectives on the international style arena—we've earned the trust and respect of some amazing people. Because I often have the opportunity to get close with these major players, I'm able to see them through a particularly intimate lens. Of course, I'm always wowed by their brilliance. But what impresses—and touches—me most is their eagerness to share their ideas and explain what drives their creative process.

Jean-Paul Gaultier consistently floors me with his ebullient nature and generous spirit. No matter how many reporters are crowded around him, vying to get a post-show interview, Gaultier will talk with each one of them. And even though he expends exhausting amounts of energy, you know that when he talks to you, he'll be just as animated and engaged as ever. Gaultier's quick wit and playfulness are a joy, and regardless of how tired I am by the time I'm finally in front of him with my microphone, I'm invariably inspired our conversations, my batteries recharged.

In the fall of 2010, Gaultier came to Montreal to begin work on a new exhibit at the Musée des Beaux Arts to celebrate his illustrious forty-year career. I was granted an exclusive sit-down interview with him, and was charmed once again by his candour. It was Gaultier's seventh visit to Montreal—he has a real affection for the city and its people. He told me that he found Canadians to be refreshing—more friendly and nowhere near as snobby as the French could be. The French, he said, were always judging people on their appearance. Gaultier talked about his own perception of beauty, and how he was always drawn to the unusual. He said that imperfection was far more intriguing to him than conventional attractiveness. He told me that he saw the world cinematically, and that theatrics were integral to his work as a designer. We discussed sexuality, sensuality, and all the subtleties of sartorial communication. Deep into our conversation, I realized that we weren't talking about fashion at all: We were discussing human nature.

By the end of the conversation, Jean-Paul half-jokingly told me that talking to journalists in this way was therapeutic for him. It was as though he could really hear himself think, he said, and thus he gained a better understanding of himself. He then began telling me that while he adored fashion, it was really only a way for him to get to people, a tool that enabled him to communicate and celebrate life. It was like hearing myself speak, and I once again realized that it's my passion for people that keeps me in this business. Basking in the glow of this designer's wonderful spirit, I silently thanked the fashion gods for allowing me the privilege of this magical moment. But I was especially moved at the end of the interview, when Jean-Paul graciously thanked me and let me know that he really "got me."

"You're great," he told me, "because you love your job."

Then there's the inimitable Karl Lagerfeld.

My relationship with Lagerfeld goes back to the summer of 1989, when I had my first sit-down interview with him at the rue Cambon Chanel couture atelier. It was a sweltering day, and I was about seven months pregnant. My crew and I had been waiting for about three hours for the Kaiser, as Lagerfeld was often called, to arrive. His assistant at the time, Gilles Dufour, was kind enough to put me out of my drab green maternity-wear misery by lending me a striking black-and-white Chanel dress (which miraculously fit, and which Lagerfeld ended up giving me!). When Lagerfeld finally arrived at the atelier, he was waving around a package of contact sheets, excited about a photo shoot he had just come from. He had taken up photography the year before and was fervent about his new hobby. We had a wonderful chat that afternoon. And ever since—having interviewed him countless times in the years that followed, in cities from Miami to Monaco—I've had a soft spot for Karl.

The great French diarist Anaïs Nin once wrote: "Life shrinks and expands in proportion to one's courage." Perhaps that explains why Lagerfeld has had such a big life: designer for three different houses (Chanel, Fendi, and his own eponymous label); photographer and illustrator; art aficionado and antiques collector; bookstore and gallery owner; publisher and author. He is fearless, and I never cease to be inspired whenever I spend time with him.

One rainy afternoon in 2003, I was invited to the elegant upstairs office of his 7L bookshop, gallery, and studio space, at 7 rue de Lille, where he was having a tête-à-tête with his close friend Ingrid Sischy, the savvy former editor of *Interview* magazine. Lagerfeld talked about his drive and relentless creativity. "The brain is something you have to train," he explained. "The more you work, the better it works. I always have the feeling—and it may be childish at my age—that the best photo will be my next one, the best collection will be my next one. I always have the feeling [that] I've accomplished nothing, that I have to start again and again and again." Lagerfeld said his biggest problem in life is that nothing satisfies him, that he always thinks he can do better. "It's hopeless," he lamented. Ingrid suggested that his generosity is the reason Lagerfeld can do so many collections. "He has the capacity to really give and really put it out there," she said. "But there's nothing else I want to do," countered Lagerfeld. "I don't want to go on holidays. I don't want to go on boats. I don't want to go to beaches. I did all that when it was time. Now I can concentrate on my work. And I'm lucky

I have people who like my work, and who I can talk to. That's very important. Otherwise, you have no echo. It's an empty thing."

In the summer of 2009, twenty years after our first encounter, he agreed to yet another exclusive sit-down interview. It was slated to take place right after the Chanel fall couture presentation at the Grand Palais. I knew I would have to wait, of course. Lagerfeld customarily chats with all the press post-show, and there are usually dozens of international crews clamouring to get to him. But like Gaultier, he always has time. If one is patient, one eventually gets to Lagerfeld. As Ingrid Sischy pointed out, the man is incredibly generous. He talks to everyone, switching effortlessly from English to French to German. Once in a while, a reporter may get snubbed—but only because he or she has asked a stupid question. Lagerfeld does not suffer fools easily and is quickly bored by people who display ignorance. That being said, he always responds to reporters backstage, often patiently repeating the same things over and over again. And he does it tirelessly and with great aplomb.

On this occasion, I was feeling quite pressured because we planned on turning our promised twenty-minute tête-à-tête into a half-hour special. We had hired an additional crew for the occasion so we could shoot the interview from two different angles. In fashion, nothing is ever for certain—things can change on a dime—so you always have to be on your toes, and just pray for the best. This is especially true when you're dealing with a volatile artist—especially one who is verging on exhaustion after sending out a breathtaking collection and then entertaining the hordes of media for about two hours straight.

It was getting close to midnight, and my crews and I were patiently standing by. Even Chanel's efficient Canadian PR head, Virginie Vincens, who had helped to orchestrate the interview, wasn't 100 percent sure it was going to happen. It was always possible that Lagerfeld would bow out suddenly if he decided he just wasn't up to talking anymore. Chanel's always-helpful Véronique Pérez, who works in the Paris office and acts as Lagerfeld's personal press handler, was doing the best she could to make sure that Karl would keep his promise, but nothing was certain. "Just make sure he sees you, Jeanne,"

Véronique told me as the media crowd started to dwindle. "If he sees you, he won't leave."

I went over to the stage where Lagerfeld had been giving his sound bites and waited til he'd wrapped up with the last reporter. He saw me and instantly came over, gave me a double kiss, and asked how I had liked the show. I was amazed that he still had the energy to do this thing and was actually up for it. We sat on a big couch (happily, the front row of that particular show was composed of these beautiful long couches), and he grabbed a pillow, cozying up to me. I grabbed another pillow.

"I like holding this pillow when I talk," he said. "But it's not to cover up my tummy, ah? I'm slim. I don't need that," he said.

"Well, my tummy does need that!" I joked.

We launched into a delightful, intimate, and very animated personal chat. Almost instantly, I forgot the cameras were even there. My only focus was Karl. It's uncanny how fast you have to be when you're interviewing him. But this exchange felt more like a conversation. My questions were totally spontaneous, though I did have a certain agenda in the back of my mind. Karl is extremely quick and constantly lobs witty remarks with lightning speed. I had to keep coming back. But I was mesmerized by him, totally captivated. And ultimately charmed, to say the least. Afterwards, as we posed together for a few post-interview pictures, Lagerfeld whispered into my ear how much he always enjoys talking with me, and how some people are just a bore to him.

A couple of months later, speaking with Karl backstage just after the presentation of his Lagerfeld label, I asked him if he'd had the chance to see our interview. "Yes, of course," he replied. "It was great. Especially because now I really know that I'm not wasting my time with you, ah?" I appreciated the compliment, especially when I thought about the frustration he must often feel, indulging so many reporters and knowing that such a limited amount of the material he gives them will likely ever be used.

SHABBY CHIC

GREAT STYLE is about much more than what we wear. If style was solely dependent on the clothes we choose and how we strut them, there would be many more inspiring people on this planet. While the lifeblood of this business may indeed be fashion's superficial side, I have learned that what's at the heart of truly great style is personal behaviour—the way we move through the world. That, and the way we treat others.

One of the most shocking and blatant displays of classless behaviour I have ever seen came in May 2006, courtesy of a prominent San Francisco fashionista and socialite who was hosting a dinner party for Alexander McQueen at the ritzy Postrio restaurant. McQueen had been invited to the Academy of Art University in San Francisco to receive an honorary doctorate, and the school, knowing that he and I had a good relationship, invited me and my cameraman to fly out for the celebration.

I had interviewed McQueen many times over the years, but the exchange we taped that afternoon in his hotel room was the most intimate conversation we had ever had. The designer had turned over a new leaf, abandoning his reckless, bad-boy image and embracing a more spiritual philosophy of growth and compassion. There was even a copy of one of the Dalai Lama's books on his coffee table. I was heartened to see Lee—as his friends called him—who had battled his fair share of personal and professional demons in the past, finally seeming so at peace with himself. We had shared a lot together. In 1996, I documented his first outrageous New York show, when he infuriated certain senior members of the fashion media by starting his American debut before they even arrived. I covered his first collection for Givenchy in 1997, when the critics ripped him apart, and he later opened his heart to me and my camera, revealing his vulnerability. And we had sat on the judging panel of the Smirnoff International Fashion Awards for a couple of years, with McQueen demonstrating his feisty side by always standing up for the most controversial design in the competition. There was a definite simpatico feeling between us, and we often shared personal tidbits of information that endeared us to each other. Lee seemed genuinely happy that I had come all the way to San Francisco to witness his proud moment, and we both looked forward to seeing each other at the dinner that evening. One of the organizers at the school told me that Lee and I were sitting together, a detail I shared with him. He was relieved, because he said he wasn't very good at chatting up strangers and was a little overwhelmed by all these fashionistas, who were so intent on schmoozing him.

My cameraman and I arrived at the restaurant early because we were only going to be allowed to shoot the first fifteen minutes or so of the cocktail portion of the dinner. The dinner was taking place in a private room at the restaurant. I went in to see the lovely, long table, formally set with placecards at each seat. Indeed, Lee and I were sitting together, and I felt quite privileged. The guests started to arrive. Our hostess—decked out in a gorgeous black McQueen number—seemed gracious and introduced me to several guests. The designer had yet to show, and I continued to mingle. When I went into the dining room a second time to put my bag on my chair, I realized that Lee's placecard was no longer beside mine: His seat had been moved a few places over. I thought that was strange but didn't ask questions.

When the shy Lee McQueen arrived, he looked a bit uncomfortable but dutifully posed for pictures and tried to make small talk to the various guests. He looked relieved when he saw me, and he said something about how great it was that we would be sitting together. I told him that unfortunately that wasn't going to be the case—someone had moved our placecards. He immediately sent someone into the dining room, and before I knew it, the placecards were back in their original position.

We all took our seats, and Lee and I proceeded to have the most wonderful dialogue—quite intense at times, but very much fun. There was some minimal conversation with the guests who sat on either side of us, but for the most part, the designer and I were engaged in an intimate discussion. Before I knew it, we were on dessert. Just as the dinner was winding down, Lee excused himself, saying that it had been wonderful to see me again, and that he was going off to a club with some friends. I told him to have a great time and said I looked forward to our next meeting. Eventually, other dinner guests started getting up from the table as well, and I decided to say my goodbyes. When I glanced down to the end of the table, I detected an unmistakably icy glare coming from our hostess. I walked over to where she was sitting, flanked by a couple of her fashionista pals, and thanked her for a lovely evening.

"Well, you can go now!" she snapped, with venom in her eyes. "You're not welcome here anymore!" Then she quickly turned away and started chatting with the women she was with.

"I'm sorry, is there a problem?" I feebly asked. But she simply ignored me.

I was flabbergasted. What could I have done to upset her so? Was it that she thought I was monopolizing Lee's attention? Did she think I'd had a hand in swapping the placecards? As I was getting my coat upstairs, with tears welling up in my eyes, the organizers from the Academy of Art University saw me leaving and asked what was up. I recounted my story, and they were outraged. They suggested that perhaps our hostess was jealous of my rapport with Lee and felt slighted by him. They told me not to worry, of course, and said that some people are simply like that. But I was totally disheartened to have been victimized by this designer-clad diva, and I will never come to terms with the crassness and cruelty she dished out that night.

The whole ugly episode made me think of the price some celebrities have to pay for their fame. I suspected that Lee McQueen was less than thrilled to have to sit at the table of some diva he really didn't care about, but that sort of social obligation comes with the territory. Some celebrities don't seem to mind having to perform on command, but others bridle at the prospect of being treated like circus horses. For those who are naturally shy or private, it can make for plenty of torment. But that's yet another layer of obligation that celebrities often are burdened with. And it's understandable that the sensitive ones are especially torn.

As much as we all strive to find a balance and live a peaceful, harmonious existence, I'm also a firm believer that complacency does not fuel creative fires. Back in the old days, when I covered the music scene, Sting once told me, "A content man can never create." I'm not sure what his personal demons were at the time, but he seemed to have come to terms with having them, and he never pretended that every aspect of his life was perfect. Certainly, some artists struggle a lot more than others. But it seems that some of the best ones—the geniuses who are almost driven mad by their desire to bring their visions to fruition—are the ones who suffer most. Blame it on their sensitivity, and on the fact that the world, as beautiful as it can sometimes be, is far from perfect.

Lee McQueen's suicide in February 2010 left the fashion world reeling. The shocking tragedy came just days after the death of his beloved mother. Undoubtedly, his close relationship with his mum contributed to the deep depression he was going through. But since our first meeting in Cape Town in 1995, I had been aware of Lee's deeply sensitive nature. I often marvelled at how he was able to come out with consistently outstanding collections season after season, and at how well he'd learned to play the fashion game.

I will never forget our conversation in 1997, just after his debut collection for Givenchy was torn apart by fashion critics. Days before the show for his eponymous label, I spoke with the wounded young talent in his London studio. Animal hides were being used for that particular collection, and McQueen pointed to a bull skin that had a gash in it. "See this?" he said, grabbing the hide. "I'm making a coat out of it. It represents the pain I went through in Paris. That's what it was like for me, this twenty-six-year-old kid, thrown into the ring and they killed me." Tears welled up in his eyes as he remembered his recent ordeal.

The following season, I interviewed him in Paris just after his second ready-to-wear collection for Givenchy. He was decidedly down and felt miffed that the crowd hadn't appreciated his fun, in-yer-face take on "Cowgirls Go Vegas." "What's the matter with these people?" he asked me post-show. "Don't they realize how much work I put into this?" McQueen never did find happiness at Givenchy. But the profile he acquired at the house did eventually help him to sell 51 percent of his own label to the Gucci Group, and he went on to create some of the most memorable and inspiring collections the fashion world has ever seen. His takes on the synergy between humanity and technology were especially profound. One of the only times I have been moved to tears by a fashion show was at McQueen's spring '99 presentation, when Shalom Harlow, wearing a huge white dress, was spray-painted by two robotic arms as she twirled on a rotating disc. Fashion's magical, trans-formational quality had never been so simply and poignantly illustrated.

Lee shunned requests for TV interviews in the few years before his untimely death. But I did have the pleasure of chatting with him one last time in October 2009, just before he sent his masterful and monumental Atlantis-inspired collection down the runway. He was outside a backstage door, grabbing a smoke, when I ran up to him and gave him a big hug.

"Jeanne, great to see you!" he said, laughing.

"I've missed you so much. How have you been?" I asked.

"I've been okay. Wait til you see this one. An underwater fantasy … all about evolution."

"Can't wait!" I told him.

"But how have you been?" he asked, looking me right in the eye. "Are you happy?"

I told him I was.

"Good, then," he said. "As long as you're happy. That's the most important thing."

I hadn't a clue how profoundly unhappy my designer friend might have been at the time.

After the incredible show—a kind of harbinger of the haunting "alien" imagery the world would see months later in James Cameron's *Avatar*—my cameraman and I stood at the door of the Paris Omnisports stadium as the chic crowd filed out. I was looking for comments about the amazing artistry that had just come down the runway. Many of fashion's most seasoned veterans had tears in their eyes as they recounted how moved they had been by McQueen's genius, and how this was the kind of show that reminded them why they had fallen in love with fashion in the first place.

SAYING GOODBYE

WE CERTAINLY WEATHERED some storms together at *FQ* magazine over the years. But none was as shocking and painful as the suicide of our executive editor, Kate MacDonald, in 2004. Kate was a dear, elegant woman with a charming demeanour, an astute eye, and a life that, in theory, seemed pretty perfect. But for reasons we'll never be completely sure of, Kate sank into a deep depression in late fall of 2003, and by the end of the year, she was no longer capable of focusing on or functioning at her job and was forced to take a temporary leave of absence from the magazine. It was devastating to see such a bright and beautiful young woman, with so much going for her, retreat to such a dark and lonely place. Kate and I were still in touch from time to time, and she was working her darndest to get back to her old self. But on April 1, 2004, I was woken up at five in the morning by my friend Bernadette Morra, the fashion editor of the *Toronto Star* at the time and a very close friend of Kate's. "Jeanne, it's Bernadette. Sorry to wake you," she said, her voice close to breaking. "But it's Kate. She—" I didn't hear another word, just gasped, knowing the worst had happened. My heart broke for Kate's three beautiful boys; for this senseless, unspeakably tragic loss; and for Kate, this sweet and generous soul who, for some inexplicable reason, had lost her desire to live.

I flashed back to a magical day in the fall of 2003, when Kate, always the fashion plate, donned a Burberry jacket, piled her three little guys into her station wagon, and headed out to visit me and the girls at Chanteclair. The Roseneath Fall Fair was on, and we spent a charmed afternoon hanging at the fair with Kate and her sons, going on rides, and playing with the baby farm animals that were on display. Back at Chanteclair, Kate's boys romped through the fields with my girls, while she delighted in taking photographs of us all, high on life. Some other friends dropped by the farm that afternoon, and amid all the laughter, Kate expertly posed us for a group photograph by the side of the house. It was a picture-perfect moment, and I remember watching Kate and thinking how vivacious and happy she looked.

Kate's funeral was bizarre, like a scene out of a stylish movie. We were going through the motions, but all were shocked at what had transpired. Michael King hired a big black SUV to transport the *FQ* team to the church. Toronto's fashion community was out in full force. I kept trying to imagine what Kate would have thought about this sea of elegant, well-dressed mourners, all coming together for this unfortunate affair that had nothing remotely to do with any sartorial celebration. I thought of Kate's great personal style, of her love of fabulous handbags and shoes and designer clothes, of how she adored and collected fashion magazines, of how impeccably groomed she always was, of how she luxuriated in her femininity, and of all her gentle, classy ways. I thought about her knack for diplomacy, the pains she took editing copy, the zeal she had for the stories we worked on, the effort she put into the shoots we produced, her passion for the industry and what she hoped it could inspire in people—what it inspired in her. I heard she was buried in her pink Chanel suit.

A couple of weeks after Kate's untimely death, I went up to Chanteclair on my own, wanting to reflect on the recent tragedy and savour some of the memories I had of my beloved colleague. One of Kate's best friends, Erin Coombs, called me that afternoon, and we engaged in a long conversation about our late friend. I was on my cellphone, walking around the property, enjoying the way everything was coming back to life in my gardens, when I found myself at the side of the house, in the exact spot where Kate had posed us all on that wonderful fall day. As my conversation with Erin continued, I looked down at the ground. I could hardly believe my eyes: There at my feet was a small, perfectly formed bird's nest that must have fallen from a nearby tree. I gently picked it up, and instantly, I felt Kate's presence. The nest seemed like a kind of personal message to me, a reminder of those happy emotions we all felt that day she and her boys came to visit the farm—feelings of home, family, and fulfilment. A wave of peace washed over me. I knew that Kate had come home.

I took the little nest inside the farmhouse, carefully wrapped it in tissue, gingerly placed it in a box, and took it back to the city with me. The next day, I dropped the box off at Kate's house with a note to her boys, telling them how I had found the nest at the farm. I hoped they too had nice memories of that special time we'd spent together.

While Kate had been with *FQ* for less than a year, her death shook us to our foundations and bonded us in a poignant way. Kate's duties were assigned to Shawna Cohen, the capable young editor Kate had helped bring on board, and we attempted to adjust our emotional blinders and carry on. The ride would endure for another five years before it all came crashing down. But while it lasted, the stint I spent with the Kontent Publishing Group, the company that produced both *FQ* and *SIR*, was filled with unparalleled creative highs, inspiring synergies, and rewarding relationships. It taught me as much as—if not more than—any of the professional or personal experiences I've ever had.

The demise of Kontent and the two publications in which we all took such pride can be attributed to several factors. Unquestionably, a major part of the problem was timing. By 2008, Geoffrey Dawe had bought out his partner, Michael King, with the intention of making the business more profitable. Few of us saw the devastating economic downturn coming. Within a few months, advertising dollars became very tight across the board, and those crucial ad pages on which we depended began to dwindle.

Production budgets were slashed, and it became increasingly challenging to pay contributors in a timely manner. We were forced to start thinking outside the box for ways to boost the magazines' revenues. Despite our best intentions, we sensed that a major downward spiral was inevitable. Frustrations mounted. This once brilliant dream factory was suddenly a dark and unhappy place. It killed me to see all our glorious creativity being smothered, and I knew the end was near.

A year after taking control of the business, Geoffrey Dawe reluctantly decided to try to sell *FQ* and *SIR*. While they had never become big money-makers, these respected titles had been built up into rather strong Canadian brands. But unloading these luxe magazines at a time when most publishers were struggling to stay afloat was difficult. And so, much to our profound sadness and dismay, *FQ* and *SIR* folded, with our tiny, talented, and dedicated team left to reinvent themselves.

Seasons come and seasons go. There's only one thing we can count on in fashion and in life: Everything changes, whether it's in small, barely discernible ways or with grand, sweeping turnarounds. We see this in the style world all the time. What's hot and desirable this spring is old news by fall. And as much as some change is wildly welcome, we sometimes abhor the way things take a turn in direction, the way our dreams go up in a puff of smoke, and the way things—and people—that were so real, so significant, so vital to our existence suddenly disappear and are gone forever.

FAITH

Bless my mother. I have always felt that she did a great job in raising me, but there was one piece of advice I could have done without. "Expect the worst," she liked to say, "and you'll never be disappointed." My mother also warned me that life is full of disappointments. Even if that is true, knowing it certainly doesn't lessen your pain and sadness when the disappointments come along, and I'm not sure expecting them really helps you to face them. Somewhere along the way, I rebelled and decided to try to see my glass as half full. If disappointments are inevitable, why aren't miracles too? And so, I continue to smother my doubts and fears in a beautiful blanket of faith that always manages to keep me feeling safe, snug, and protected.

BELIEVING

"DON'T BE AFRAID. And never give up." That's the one motto that continually resonates through my head. From the beginning, it was the principle I relied on to launch the career I enjoy today. It was the refrain that helped me deal with the daunting uncertainty of my first audition at the age of sixteen. It gave me the gumption at nineteen to leave home and move to New York to pursue my dreams. It propelled me to take off for Newfoundland and find work as a mime in my early twenties. And it inspired me to move back to Toronto in 1978 and attempt to make my mark in big-city media. "Don't be afraid. And never give up." Those were my father's words, the words he said to my mother when he so gallantly rescued her from her Nazi-ravaged village. It became his personal motto, the maxim that saw my parents through the war and all its horrors, until eventually they boarded a ship in 1948 and began the brave voyage that would transport them to a new world.

"Don't be afraid. And never give up." It's no wonder I grew up with those words ingrained in my psyche. I fed off them as a kid when I started taking swimming lessons, terrified to jump off the diving board; when I put on my first pair of skates and wobbled over to hang on to the boards for safety; when I courageously careened down neighbourhood sidewalks as my dad held on to the back of my bicycle seat. Years later, I relied on the motto in my darkest hours, when Denny left and I fought to establish a new sense of myself in a life that had suddenly turned bleak and desperately lonely.

I can't count the number of times I have heard my late father's words in my head. I hear them even when I'm out in the field, running around backstage at some fashion event, trying to find the designer for a quick interview or pushing my way through the media throngs and the hordes of paparazzi, chasing after some high-profile celeb in the hope of grabbing a few precious seconds on camera. My father's advice still serves me well, instilling me with the nerve, tenacity, and blind faith required to do my job ... and live my life.

I have also learned that sometimes, just when I'm about to give up, miracles do happen. Covering Stella McCartney's first Chloé show at the old Paris Opéra in October 1997 was an amazing experience. I'd first met Stella in London the year before, at her small Notting Hill studio, just after she graduated from Central Saint Martins College of Art and Design. Fashion arbiters were already buzzing about her, and we at *Fashion Television* were keen to see what all the hype was about. I wasn't disappointed. From the moment I stepped into her unassuming atelier, I felt a wholesome, good-vibe feeling, and Stella could not have been friendlier or more accommodating. She was in between appointments with buyers—the word was out, and retailers were scrambling to get her on board. Warm and down-to-earth, she took me through each of the garments on the rack, and I was charmed by the collection. The clothes featured romantic details, like vintage buttons and ribbons, and there was a femininity to her vision that soon became her trademark.

I talked to her about what she had learned from her famous parents, and I was pleased to see that the daughter of my personal teenage icon had turned out to be such a lovely young woman. Having had the joy of actually meeting and interviewing Paul McCartney several times in the 1980s, when I was an entertainment reporter, I was heartened to see that he was the "real deal"—charming, personable, and very present. My old hero hadn't let me down! Paul struck me as incredibly grounded, and someone who really loved people. The same went for

Linda, whom I'd had the chance to meet and interview years before. I asked Stella about the most valuable lesson her parents had taught her. She reflected for a moment, then said, matter-of-factly, "They taught me to be normal."

The very next year, Stella was appointed creative head of the French label Chloé, controversially ousting the venerable Karl Lagerfeld. Anticipation was high as the press and invited guests filed in to her first show, in one of the regal gilt salons of the Opéra Garnier. As the room began to fill up, I spotted Paul and Linda McCartney in the front row, beside Ringo Starr and his wife, Barbara Bach. For an old Beatlemaniac like me, this was huge. Of course, cameras weren't allowed anywhere near the luminaries, so I just prayed I would get lucky when I tried to grab them after the show. In the meantime, I rushed over to the bank of cameras assembled at the end of the runway and asked my cameraman, Pat Pidgeon, to at least get a long shot of the illustrious couples in their front-row seats.

The presentation was an unmitigated success, with Stella's first Chloé collection the best that house had seen in years. When it was over, Pat and I made a mad dash backstage so we could record a few words with the happy designer. Stella was standing at the door of a crowded dressing room, her people attempting to stave off the scores of reporters. Pat and I pushed and shoved our way towards her, and miraculously, I caught her eye. She seemed overjoyed to see me, instantly remembering me as someone who had taken an interest in her before all this hoopla began. "Ah, it's you!" she called out, playfully pointing her finger at me. "You were there from the beginning!" And she laughed. I told her how much I'd loved the show and congratulated her on a job well done. Then I began asking around for Paul, but I was told he had already made a quick getaway.

I was crestfallen that my hero had escaped me. After all, wouldn't I—the devoted fan who had slept with a poster of the former Beatle over her bed for years—be the perfect one to score a quick sound bite from Big Daddy? Well, I had done my best, I began to tell myself. I would just have to accept that I had missed the most exciting person ever to grace the front row of a fashion show. Still, I was uneasy with defeat. Could we not at least try to discover if Paul and Linda were still in the building? Surely we would have nothing to lose by staking out another door—a less obvious exit—in hopes of catching him on his way out of the opera house. Pat agreed it was worth a try, so we explored a little and found an empty corridor that led to another rear exit. We had just started walking down this deserted hallway when we suddenly became aware of a bit of a kerfuffle. Half a dozen security types were escorting Paul and Linda down the corridor! They were walking briskly, so I fearlessly kicked into gear and called out to Pat to start rolling. Heart pounding, I ran over to the McCartneys and, mic in hand, attempted to engage them.

"You must be pretty proud of that girl of yours," I said, hoping to heck they wouldn't brush me aside.

To my unfathomable delight, they turned towards me, slowing their pace. My perseverance had paid off! Could it be that they recognized my face from our past interviews? Or perhaps they had seen the *FT* piece we did on Stella? There definitely seemed to be a hint of recognition. I will never forget their gorgeous, smiling faces and the dazzling light they generated. It was easy to see they were exhilarated by their daughter's sudden success.

"Proud, proud, proud," chirped Paul.

"And who do you suppose she gets all this talent from?" I fired back.

"Oh, no doubt. It's her mum," he said, turning lovingly to Linda. I was moved to see the incredible bond between those two.

Now, whenever I see Paul at one of Stella's shows—when he was with the infamous Heather Mills, or more recently, with the chic Nancy Shevell—I think how much that whole family must miss the lovely Linda, who was such an amazing spirit. But happily, even though it took him a while to figure it out, Paul looks as though he's finally found the right partner again. The man's a true romantic, all right. I see it in him clearly because I am one as well. I, too, had been looking for the right kind of love again—something that I feared had eluded me. And my hope was eroding. Once again, I dug deep and made up my mind to keep faith. I believe in fate, and every so often, serendipity rears its fabulous head, reminding me why it's imperative not to be afraid, and to never, ever give up.

In February 2007, I took a trip to St. John's—my beloved old stomping grounds—with my friend Mary Symons. We heard that the celebrated Newfoundland singer/songwriter Ron Hynes was performing at a downtown club, and since we were both big fans of his, we made it our business to check him out. Ron seemed delighted to see me. He told me he was slated to perform in Toronto the following month, as part of a literary/music festival called the March Hare. The weekend event was taking place at Brass Tapps, a funky Newfoundland-themed bar owned by David Michael, a musician I had known from my old days in St. John's back in the 1970s. I made a mental note to get tickets to the festival.

The first Friday night of the March Hare, I dropped by Brass Tapps with my daughters, and had a fun time listening to readings and hearing some great music at the crowded, intimate club. It was wonderful to see some of my old acquaintances from that memorable time I spent on The Rock. I knew it would be just the kind of thing my friend Mary would love, so I planned to surprise her the next day by picking her up and taking her to the March Hare's matinee. It would be a special treat, the kind of thing she would never do herself. In fact, as charming a place as Brass Tapps was, it wasn't really on either of our radars. But being there that evening somehow made me feel at home again. It was cozy, unpretentious, and brought me right back to that beautiful culture I so loved.

The next day, I picked Mary up, having told her she was going on a surprise outing. She was puzzled when we pulled up in front of the little College Street bar. But the minute we got inside and heard that rollicking Newfoundland music, she was tickled to be there. We made our way towards the back of the room and found a couple of empty chairs squeezed in beside one of the tables. Shortly after we got settled, someone tapped me on my back. I turned around and saw a handsome guy with greying hair, sparkling blue eyes, a strong jaw, and irresistible dimples. He looked vaguely familiar.

"Jeanne, hi! It's Barry Flatman. What are you doing here?" he asked.

I'd last seen Barry about ten years earlier, on a summer weekend on Martha's Vineyard, at the bar mitzvah of the son of our mutual friends, Fred and Deenah Mollin. It was a sad time for both of us: Barry had just lost his beloved girlfriend to cancer, and although I was still with Denny, he was battling depression. Little did I know then that our marriage would come to an end a few months later.

"Well, I'm a big fan of anything to do with Newfoundland," I explained. "You know, I used to live there! What are *you* doing here?"

"Oh, I love Newfoundland!" he told me. "I've been there a few times. Besides, the owner's one of my closest pals."

When the set ended, Barry and I got up to resume our chat near the bar. I had known Barry, a talented Canadian actor, since 1971, when we were both involved with Toronto's Young People's Theatre, a company that toured children's productions throughout Ontario. Although we were with different groups under the YPT umbrella, I had seen Barry perform. He was a great improvisational talent—funny, irreverent, and quite amazing looking, with long red hair down to his shoulders and a wild red beard. I remember thinking then that he looked like a bona fide rock star. I actually had a mini crush on him. Barry went on to have a successful career in film and television, and I heard about him only in passing over the years. But here he was, obviously having remembered me, and he struck me as incredibly engaging and engaged. I felt something clicking and, without even knowing if he was single at this point, decided to take the plunge. "Great chatting with you," I said as our conversation was wrapping up. And then I gave him my card. "Maybe we can get together for coffee sometime." Yeesh! I could hardly believe my ears! Being this forward with a guy I had just met—or re-met—was not something I usually did. But strangely, it felt right. Barry promised to call. I looked forward to hearing from him.

A couple of months went by without a peep. I told Deenah that I had run into Barry and was hoping to hear from him again. "He must have a girlfriend," I said. She assured me that he didn't. But she told me he might be going through a tough time: Barry had been diagnosed with oral cancer the year before and had to have about 20 percent of his tongue removed. He had rehabilitated himself and learned to speak again, but he was trying to get back on the work track. I was amazed to learn all of this. I couldn't begin to imagine the challenges this guy must have faced. "I'm going to try to get him to go out for lunch with us," Deenah said. She sensed we might be right for each other too.

Another couple of months went by, but the timing never seemed to work. Apparently, Barry let Deenah know that he would love to get together with us, but now he was out of town, shooting a miniseries in western Canada. I was glad to hear he was working but decided that my interest in him wasn't being reciprocated. I wrote him off and tried to keep my eyes open for more potential dating material.

By early fall, my loneliness was escalating. I still hadn't met anyone remotely intriguing, and I was feeling a little sorry for myself. I was sitting at my computer one day when my phone rang. It was my friend Kate with a query. "Jeanne, do you know a guy named Barry Flatman?" In the name of friendship, sweet Kate had been on a sort of manhunt, asking who might be available and a suitable match for me. Apparently, her pal Liz Ramos, another old acquaintance, suggested her dear (and, thankfully, single) friend, Barry.

"Forget it. I know him, but he's not interested. I gave him my card and he said he would call months ago, but he never did," I told her.

Suddenly, Liz got on the phone. "Honestly, don't judge the situation by that. He's been crazy busy. He's still not even in town. He's in New York, rehearsing a show. I'm going there next week, and I'm going to suggest he call you."

By now, I was feeling like quite the loser: These two gals actually sounded like they were going to coerce the old boy into contacting me!

"Please don't bother. I really appreciate it, but he's just not interested," I protested. But Liz wouldn't take no for an answer.

About a week later, she contacted me with the news. "Well, I saw Barry, and he said he had been meaning to contact you but was just too wrapped up getting his life back on track. He says he's definitely going to call you when he comes back to town in November."

I didn't believe her for a minute but thanked her anyway. I certainly wasn't holding my breath.

By the beginning of December, I was on some kind of streak. I had gone to a couple of early Christmas parties and had met a number of interesting men who were asking me out on dates. While I certainly hadn't found Mr. Right, it was all good for the ego. On December 11, I was sitting at Il Posto restaurant in Yorkville with my mother, as well as my sister and my brother-in-law, who were in from L.A. It had been my mum's birthday a couple of days before, and we were celebrating over lunch. My sister asked if I knew of anything fun she could do with my mother that week. I told her I had heard that the splashy Gershwin musical *White Christmas* was in town, and I would arrange to get her tickets for the following Friday. I got on the phone and ordered the tickets right then and there. As soon as I hung up, my phone rang. It was Deenah.

"Jeanne, are you still interested in Barry Flatman?" she asked coyly.

"Would you please just forget about him! Someone else already tried to set us up, and it's just not happening!" I snapped impatiently.

"No, he is interested in you! Actually, Fred is in town, and Barry asked Fred about you! We're all having dinner out tomorrow night. Want to come?"

I was happy to be able to tell her that I already had a date for the following evening. "Maybe some other time," I said wistfully, secretly sad that the Barry Flatman fantasy might never come to fruition after all.

When I got home at the end of the day, Deenah called again to tell me that their plans had changed, and they were all going out to dinner that evening. "I know it's last minute, but can you make it?" she asked.

Knowing that Deenah's kids would be coming along, I asked Bekky if she would be up for dinner with the gang. She acquiesced, and I ran upstairs to get ready for this long-awaited rendezvous with the mysterious Mr. Flatman.

The atmosphere at Vittorio's, a cozy family-run Italian eatery, was lively and inviting as Bekky and I made our way to the back of the restaurant where the Mollins were seated. As I approached the long wooden table, Barry got up and walked towards me, opened his arms, and immediately gave me a big bear hug. "Well, all these yentas are trying to get us together. Guess we're going to have to do something about it!" He was laughing. I was taken aback and a tad embarrassed by all the plotting and scheming that had gone on. But at the same time, I was totally charmed by this guy's candour and affability. We took our seats next to each other at the end of the table. Right off the bat, I told Barry I had heard he was rehearsing a show and asked which one. "It's a big musical," he said. "*White Christmas.*" I laughed out loud. Serendipity! I told him I had just booked tickets to that show for my mum that afternoon. Barry and I spent the rest of the dinner locked in conversation, oblivious to everyone else at the table. The electricity was unmistakable: It felt like coming home.

Two days later, we met for lunch at Allen's on the Danforth and spent a solid four hours talking over chamomile tea and honey: kids, relationships, art, work, life, and death. I was enthralled by his passion and honesty, his strong family values, and the deep love he had for his many friends. We had both endured painful marriage breakups, learned to live with loss, and wore our scars like badges of honour. We were survivors. And as the afternoon rambled on, it was apparent we were on to something.

I spent the next few weeks revelling in this most romantic court-ship. The first time he brought me flowers—three gargantuan bouquets of the most exquisitely fragrant lilies imaginable—he literally floored me. I sank to my knees, then playfully sprawled on my new hardwood kitchen floor, grinning from ear to ear, my arms filled with giant lilies, luxuriating in this new-found joy that had been so long in coming. I couldn't wait to take Barry to the farm so he could experience that other important aspect of my life. We arrived there on a misty January weekend, just about a month into the relationship. We danced in the dining room, and I cried. It was as though I had conjured this guy up! I thanked God I had never given up on finding someone who not only got the music but also got me.

GETTING OVER IT

THE FASHION WORLD is filled with some of the most outlandish egos imaginable. After all, personal vision dictates creativity in this arena, and those with the biggest egos often are the ones who make the biggest mark. You have to have a strong sense of yourself to forge ahead, ignore all naysayers, and pursue a dream. And sometimes, as a matter of self-preservation, you do have to look out for yourself. But for the sake of progress, ego often has to be put on a back burner.

I can't tell you how many temper tantrums I have seen over the assignment of a less-than-ideal seat at a fashion show—sometimes from some otherwise classy people. Often in these cases, the individual's self-image has been challenged, his or her sense of entitlement crushed. Sometimes, it's all very understandable. The fashion arena—and the world at large—can be a crazy-making place, with little respect and even less justice. But I have learned that by sublimating ego, a lot of grief can often be spared.

One afternoon, I was preparing to leave my much-loved hair salon, Rapunzel, having just been coiffed by the fabulous Gregory Parvatan, who'd been my hairdresser since I first started working in television in 1979, more than thirty years ago. (There's something to be said for loyalty!) I was feeling reasonably chic and ready to take on the world once again, now that my colour had been done and my hair blown dry by the master. One foot was out the door when Gregory rushed over and told me, slightly apprehensively, that there was someone in the salon who was dying to meet me.

"Oh, really?" I asked, flattered. "Who?"

Gregory hesitated for a moment, then blurted out, "Denny's girlfriend!"

A bizarre mix of emotions swept over me: fear, excitement, fear, jealousy, fear, curiosity, fear, anger, fear. But mostly dread. Gregory had been Denny's hairdresser for years too. I had heard that he'd sent his new girlfriend to see Gregory a while back, and I was a little incensed. After all, with all the great hairdressers in Toronto, why would she have to invade my inner sanctum? Gregory admitted that her visit had made him a little uncomfortable as well, since he and I were so very close. I asked if he would mind telling Denny that it made for an awkward situation, and he promised he would. Evidently, he didn't.

So there I was, being asked if I would like to meet the gal who had been living with my ex-husband for the past year or so, a woman I had heard about in bits and pieces from my girls, but never once from Denny himself. Of course I was curious to see this young woman for myself, and to try to assess what it was that Denny was so attracted to these days. Perhaps I could gain a little insight into him in the process. But was I finally meeting this mystery woman right here, right now?

Most women would agree that our hairdressers are among our closest confidants, and a salon is tantamount to a port in a storm. This is where many of us truly "let our hair down," gab and gossip, and don't feel horrid about looking like something the cat dragged in, with gobs of dye in our unruly tresses, sans makeup, and frequently clad in schleppy attire. This is a kind of limbo, a place where we can allow ourselves to feel vulnerable. It's the last place you would ever want to be judged, assessed, or presented. A deep wave of insecurity washed over me.

"How long has she been here?" I asked, worried that the young woman may actually have witnessed my roots being done.

"Oh, she just sat in my chair a minute ago," Gregory reassured me.

My eyes darted over to the familiar station. And my worst fears were confirmed. The person sitting in Greg's chair was very tall. And very thin. And she had lovely, long hair that even looked good wet. I took a deep breath and mustered all the courage I could. "Sure," I said. "Let's go over."

The moment I got to the chair, the young woman flashed a big smile and instantly stood up. Okay, I thought. At least she's respectful. But God, she's so young! My heart was beating like crazy. Gathering every ounce of grown-up in me, I stuck out my hand and said, "Well, hi there! Nice to finally meet you ... I've heard so much about you!" This, in fact, was not true. I had hardly heard anything about her. But I had to say something.

"Oh, and I've heard so much about you too!" she said, sounding especially nice and sincere.

I guessed she had heard "so much about me" from the girls. It's unlikely Denny would be very chatty about me. And then came that particularly awkward moment when we both just stood there grinning, with Gregory uncomfortably looking on. My mind was racing with thoughts of how preposterously young this woman looked and questions about what she could possibly have in common with Denny. Are they truly happy? I wondered. And does he treat her the way he treated me? Honestly, I just felt I had nothing to say to this woman, who actually struck me as kind of a girl, just because she really did look so ... well, young. She also wasn't wearing a stitch of makeup. Which made me feel even older. She looked like someone who could be Bekky's friend. She looked like my boyfriend's daughter. She looked like a schoolgirl, a child, a fetus, an embryo, a zygote. I marvelled at how there wasn't a single line on her face. It was fresh, wholesome, and squeaky clean. I suddenly felt like somebody's mother. And then I reminded myself that I *was* somebody's mother.

"Well, so ... are you just ... around?" I asked, trying to make conversation. As soon as the words were out of my mouth, I realized they made no sense at all. I was so shocked to see her in the salon, sitting down for a haircut in the middle of the afternoon. Shouldn't she be in school or something? Okay. Carried away again.

"Oh, I just took the afternoon off work," she informed me, then she went on to say something about going on a vacation.

"So!" I said, not knowing where I was going at all. "You certainly have a really great hairdresser here." I turned to Gregory. "Greg's been doing my hair, for ... uh, well ..."

And quick as whip, dear Gregory piped in, "Since before you were born!"

We all laughed out loud. And that was my cue to get the heck out of there.

"Well, nice meeting you. Take good care," I said, and quickly turned, making a beeline for the door.

My heart was pounding hard, as if I had been hit by an adrenalin rush. I got into the car and looked in the mirror. I had to be honest: I kind of looked old, especially compared to the fair young woman I had just encountered. I knew it wasn't right or smart or mature of me to feel this way. But that's how I felt. (She wasn't even the one who had broken up our marriage. That ended years ago.) And to top it off, even though I knew I had acted classily, I felt totally goofy about the dramatic royal blue cape I was wearing. I wondered how I must have come off to her.

I'm not sure, even now, why any of this mattered so much. But it did. I called my best friend, Penny Fiksel, to share what had just happened. And we had a bit of a laugh over it. About an hour later, I called Gregory. "Oh, you wouldn't have believed it!" he said. "After you left, she kept saying how thrilled she was that she had finally met you, because she grew up watching you and always looked up to you. And then she kept saying what a lovely woman you were."

I was happy I hadn't disappointed her. Nevertheless, I cried. And once again, I'm not sure why any of this mattered so much. But it did.

A couple of months later, Bekky, who had been studying theatre at university in Montreal for four years, was giving her end-of-term performance, a big circus-style show that she had written. Obviously, she was keen for both Denny and me to see it. I made plans to fly to Montreal with Joey, who was still living at home with me. I told Bekky when I was coming in and what flight I would be on. "Oh," she told me, "that's the flight Dad and his girlfriend are taking too." I hadn't figured on his bringing her, but there you have it. It crossed my mind to change my flight, but that seemed foolish. And so, we all made the trip to Montreal together—Denny and his pleasant young girlfriend, me and Joey. And as fate would have it, Jo and I ended up right across the aisle from the other two. It was freaky watching this "couple" travel together, this guy with whom I shared so much history, now totally involved with someone else.

We all had a good time in the end, and after Bekky's show, I invited Denny and his girlfriend back to my hotel for drinks. We sat around a big table at the hotel's glamorous restaurant, drinking Champagne, telling stories, and taking pictures. It all felt very cozy, and I made a concerted effort to be as upbeat and charming as I could, feeling proud of myself for handling all the weirdness with such aplomb. I kept looking around the table, watching our girls enjoying themselves, just relishing all the love and laughter and knowing how important it was that both parents could be there for Bekky on such a special night. When Denny and his girlfriend left, I actually gave them both a peck on the cheek. Then I turned to Bekky, who was sitting beside me, and said, "Okay, Bek, I'm going to give myself a medal for getting through all that." She smiled and gave me a hug, understanding exactly what I meant.

Back in Toronto a few days later, I received a handwritten note in the mail. It was from Denny's girlfriend, saying how wonderful it had been to spend time together, and hoping that we might do it again someday. I doubted that would happen any day soon, but I appreciated her warmth, thoughtfulness, and sweet sincerity. Most of all, I was pleased with myself for successfully wrestling my neurotic ego to the back burner, and allowing myself to open my mind and my heart to possibilities that could take us all forward.

OH, CANADA!

I'VE ALWAYS MAINTAINED that the best part of any trip is the taxi ride home from the airport. That's when I feel the most fulfilled—tuckered out, yes, but infinitely richer for all the experiences I have had, and always comforted to know that I have an exquisite life to return to.

Coming home to Canada after my global jaunts is particularly soothing. There's a wholesomeness to this country, an unassuming purity that's light years away from the pomp and pretension of some of the high-style circles I'm obliged to run in. And while there are times when I have castigated Canada for being too conservative, small-minded, limiting, or petty, I know it's because of this country that I have achieved my level of success and have been able to thrive in an industry fraught with hype without falling victim to the phoniness and superficiality. I am who I am because of this country.

My pride in Canada goes back to my early childhood. One of my most treasured possessions is a small plastic RCMP doll that stands on guard on a shelf in my farmhouse dining room. The wee officer is a souvenir from my first road trip to Ottawa with my parents in 1960, when I was about eight years old. My mother still delights in telling how that little Mountie captured my heart when I spotted him in a

Parliament Hill souvenir shop. Though I desperately wanted that little doll, my parents refused to indulge me. To them, ten dollars was simply too much to spend on such a frivolous thing, and they felt I'd had my share of gifts that week. As we left Ottawa, I cried myself to sleep in the backseat of our 1953 Buick, heartbroken that the little treasure wasn't coming home with me.

When I woke up about an hour later, I was surprised to see that we were back in Ottawa, in front of the souvenir shop where the Mountie lived. Moments later, my mother emerged with the coveted doll. I was flabbergasted when she presented it to me. Apparently, my parents had felt so bad about denying me that they turned around and drove back to get it for me. I was enthralled. The little Mountie spoke of the grandeur of what my family had experienced in Ottawa, touring those splendid Parliament Buildings for the first time, and was emblematic of the intense pride we all felt in being citizens of this great and glorious country. Every time I see my Mountie, I applaud my parents for having the courage and good sense to immigrate to Canada to rebuild their shattered lives.

No matter how much fame or fortune you win, I've found that Canada has a funny way of keeping your feet on the ground. Maybe it's because we've all got to work at least twice as hard to make it here. Or maybe it's just because the people who leave this country—especially those in the entertainment business—are often rewarded for doing so. Those of us who choose to stay, and make it despite the odds, somehow aren't ever as celebrated as those who abandon ship. And maybe it's that lack of celebration that keeps us humble. I suppose it's a good thing. The humility this country breeds has put it on the map, in a sense. In my mind, it's made us a nicer, less aggressive, gentler, and generally more compassionate people. The rest of the world seems to associate these qualities with Canadians. And while I admit that I sometimes envy those who had the guts and determination to leave this country in pursuit of their dreams, deep down I'm proud that I managed to make so many of my own dreams come true while staying in my own backyard. I became a success both thanks to Canada and in spite of Canada. And I wouldn't have wanted to do it any other way.

Recently, I had the chance to bask in the glow of this country in even more enviable ways. In February 2010, I was given the heart-swelling honour of being chosen an Olympic torchbearer. In their infinite wisdom, CTV head honchos Ivan Fecan and Susanne Boyce decided that style should be represented in the network's Olympic coverage, and I was assigned to report on fashion at the Vancouver winter games. My sports-meets-style stint began the moment I donned my white nylon torchbearer's uniform and headed out to the suburb of Ladner, B.C., one of twelve thousand Canadians privileged to participate in the mammoth cross-country torch relay. As I sat on the torchbearers' bus, which was transporting me to the drop-off point where I would start my three-hundred-metre torch run, my heart pounded with anticipation.

It was a perfectly sunny day, and Ladner Trunk Road was lined with hundreds of the most beautiful smiling faces I had ever seen. People of all ages had gathered to watch the torch parade, and many were decked out in patriotic red and white, some waving flags, all eager to see this powerful flame that was igniting the passion of an entire nation. My red-mittened right hand waved like crazy through the bus window while my left clutched my sleek white Bombardier-designed torch, the precious implement that would link me to the Olympic experience.

As I approached my drop-off point, I began to see familiar faces by the side of the road—friends and family who had come out to see me run. My boyfriend, Barry, was there with his sister, Joyce, and her husband, Pat, both wearing jackets emblazoned with the words "Team Beker." My dear old friend Mark Labelle came out. And perhaps most touchingly, Denny's two sisters and their kids—still family, despite all that heartache long ago—were there, holding signs that read "Go, Auntie Jeanne!" I was overwhelmed with happiness.

The bus dropped me off at my starting point by the side of the road, where I cheerfully posed for photographs with assorted fans all craving a piece of the torch relay's magic. After a couple of minutes of sheer exhilaration, dancing to the strains of "Build Me Up, Buttercup," which was blaring from a promotional Coca-Cola truck in the convoy, I was escorted to the middle of the road and suddenly surrounded by other runners. I was jumping up and down with excitement! My torch was ignited, and we all began following a truck with a camera on the back of it, which was beaming my image live on the Internet to the rest of the world. I knew my girls and Penny would be watching together back home in Toronto, my sister would be watching in L.A., and even my dear mum would be sitting at her new computer, transfixed by the technology that allowed her to share this special moment with me. And as I gazed up at that beautiful flame dancing above my head, I saw my whole life in an instant—felt the love and the pride and the passion of my parents and my children, remembered the dreams of my past, and kindled new hopes for my future. The side of the road soon became a blur of red and white and smiles and waves as my heart glowed. For three hundred glorious metres, the little kid in me just couldn't stop smiling as my inner voice shouted, "I love you, Canada!" over and over and over again.

DRESSING UP

FORTY-EIGHT YEARS after our first Ottawa trip together, my mother, at the age of eighty-seven, was invited back for a special Holocaust remembrance ceremony on Parliament Hill. She had been asked to lay a wreath in memory of her own family and the six million other Jews who were annihilated. About fifty Holocaust survivors from Toronto and Montreal were set to participate, and the plan was to bring them to Ottawa for the day by bus. As excited as my mother was about the trip, my sister and I felt that all those hours on a bus would be too tiring for her. I realized that if my mother was going to go to Ottawa, I would have to accompany her there by plane, and it would be best if we spent the night there, since the journey would undoubtedly be exhausting. She was exhilarated by the prospect of not only travelling with me but also making the pilgrimage to our capital city to honour those she had loved and lost.

I mentioned to my friend Mitchel Raphael, the Ottawa society columnist for *Maclean's* magazine, that we were considering making the trip. Immediately, the cogs in his brain started turning. A couple of weeks earlier, Mitchel had reported that the prime minister's wife, Laureen Harper, was a huge fan of *Fashion Television* and had been following my career closely for years. Mitchel decided to let the personable Mrs. Harper know that I was planning a visit to Ottawa with my mother. Perhaps she would like to meet us for tea? No sooner had he informed us of his plans than we were invited to 24 Sussex Drive for dinner! We were flabbergasted. My mother marvelled at how a girl from a tiny shtetl, who was once forced to run for her life, could ever be invited to such an illustrious place. Armed with perhaps the most prestigious invitation my mother had ever received, she and I made the trek to Ottawa. Like a child, she was thrilled by the view of Parliament Hill outside her hotel room window, and she wondered if she would actually get the chance to meet Stephen Harper himself.

It was the eve of the Holocaust memorial service, and our anticipation mounted as we were picked up at the hotel by Environment Minister John Baird and Jason Kenney, the secretary of state for multiculturalism, who were also invited to dinner. Mitchel was on board as well, toting a huge bouquet of flowers for Mrs. Harper. He was thrilled to be included, having never been invited to 24 Sussex for dinner before. Entering the front gates was a fantasy. But reality set in when the great front door opened and we saw Mrs. Harper standing there, dressed simply in white slacks and a black-and-white top. "Hey! I thought this was going to be a casual dinner!" she quipped, taking in my dramatic Louise Kennedy embroidered coat and chic David Dixon navy crepe dress. My mother had opted for an elegant black silk jacket and skirt. Apparently the prime minister's wife had expected us to show up in jeans.

But although it was merely another cozy home-cooked meal for Laureen Harper, it was for us the height of splendour. Unfortunately, the prime minister had had to fly to Calgary that afternoon, so the super-attractive Mrs. Harper was hosting solo. I had heard it was the prime minister's birthday, so I brought him a whimsical Ferragamo blue silk tie decorated with tiny dragonflies. (Doubt that he's ever worn it, but he did follow up with a lovely thank-you note a couple of weeks later.) As for the lady of the house, she was warmer and more affable than we ever could have imagined. Laureen Harper had grown up on a farm outside of Calgary, and she jokingly kept referring to herself as a mere "farm girl." Shortly after we arrived, she began regaling us with tales about Nicolas Sarkozy and Vladimir Putin, joking that now she would have to keep up with the French president's fashionable wife, the former model Carla Bruni.

We could hardly believe we were sitting around a table where such dignitaries had sat before. Yet there, telling her own story, was my diminutive, starry-eyed mother. It was a story I had heard countless times. But to hear the saga relayed at the home of the prime minister was especially powerful. My mother was particularly moved. She had grown so used to hiding her identity as a Jew that it seemed at once frightening and liberating to be discussing her past so openly. "If you live long enough, you get to do everything," she said.

The next day, in the bright Ottawa sunshine, in front of an impressive audience of government dignitaries and Holocaust survivors and their families, my mother placed a wreath at the base of the war memorial on Parliament Hill. I watched the tears well up in her eyes as the memories of that dark chapter in her life came rushing back. But moments later, we were posing for cameras and meeting the Israeli ambassador, and all the sadness seemed to dissipate. My mother was a survivor, and life in the here and now was remarkably sweet.

At dinner the night before, Laureen Harper and I had bonded as I luxuriated in my own "proud Canadian" moment. I was especially impressed by Mrs. Harper's down-to-earth, candid nature and her curiosity about the fashion world. She admitted that she didn't know much about the subject, and she said she was hardly familiar with any Canadian designers at all. I told her how important I thought it would be for her to start wearing Canadian fashion, and offered to take her on a shopping spree in Toronto and introduce her to a handful of our top designers. She was game, and a couple of months later, we hatched a plan for her to visit Toronto to familiarize herself with some of our best talent.

Mrs. Harper's wee shopping spree had to be kept a secret: She didn't want everybody thinking that she was spending too much on designer duds at a time when the economy was hurting and her husband was implementing so many cutbacks. Of course, I was dying to bring my cameraman along to capture the excitement of turning the PM's wife on to Canadian designers. What a great story that would have made! But it was obvious that she regarded this type of publicity as inappropriate. So I had to settle for an intimate experience, and I began calling various designers to arrange for a showroom visit.

Toronto's Lida Baday, whom I had been wearing for years, was at the top of my list. She had cultivated a strong following for herself, both at home and in the U.S., with her highly wearable, clean, modern lines and sophisticated styling. The veteran designer Wayne Clarke, often referred to as Canada's "King of Glamour," was also a must. Wayne, originally from Calgary, is a legend in Canada for his fabulous red-carpet designs. I also wanted to introduce Mrs. Harper to Joeffer Caoc—a solid Toronto designer whose slightly edgy and urbane creations would be perfect for the spirited prime minister's wife. Greta Constantine's Stephen Wong and Kirk Pickersgill were also on my list, for their avant garde but glamorous creations, as was R.U.'s Rosemarie Umetsu, who designs striking and memorable frocks for many Canadian women in the arts. An accessories designer was also in order, so I invited Toronto's Rita Tesolin into the mix as well. I knew her innovative, affordable costume jewellery would be a hit.

Laureen and I had a grand time running around to the different showrooms and meeting with some of the designers. (Unfortunately, Lida and Joeffer were out of town that day.) It was especially fun encouraging the prime minister's wife to try on various looks and listening to her speculate at just what occasion she might wear some of these creations. The petite Mrs. Harper looked smashing in just about everything, and I was delighted to see that despite her insecurities, she tried on items that were initially out of her comfort zone, sometimes with delightful results. She was a great sport, and charmed everyone we met with her honesty and unpretentiousness. "I'm not one of those women who dresses effortlessly," she said. "I wish I was. I'm very jealous of those women who throw something on and look great. That is definitely not me. By day I'm the fleece-wearing mum, and a few times a year I get to dress up and go out with my husband." Everyone agreed that Laureen Harper was likely the prime minister's best asset.

In the months that followed, I was thrilled to see Mrs. Harper out and about in some of the outfits she had ordered that day in Toronto. And once America's new first lady, Michelle Obama, started getting attention for some lesser-known American designers, Laureen decided to step up and make a little more noise about her own patriotic foray into the fashion arena. In the summer of 2009, she asked me to help her choose a dress to wear to a fancy dinner she would attend at the G8 Summit in Italy. She was eager to make a Canadian fashion statement, knowing she would be photographed alongside the likes of Michelle Obama and Carla Bruni. "I think both these women are beautiful," she said, "and great ambassadors for their fashion industries." And she had come to appreciate just how crucial this sort of attention can be for a designer. (Jason Wu was catapulted into the media spotlight when Michelle Obama started appearing in his creations). I suggested Andy Thê-Anh might be the ideal designer for this outing, so we agreed to meet in Montreal to visit his Peel Street boutique. It was there that Mrs. Harper fell in love with a fab red cocktail dress. As it happened, there was no swank dinner party at the G8 after all, so she was forced to delay her dress's debut until a National Arts Centre gala in Ottawa later that fall. "I love the colour of the dress. Like every other woman, I wear lots of black, so this is a bit out of my comfort zone," she admitted. She was also taken with the garment's beautiful beaded straps. "That took the stress out of picking jewellery, as I didn't need any," she said, revealing again her innate practicality.

The biggest kick for me was the email I received from Laureen after the dress's debut. "You've really inspired me to try some new things and step it up," she wrote. As a proud Canadian, I couldn't have been more pleased. And I'm still amazed and flattered that the wife of Canada's highest official asked *me* to help her dress.

But it's not like Mrs. Harper's brush with high style heralded a grand fashionista-in-the-making. "Most Canadians wouldn't know me if they ran into me on a sidewalk," she explained with disarming humility. "I'm very rarely recognized, and I like that. The wife of the prime minister has no official role or title. I'm usually just another mum running around after kids. But once in a while, I get to go to an event and dress up, and

I find that's lots of fun." It seemed that "dressing up" was something Laureen Harper was beginning to enjoy more and more, even though she continued to harbour a few insecurities, especially when it came to the challenge of "keeping up" with her powerful hubby. "My husband walks very fast, and I have to run after him in three- or four-inch heels," she told me. "I have to remind him ahead of time to slow down. It isn't very ladylike to yell at him to slow down," she added.

I have often wondered about the women behind some of the world's most powerful men and just how much they inspire, enable, cajole, and cheer them on. My friendship with Laureen Harper has been a revelation to me—but I suppose I'm most impressed with her accessibility and characteristically Canadian lack of pretension. Ultimately, she has helped remind me what this country is all about, and why I'm so lucky to call Canada home.

ROUND AGAIN

TRUTH BE TOLD, I'm not too preoccupied with thoughts that life is passing me by, that I'll never achieve certain goals or get the chance to recapture a certain happiness. By now, you probably understand why I have so much faith, and why I'm so tenacious. I'm living proof that dreams come true if you focus and don't let go. Happily, as I write this book, I'm still on a roll in this magical life of mine. In addition to my career as a broadcaster and journalist, I'm getting a second chance to create a line of stylish pieces for women who love fashion and are looking for an easy and affordable way to put their wardrobes together. Since September 2010, "EDIT by Jeanne Beker" has been available exclusively at The Bay department stores across Canada. And it all came about in a most serendipitous way.

In the spring of 2008, I was invited to a luncheon at Jamie Kennedy's restaurant at the Gardiner Museum in Toronto. It was hosted by a Montreal company, Levy Canada, which I knew as a producer of quality sportswear. Levy Canada produces the outerwear for such well-known international brands as Liz Claiborne, Betsey Johnson, Perry Ellis, Nautica, and Laundry. Although I wasn't familiar with anybody at Levy Canada, I was still editing *FQ* magazine at the time and felt this might be a good relationship to cultivate. After all, whenever a Canadian company is behind an international brand ... well, that's impressive. But I also had another motive in mind. My dear old pal Bonnie Brooks—who was once editor-in-chief of *Flare* magazine and subsequently moved to Hong Kong, where she ran the hugely successful Lane Crawford department stores, becoming one of the industry's most respected retailers—was coming back to Toronto to become president and CEO of The Bay. Bonnie and I were eager to work together somehow. It seemed like a no-brainer for me to come up with a fabulous new clothing line for the stores, but Bonnie had informed me that she wasn't doing any "private labels" for the time being, and that if I wanted to sell them a clothing line, I would have to find a manufacturer and pitch her the collection. So that was all at the back of my mind as I went off to the Levy Canada luncheon.

Oddly, I remember going back and forth on whether I had the time that week to attend this press event. It seemed like a luxury to be able to sit back and schmooze with other editors over lunch and a small fashion presentation. In fact, I decided at one point that I would definitely decline the invitation. But for some reason, I relented the night before, contacted the PR company that had invited me, and said I'd be there. I don't know why I suddenly changed my mind. Evidently, the fashion gods had something to do with it.

Levy Canada's presentation at the Gardiner was swank and sophisticated. The VP of marketing (and the woman behind it all), Linda Legault, was warm and down-to-earth, and we instantly connected. She struck me as a no-nonsense businesswoman, with years of experience under her belt and a realistic view of the industry. I told her how impressed I was with the presentation, and she suggested I come to Montreal to check out the showrooms of Levy Canada and their partners, the Corwik Group (which was behind a number of diverse sportswear collections) and FDJ French Dressing (a successful jeans label). I told Linda that I came to Montreal regularly because Bekky was attending university there. On my next trip, I would give her a call.

I made it to Montreal a few weeks later and visited Linda's showrooms. I was immediately impressed by the eclectic sportswear collections I saw there, and once again the cogs started turning. What if I could cull a line by choosing a variety of affordable pieces from all the different collections produced by these companies? That way, I would work as a kind of editor with their stable of designers and stylists. Of course, we would tweak the pieces to make them original. And the line could be called "EDIT by Jeanne Beker." Linda and her team loved the idea.

A couple of months later, I was standing in front of Bonnie Brooks and her team, pitching our focused little collection of wardrobe essentials. It felt right from the get-go, and with each piece I talked about, the enthusiasm in the room grew. Before I knew it, the team was talking marketing strategy, and we had a deal. I was stepping onto a new platform once again. It wasn't my first foray into putting out a collection, of course, but this time, it felt better. Bigger and more solid. I knew my partners and I were in this for the long haul. The Bay gave us a huge vote of confidence by ordering EDIT for sixty-five stores across Canada. And Linda and her team began making plans to launch the label internationally. I felt as though I was off to the races once again.

EDIT launched in September 2010 and was an instant success, with some pieces selling out within the first week. The Bay started reordering within days, and the positive feedback from the press and customers was dizzying. Women of all ages, shapes, and sizes were snapping up these chic, wearable basics. Soon, The Bay started talking about a plus-size collection, as well as the possibility of EDIT accessories and bags. While I was careful not to get carried away by these developments, I was happy to think that if things continued to work out, I might have a lucrative and stimulating project to keep me busy long after I stopped running after Karl Lagerfeld in my stilettos—though retirement from that particular scene still seems miles away.

A few months earlier, in February 2010, I was nestled in the luxury of the gleaming bird's-eye maple and cream leather interior of a plush little Gulfstream jet. As I nursed my third glass of Veuve, I contemplated the mysterious way we sometimes get to return to places, people, and situations we knew at an earlier time and in dramatically different circumstances. "Do you want to go up to the cockpit for landing?" my host asked. I knew the fog on the ground in St. John's that morning was as thick as pea soup, but even though my vision would be limited, I welcomed the opportunity to observe the pilots in action. I went up front and was strapped into the jump seat alongside a panel of gauges and buttons and switches. Soon, a fascinating buzz of technical jargon was coming through my headset.

I had been to Newfoundland so many times since I moved there in 1975, the day after I married my first husband, Marty. For our big adventure, my dad generously presented us with his old 1959 Chrysler, which we playfully dubbed the Golden Slipper, since it was my dad's slipper business that had allowed him to purchase the vehicle in the first place. The grand old jalopy barely made it across the island from Argentia, but we savoured every second of that romantic ride. I was brimming with idealism back then, certain I was embarking on an exhilarating journey that would change the course of my life forever. And I was right: It was in this magnificent province that my thirty-five-year affair with media began. In a funny way, Newfoundland has acted as a kind of catalyst for me more than once. First, it was where I launched my media career. Then I came back to St. John's in January 1998, after a twenty-year absence, to produce a TV special on Canadian fashion. I wanted to include a story on a St. John's retailer, Wenches and Rogues, whose Water Street boutique sold Canadian labels exclusively. Besides, who could resist a fashion shoot on Signal Hill? I was by then leading a much different life than the one I had left behind in 1978: I was married to somebody else, the mother of two little girls, and enjoying a successful, bustling career. When I arrived in town, I immediately reconnected with old friends, visited the streets where I had lived and worked, dropped by some of the shops I had frequented, and spent a lot of time just marvelling at how far I had come. I felt ready to take on the world! When I returned home from Newfoundland that weekend, I got the brutal news that my husband, Denny, was leaving me, and my world came crashing down.

I spent the next few years struggling to rebuild my life, and during that time, I made several trips back to The Rock. My dear friends Chabela and George Ayoub had purchased a little saltbox house in the fishing village of Bauline, about forty-five minutes outside of St. John's. Their precious seaside home was always a great source of comfort to me, and I visited Bauline several times with my girls, taking great delight in the charm of the Newfoundland people and the cozy quiet of outport life. This province possesses a brilliant community spirit that has never failed to restore my faith in myself and in life's possibilities. There's a precious rustic quality to life here, a sense of innocence and adventure that I hold very dear, and that is light years away from the trenches of fashion.

And now another homecoming—this time in the cockpit of a glamorous private jet, with my beautiful twenty-year-old daughter, Joey, in tow. She's a musician/singer/songwriter, and I jumped at the opportunity to bring her to the Juno Awards—Canada's version of the Grammy Awards—which were being held in Newfoundland for the first time in a decade. CTV was producing the show, and the weekend would give us all a chance to hear some great music and connect with some very talented songwriters. I also brought along my producer, Christopher Sherman—one of my closest friends and confidants. He had never experienced Newfoundland before, and I knew we would have a stellar time.

My host—a prominent Toronto businessman with whom I was discussing extending my personal brand—invited us to stay in Beachy Cove, at the splendid country home of one of Newfoundland's most legendary families. The sojourn was a fantasy from beginning to end. But one of the greatest thrills was walking the red carpet in my fringed Armani dress, which I'd teamed with a little leather shrug by Abbyshot, a local St. John's label that had generously gifted me the garment on a previous trip, when I had hosted a charity fashion event. No sooner did my Louboutin boots hit the crimson rug than a host of kids, no doubt fans of *Canada's Next Top Model*, started calling my name. I joyfully signed autographs and posed for pictures, lapping up every second of my big minute in the spotlight, pleased to be the momentary centre of attention at such a monumental event.

A few weeks later, I had the privilege of attending a special luncheon at Toronto's CN Tower. Hosted by Laureen Harper, the event was in honour of the spouses of the G20 Summit. Sixteen wives of world leaders attended, as did ten Canadian "Women of Distinction," handpicked by Mrs. Harper. I was among the highly eclectic, successful bunch. Others included the Olympians Joannie Rochette and Silken Laumann; Julie Payette, the astronaut; the journalist Christie Blatchford; and Senators Nancy Greene Raine and Pamela Wallin. It was an impressive gang, to be sure. Mrs. Harper was at the table's head, with the incomparable Michelle Obama at her right, while I was seated at Mrs. Harper's left— directly across from Mrs. Obama. I stood at the table, looking down at the placecards before we all took our seats. And for one moment, overwhelmed by this phenomenal honour, I got misty-eyed. All I could think of were my parents, and how proud my late dad would be if he could see this. And I kept asking myself how a kid from Downsview— who simply dreamed, believed, and worked really hard—had managed to find herself sitting among some of the most prominent women in the world.

In person, Michelle Obama was even more gorgeous and gracious than I had imagined. Her sheer physical presence was striking enough. But coupled with her generosity of spirit and inimitable "comfortable in her own skin" style, it gave her a larger-than-life quality the likes of which I had never seen. Wearing a Rachel Roy brocade ensemble and pointy-toed high-heeled pumps, Michelle Obama was the last one to arrive at the luncheon and the first to leave. But not for a single instant did you get the impression that she didn't want to be there. When Laureen kindly introduced me to her as "my good friend Jeanne Beker," she stretched out her hand, looked me right in the eye, and said, "So nice to see you!" flashing her infectious smile. It was as though she actually knew me, remembered me from somewhere, perhaps had watched me on TV for years! Of course, I knew that probably wasn't the case, but it was flattering and I warmed to her right away.

At the table, the conversation ran the gamut from designer clothes to diets and working out to raising children. We discussed the pressures of keeping up appearances, and the challenges of instilling good values in our kids. It was the kind of girl talk one would expect among close friends, and the wonderful warmth of the exchanges was heartening. I came away feeling high on the spirit of sisterhood and savouring an awareness that had come to me so many times before: We're really not that different from one another.

I had barely come down to earth from the excitement of that memorable afternoon when another wonderful opportunity came my way. I was asked to appear in a month-long run of *Love, Loss, and What I Wore* at Toronto's Panasonic Theatre. This stage play, written by Nora and Delia Ephron, had been showing to packed houses in both New York and L.A. for months. Like *The Vagina Monologues*, the show was based on interviews with a wide range of women, and was performed on stage by a handful of actresses sitting on stools and reading from a script. The stories revolved around fashion and clothing, and how certain pieces of our wardrobe help define us at different stages of our lives. Essentially, it's a show about sisterhood and heart, and I had the privilege of being cast with an extraordinarily talented group of women: the veteran broadcaster and former Stratford actress Barbara Budd; Luba Goy, of Royal Canadian Air Farce fame; the brilliant actress Sheila McCarthy; and Jane McLean, whose star was beginning to rise in Hollywood. It was a hugely rewarding experience, and I got to deliver a range of compelling, bittersweet monologues dealing with everything from wearing a blowup bra to having a mastectomy.

The connection we all felt with the women in the audience was profound. We laughed, we cried, we mused, we remembered. But most important, all of us—cast and audience members alike—admitted our fears, our vulnerabilities, and our passions through these reminiscences about clothes. It got me thinking a lot about how fashion brings people together, and how it can even bring us closer to our own personal truths. And I got to thinking as well about how this enigmatic sartorial arena had served me so well, in so many ways, by giving me a voice, an identity, and a unique way of touching people.

As I travelled across Canada that fall, promoting my EDIT line, I had the privilege of meeting hundreds of fashion fans, from young girls to little old ladies. Grandmothers, mothers, and daughters—and even some men—came out to meet me, and to hear me talk about fashion and the glamorous world they saw on *Fashion Television* every week. At every event, I would start out talking about fashion trends and personal style. But by the end of each session, during the audience Q&A, I invariably found myself addressing life's larger picture, talking about confidence, courage, passion, and tenacity.

I then had the pleasure of meeting fans one on one. The exchanges were always fleeting, but each one seemed so sincere, so full of deep feeling and appreciation. People told me how they'd grown up watching me, some in faraway places where *FT* became their window onto a world filled with possibilities. Some people said they were moved to pursue careers in fashion because of my work. Some just said they found me inspiring.

My final "launch" appearance was at The Bay store at Yorkdale—the Downsview mall where, as a sixteen-year-old, I got my first weekend job in fashion, selling on the floor of a womenswear retailer. I even had my sweet sixteen party in the basement of a Yorkdale restaurant. And as I signed autographs and chatted, taking a moment to look into the eyes of all these gorgeous faces who had come out to see me, a realization came to me: I was passionate about fashion, but only because it had become such a perfect means to this gratifying end—this way of communicating, getting to people, studying human nature, and learning about life. I knew I had found my calling.

ACKNOWLEDGMENTS

The late, great Alexander McQueen once told me that everything in life is a lesson. While that may not be an original notion, it's one that resonates with me loud and clear. Originally, I wanted to call this book *Life Lessons in Fashion's Trenches*, spelling out each valuable "lesson" I'd learned. But my brilliant editors, Diane Turbide and Jonathan Webb, convinced me that simply telling the story of how I found myself—and continue to find myself—in this fantastic arena might be more concise and compelling for readers. The lessons learned are obvious.

My wondrous and edifying journey—especially these last dozen or so years, since I wrote my first autobiography, *Jeanne Unbottled: Adventures in High Style*—has been inspired and enhanced by so many amazing people. Thanks to those in my *Fashion Television* family, past and present, who've helped me tell so many stories: Jay Levine; Howard Brull; Marcia Martin; Mary Benadiba; Luke McCarty; Shane Hogan; Claire Caillout; our Paris driver, J.F., and our New York driver, Sam; and all the talented writers, producers, editors, interns, and cameramen. I must especially thank my dance partners in the field: Arthur Pressick, Martin Brown, Jeff Brinkert, Patrick Pidgeon, Jim Needham, and Basil Young. A special thank-you to the one and only

Christopher Sherman for taking such good care of me, and to CTV publicists Matthew Almeida and Ellery Ulster for helping get the word out there. Heartfelt appreciation also goes to CTV's head honchos, Susanne Boyce and Ivan Fecan, for their vision and support; to David Greener for being relentless; to Geoffrey Dawe, Michael King, and Shelagh Tarleton for enabling my big magazine adventures; to Ed Matier, Linda Legault, Noah Stern, and Ayal Twik for seeing the power of the brand; to Gregory Parvatan for coiffing me; to Lida Baday for dressing me; to Dr. Trevor Born for tweaking me; to Steve Hudson for trimming me; to my pal Bonnie Brooks for inspiring me; and to Eden del Pilar and Emma Madriaga for helping me run my home.

Thank you to my *Globe and Mail* editors, past and present—Sheree Lee Olson, Debra Fulsang, Danny Sinopoli, and Maggie Wrobel. And much gratitude to all the people at Penguin Group (Canada), especially Diane, Jonathan, Mary Opper, Sandra Tooze, and Trish Bunnett, as well as freelance editor Janice Weaver.

More big thanks to all my beloved friends, who keep me cozy and help me hang in there, especially Penny Fiksel, Jackie Feldman, Deenah Mollin, Carol Leggett, Louise Kennedy, Melanie Reffes, Dawna Treibicz, Kate Alexander Daniels, Chabela and George Ayoub, Mary Symons, Andrée Gagné, Diti Dumas, Vivian Reiss, Melanie Chikofsky, Carl Lyons, Joyce Roney, Robbie Cooper, Sandy Kybartas, Jaleh Farhadpour, Kyra Harper, Wendy Natale, Sue Brunt, Max Gotlieb, Steven Levy, Stephan Argent, Mark Labelle, Virginie Vincens, Alan Gratias, the Oundjian family, Melissa Chepa, Dan Duford, Luigi Carruba, Marion Perlet, and the inimitably colourful Toller Cranston. Much gratitude also goes to Denny O'Neil for fathering my two exquisite beauties; to Jack Steckel for helping me through such a trying time; and to Barry Flatman for the passion. Finally, thank you to my immediate family for all the love—Marilyn Beker; Greg Rorabaugh; Keith Del Principe; Bekky; Joey; my mum, Bronia; and my late dad, Joseph, who's still with us every day. You all mean the world to me.

INDEX